MY FATHER'S BUSINESS

A BIOGRAPHY OF
His Eminence G. Emmett Cardinal Carter

Michael W. Higgins
&
Douglas R. Letson

MACMILLAN OF CANADA
A Division of Canada Publishing Corporation
Toronto, Ontario, Canada

Canadian Cataloguing in Publication Data

Higgins, Michael W.
  My Father's business : a biography of His Eminence G. Emmett Cardinal Carter

Includes bibliographical references.
ISBN 0-7715-9108-X

1. Carter, Emmett Gerald, 1912-   .   2. Cardinals –
Ontario – Biography.   I. Letson, Douglas Richard,
1939-   .   II. Title.

BX4705.C37H53 1990   282'.092   C90-094605-9

The authors express their gratitude to the following for permission to reprint previously published material: Conrad Black, for an excerpt from "Unholy Economics" in *The Globe and Mail Report on Business*; George Bull, for a passage from *Inside the Vatican* (St. Martin's Press); Faber and Faber, for a passage from *Selected Essays* by T.S. Eliot; John Fraser, for a passage from *Telling Tales* (Collins); Francis J. Leddy, for passages from "The Keys of St. Peter and the Cross of Malta: and from "May There Be No Dust Upon Our Banner"; *The Catholic Register*, for various excerpts from *A Shepherd Speaks: Occasional Writings, Sermons, and Papers by Gerald Emmett Cardinal Carter*; Anne Roche Muggeridge, for passages from *The Desolate City* and *The Gates of Hell* (both published by McClelland and Stewart), and from "What Do You Do When Your Church Leaves You?" (*Saturday Night*); the *New Catholic Encyclopedia*, for excerpts from "The Church in Canada," v. 18; Brocard Sewell, for a passage from *The Vatican Oracle* (Duckworth); and to various individuals who kindly granted permission to quote from personal correspondence.

1 2 3 4 5 FP 94 93 92 91 90

Jacket design by David Montle
Jacket photo by Karsh, Ottawa

Macmillan of Canada
A Division of Canada Publishing Corporation
Toronto, Ontario, Canada
Printed in Canada

To our children:

Rebecca, Andrew, Sarah, and Alexa Higgins
Nadine, Rick, and Cheryl Letson

THE NIGHT IS LONELY

The night is lonely and the silence
Broods as the waves speak as they reach the shore.
The dog lies stretched across the threshold
Faithful in sleep, the faith image of a Lord
Who sleepeth not nor yet grows old.

But I grow old and do not comprehend
How youth and strength can fail so soon.
No more the swish of the snow on the skis,
The whistle of the wind, the steep descent
The thrill of swing and turn and check.

No more, the dominance of muscle and eye
O'er motion and reflex, o'er competing skill
We die so slowly, friends we do not see
The silent approach, the thief in the night
Who takes from us what we cherish most
And never feel it go. Until 'tis gone.
We reach for it and lo 'tis no longer there.

Kind friend, let not this silent marauder
Make you an accomplice.
My heart is still my own, my love untouched
This is the treasure, heaven taught,
Which thieves steal not, nor rust destroys.
Take it, it's yours, yet giving it
I lose it not. It grows not old.

G. Emmett Carter

CONTENTS

Acknowledgements   /   vii
Preface   /   ix
Prologue   /   1

PART I   MONTREAL (1912-1961)

Chapter One: Youth   /   7
Chapter Two: Seminarian and Newman Chaplain   /   19
Chapter Three: Educator and Theorist: Carter the
    Writer   /   33

PART II   LONDON (1961-1978)

Chapter Four: Emmett Carter and Vatican II   /   57
Chapter Five: Reshaping Catholic Education in
    Ontario   /   79
Chapter Six: *Humanae vitae* and the Struggle over Personal
    Conscience   /   101
Chapter Seven: Reflections on Women and the
    Priesthood   /   115
Chapter Eight: The 1970s: Who Speaks for the
    Church?   /   125

PART III   TORONTO (1978-1990)

Chapter Nine: The Toronto Challenge   /   149
Chapter Ten: Educator and Lobbyist: Carter the
    Politician   /   171

Chapter Eleven: Women and the Church: The Controversy
    Continues   /   179
Chapter Twelve: The Modern Family in Crisis   /   197
Chapter Thirteen: End of an Era   /   207

Epilogue   /   231
List of Persons Interviewed   /   235
Endnotes   /   237
Index   /   247

ACKNOWLEDGEMENTS

No book springs full-blown from the heads of its authors. *My Father's Business: A Biography of His Eminence G. Emmett Cardinal Carter* is the product of many minds and many willing hands. For the assistance of all of them, we are unabashedly grateful.

No one has been more helpful in the pursuit of this project than our wives, Krystyna Higgins and Donna Letson, for whom Cardinal Carter became not quite a member of the family, but at least a comfortably entrenched house-guest who was somewhat reluctant to leave: the researching and the writing of his biography consumed most of our nonteaching, nonadministrating free time over the past three years. Nonetheless, Krystyna and Donna accepted our absences and periods of seclusion with relative cheerfulness, being willing also to lend their expert services to the critiquing of the texts and the proofing of the galleys. For all of this, we are in their debt.

We are, of course, especially indebted to the numerous individuals who willingly gave of their time and of themselves to cooperate in providing the background interviews which helped to introduce us to the complexity, achievements, and shortcomings of the man. Good friends and thoughtful critics of the Cardinal, their names appear both in the text and as an introduction to the endnotes which accompany the text. Meeting with them, talking with them, and enjoying their hospitality has been both an honour and a delight. We trust that we have reported their ideas accurately, though we do not attribute the argument or the opinions contained herein in any way to them; the opinions contained in this book are the joint responsibility solely of the authors.

We are also sincerely indebted to the staff at the Toronto Archdiocese who helped us gain access both to Cardinal Carter's personal archives and to the parking lot; special thanks to Father Brad Massman, the Cardinal's Director of Communications at the beginning of this project, whose ebullient good nature and willing assistance made our days in Toronto a real delight; to Margaret McLaughlin, the Cardinal's Assistant to the Director of Communications during our early visits to the Chancery, whose trust and generosity proved to be particularly valuable in facilitating our original research on the Cardinal; and to Vicki Garnett, Cardinal Carter's immensely helpful administrative assistant, whose assistance in coordinating our activities in Toronto expedited the use of countless hours there. Our thanks, too, to Cardinal Carter's housekeeper, Araceli Echebarria, for her warm welcomes and hot meals.

Other people have been of incalculable assistance to us as we pursued our research, especially Gary Draper, the librarian at the University of St. Jerome's College. A host of others have helped us to locate materials and amass data — people like Joe Barnicke and Charles Wayland, who made available to us a number of pictures of the Cardinal during moments of relaxation; Sisters Lenore and Mae Carter, who provided us with invaluable cartons of personal Carter memorabilia; Lenore Duggan, a niece to the Cardinal, who provided us with a cache of family photographs and patiently verified details concerning the family history; Edward Jackman, o.p., historian for the Archdiocese of Toronto, who facilitated a number of interviews and was generally helpful; John MacPherson, Professor of English at St. Francis Xavier University in Antigonish and President of the Canadian Association of the Knights of Malta, who has several times opened his home to us and who assisted in arranging interviews down east; Mary Malone, professor of religious studies at the University of St. Jerome's College, who unearthed for us various collections of information; and Phil Mueller, the Principal of King's College, who helped us gather information with respect to the College's history during the Carter days; and Charles Van Alphan for painstakingly pulling together a set of the all-but-extinct Come to the Father texts.

The Jackman Foundation and the Academic Development Fund at the University of St. Jerome's College have provided generous and essential financial assistance to this project, assistance without which the breadth of our research would not have been a fiscal possibility.

Michael Higgins
Douglas Letson
Waterloo, Ontario
August 15, 1990

took her about one second to figure it out, but you should have seen the look of consternation on her face."

It's the spontaneous type of jest Carter loves. Rather like the prank he pulled the day we were visiting him at Lake Simcoe. His dog Kelty had a running sore, and Carter had put a pail over her neck to prevent her from scratching the infected area. The pail soon became the centre of attention. So partway through the morning, Carter excused himself, soon to return from the cottage with a pail over his head too.

The Gang of Five — Alex Carter, Emmett Carter, Philip Pocock, George Flahiff and Joseph-Aurèle Plourde — have developed their own history and their own mythology, complete with their own gag book. Plourde, for example, tells the story about a game of bridge in which the two Carters were partners, Plourde and Pocock being their opposition. Alex opened the bidding with something akin to one heart. Pocock doubled. "He had less experience than the rest of us, but I was mad. I said, 'One does not double one heart!' I passed. Alex redoubled. Finally, we played the hand and they went down, two or three in the hole, which was absolutely unimaginable. They were ahead of us up to that time, but because they went in the hole, we were ahead. Emmett was so mad that he left the table and went up to sleep." Carter is competitive, even at cards.

Long-time friend and travelling companion, Joe Snyder, speaks with genuine affection for the Cardinal; he also has his share of humorous anecdotes which put the finger on the character of the man. Snyder first got to know Carter well while he was studying canon law at St. Paul's in Ottawa. One evening Snyder got an invitation to dinner, a dinner at which Carter ordered escargot, which Snyder declined, never before having seen the delicacy. "I said they looked like snails. They were in snail shells. So we had roast beef, and that is where he started to teach me how to eat roast beef. Then he ordered a bottle of wine. And about halfway through the meal he said, 'Don't you like the wine?' I said that I did, and he replied, 'Well, you better start drinking or you'll be looking at stewed bishop.'" (Snyder adds for the record that he has never seen stewed bishop all the time they've lived and travelled together.)

Snyder also talks about their visit to Spain. "That's where he taught me to use the camera." Snyder had never used a slide camera before, so Carter loaded it for him, and Snyder blithely snapped away, capturing dozens of gorgeous pictures. Only much later did they realize that the film was not advancing. "I was so happy that he had somebody's throat and go to bed and sleep like it doesn't bother them. You've got to have people like that in the church. If you have all guys like me, you know. ... The church has a human dimension, a sociological dimension, so that every now and then somebody has to come in and shake her up and straighten her out again. The church has had some popes who were real buggers and some who were saints: I'm sure the buggers cleaned up all kinds of things the saints couldn't have done." (Strong words, whose sentiments are shared by not a few; yet, very close friends like John Sherlock, Brad Massman and Joe Snyder insist that the Cardinal is actually quite shy.) When all is said and done, nonetheless, Power concludes: "I think we are very gifted to have a guy like Gerald Emmett Cardinal Carter in Toronto at this time."

Not everyone takes the Cardinal so seriously, of course. James McConica, for example, tells a story whose origin he attributes to Alan McCormack, the archdiocesan Chancellor for Spiritual Affairs and personal assistant to Carter. As McConica tells the story, McCormack had just concluded a November noonday mass at the cathedral when a woman approached him to ask whether the Cardinal would be present at the carol service for Christmas. McConica explains that it is an occasion "Where he wears the cap and gown and the whole bit, you see, and sits in the sanctuary. And Alan said, 'Well, I think that is his intention, although it is not clear whether he will be well enough. I know he wants to.' To which she replied: 'Oh, I do hope he comes, he looks exactly like a big poinsettia.'" So much for pomp and circumstance, so much for awesome authority.

The stories people tell when asked to recount an anecdote which shows Carter's human side are decidedly instructive. While we were in Winnipeg, for example, interviewing Emmett's sister Mae, who is a nun, her neighbour and good friend Arnold Rogers, a Jewish medical doctor, dropped by intent on passing along a human interest story about Mae and Emmett. "Emmett Carter was visiting here at the time nuns were not allowed to eat with people aside from their own order. They brought Emmett and me a little coffee and some goodies, and a few salad greens. Mae had made the tray look very nice. In the middle of the tray was a vase with a rose in it. So Emmett and I had decided that this looked far too formal and that we should tease Mae a little bit, so we took the rose and hid it, and replaced it with a piece of celery. When Mae came back we asked her what she meant by this sort of desecration of such a fine salad tray, using celery as a decoration. It

Carter is a complex man. Though some would describe him in simple terms (one of his fellow bishops characterizes him in a single word: "megalomaniac"), most see him as a man of the church, dedicated, intelligent, contradictory: human. His brother Alex assures us that Emmett is no saint. Nor would he pretend to saintliness. In fact, despite the Carter brothers' mutual assurance that humility is not a family virtue, Emmett Carter asked us honestly and bluntly for a portrait which captures him "warts and all". True to his word, he has been helpful without being intrusive.

Carter is often criticized for gathering yes-men about him; the less critical see him surrounded by weak advisors. Yet no one calls Aloysius Ambrozic weak or pliable, and no one depicts Carter as a weak leader. Indeed, his biographers are generally caricatured as being left of centre, and his willingness to cooperate with them has been received with some puzzlement in a few quarters: one bishop is reported to have wondered out loud whether the Cardinal had taken leave of his senses. No one saw the biographers as yes-men. For his part, Carter eschews tags like left and right, conservative and liberal, preferring rather to react to issues than to be programmed into a paradigm. Despite the apparent complexity of the man, despite the apparent contradictions, the image is clear. Gerald Emmett Cardinal Carter is before all else a man of the church, a man willing to sublimate his personal well-being, personal will, for the good of the institution and the will of his legitimate superiors. He sees the necessity for unity in those things which are essential to the faith, for latitude in doubtful matters, and for charity in all things (*in necessariis unitas, in dubiis libertas, in omnibus caritas*). He deals with others in charity and with fairness; he expects no less in return.

The best approach to an introductory overview of the Cardinal, his whims and his instincts, is through the eyes of some of his colleagues. Indeed, although Bishop William Power wondered, "Is he going to read this biography before or after he is buried?", he, like the majority of those whom we interviewed, was quite candid. Reflecting on the pomp and circumstance of Carter's seventy-fifth anniversary celebrations in Toronto, Power notes that there has never been a gathering like it in the history of Toronto, and only Carter could have pulled it off. "I have such admiration for him; yet, I disagree violently with his manner. But that is Gerald Emmett."

And what of Carter's administrative style? "Every now and then in the church there have to be Gerald Emmett Carters that can slit

PREFACE

My Father's Business: a designation which will no doubt evoke a host of differing responses, depending on the dispositions the reader brings to this biography. For many, Gerald Emmett Cardinal Carter is a businessman rather than a man of God; for many others, he is pre-eminently the churchman. For some he is the unyielding pedagogue with the razor-like wit; for others he is a man of sensitivity and genuine compassion. To most he is "Your Eminence"; to the few, he is "Min", a nickname born of a nephew's inability to pronounce the word "Emmett". He is a man who enjoys a good laugh, but one who Jesuit priest William Ryan says "enjoys intellectual conversation; somehow if he meets with you, even in a relaxed way, it's always a challenge." *My Father's Business* is meant to capture the complexity of the man.

"Did you not know that I must be about my Father's business?" (Luke 2:49) According to traditional biblical insights, it is with these words that Jesus began his public ministry, asking questions and instructing the teachers at the temple in Jerusalem. The title of our book is meant to describe the churchman whose fifty years and more have been characterized by an educational apostolate as teacher, as inspector of schools, and as bishop charged with the responsibility of being the principal teacher in his diocese. The title also recalls Carter's emphasis on Christ as the modern hero, a hero in whose footsteps all christians are called to walk, be they cardinals or bishops, women or men, cleric or lay, students or teachers. The title also echoes the words of Christ to his mother as he prepares her for his leaving home, father, and mother in pursuit of his ministry. As the words are also spoken by man to woman, they anticipate the crucial contemporary issues of the enabling of woman and of the contested maleness of priestly ministry. It is a title which plays on the ambiguity of the word "business", an ambiguity describing a man who is himself somewhat of a conundrum and an orator with a predilection for playing with words.

loaded it rather than me. Because he didn't want to admit it. That would be a wart. He doesn't tolerate stupidity. But he owned up. He had to."

"He also doesn't tolerate tardiness. That would be another wart. One time I had to drive over to the airport in Detroit to pick him up and the traffic in the tunnel from Windsor was backed right up onto the street. So when I got to the airport I was very late. That was the only time I've seen him that I could call him forlorn: sitting on his bag outside the airlines door. And really looking mad. So I jumped out of the car, picked up his bag, and threw it into the trunk. And he got into the car without saying anything to me. I got back into the car, and he said 'Nice of you to come.' And I said, 'I'm sorry, but you won't believe it. The traffic in the tunnel is atrocious.' 'Sure.' So we drove in silence until we got back into the tunnel. And thank God they were still lined up. He says, 'I see what you mean.' But he never says, 'I'm sorry.' That would be the closest you would get." (Massman agrees, adding that one is more apt to receive a friendly invitation to dinner than an actual verbal apology.)

Joe Snyder has a battery of amusing stories, all told with love, and all confirming in their own way what many have said in less anecdotal fashion.

Asked for a story that would give an insight into the human nature of the man, John Sherlock paused for a short time, then described a dog that Carter had owned while he was Bishop of London. (All his life, Carter seems to have enjoyed canine companionship.) Sherlock described the animal as a "fierce attack dog, slim and black."

"If the Cardinal were having a drink he would toss up an olive stone and she would leap up, catch the stone, and proceed to grind it with her teeth. But she was as gentle as could be. One day I was up at Grand Bend where he had a cottage and where he did a lot of his correspondence and a lot of his writing. And he was a great athlete, you know. He loved to ski and swim and play tennis. Played tennis with him once. He was testing me out. I had fiddled around with tennis but did not take it very seriously. He did. I won one game in a set. He never asked me again. I understood. But he would be in the water, and he would actually have a hand dictaphone, and would dictate letters while he was in the lake. One day we were sitting there talking about things in the diocese when all of a sudden the dog, Heidi, stood up beside his chair. She just stiffened herself. And then she shot into the bushes and grabbed a rabbit and proceeded to snap its neck and eat the whole thing. She was absolutely gentle, you know. But she had the capacity for fierce action." "A bit like himself?" we wondered. "Yes, a bit like himself. Yes."

Carter is also known for his quick wit. Sherlock tells the story of a priest "who had gone off in high dudgeon, sort of abandoned the priesthood, and in the process criticized the Cardinal quite bitterly." When, at the priests' diocesan picnic, one of the priests pointed out that the priest in question was rumoured to be saying mass in private homes, Carter responded, "I suspended him, I didn't shoot him."

Carter can also take an appropriately light-hearted approach in a difficult situation. In August 1982, for example, facing the proposed cancellation of the traditional Santa Claus parade in downtown Toronto, Carter claimed that he had accepted the role of mediator and passed along to the media Santa's plea for a reconsideration. Carter accepted the role willingly, assuming he had been approached by Santa "perhaps because he wears the same colour as I do, or again perhaps because he was and is a Catholic saint."

A quick wit and a sense of fun, however, can be a curse as well as a gift. Carter has been burned so many times by public reactions to his jokes that he devoted his 1984 presentation to the Metro Toronto Police Commission Communion Breakfast to the theme "On Having a Sense of Humour". He dedicated the talk to "the self-righteous journalists of this world. Especially one local paper." Risibility, he pointed out, is related to subtlety and is a human characteristic not shared with the animals. Mockery is not funny if meant to hurt or deprecate; racist humour or humour based on physical defects is not funny if it is meant to belittle. But there has to be room for good natured teasing: "Teasing is the flower of friendship," he said.

Carter's jest that "an Irishman's idea of a queer is a guy who prefers women to whisky" prompted a barrage of complaints from the local media, as had his Jewish joke about a burning bush providing a steady source of fuel. So when he began one of his Cardinal's Dinners by alluding to a politician who had commented, "The only time I get into trouble is when I try to be funny," Carter was speaking from unhappy personal experience. And yet, he has also provided many an audience with marvellously good material. Carter is a serious man with a genuinely light side.

In his biography, therefore, we have tried to present all sides of the man, though it is the serious side which, no doubt, will prevail. For our part, we have tried to be honest recorders of history, mindful of

Pope Leo XIII's advice as quoted by Canon Carter: "The first law of history is to tell no lie; the second to say the whole truth without any fear whatever. . . . If the Gospels were written in our day, the denial of St. Peter would be justified and the treason of Judas would be suppressed on the grounds that they impaired the dignity of the Apostles."[1]

Prologue

It was a moment of high grandeur, befitting the office and the man. It was a day for a prince.

At four o'clock in the afternoon, mass was celebrated in the Cathedral Church of St. Michael. Attendance was by invitation only. Many of the senior bishops of Canada were present in the sanctuary, and many of the senior political leaders were present in the pews. It was a supremely grand ceremony. The music of the baroque masters Gabrieli, Johann Sebastian Bach and Henry Purcell, jostled with the more modern tones of Gallus, Somerville, Franck and Bruckner, and there were, of course, the sublime cadences of plainchant. An eclectic affair, but stately. The magnificence of the concluding Te Deum captured the style and the ambition of the prelate in scarlet.

On May 26, 1987, the Lord Cardinal Gerald Emmett Carter, Archbishop of Toronto, celebrated a triple anniversary: his seventy-fifth birthday, his fiftieth year as a priest, and his twenty-fifth year as a bishop. *Ad multos annos.*

As the packed cathedral gradually emptied, its honoured occupants climbing into their limousines, the less prominent into vehicles of more modest bearing, the police held the curious and the devout at a respectful distance. And then all the congregation, with the more hardy walking, moved toward the cavernous Metro Convention Centre. It was here, with more than three thousand people gathered to pay homage, that the secular festivity would complement the earlier sacred ceremony.

Here were assembled the current Prime Minister, former prime ministers, premiers and ex-premiers, royal representatives of both provincial and federal governments, along with numerous municipal politicians, regional potentates and scores of Roman Catholic hierarchs, and the customary ecumenical and interfaith sprinkling of officials, with a generous body of delegates from the common order, to pay tribute to Canada's most accomplished and public church leader. It was Carter's hour.

Amidst the Byzantine commendations and predictable congratulations, there were genuine expressions of affection and admiration. Pierre Elliott Trudeau recognized an equal, William Davis a friend, and Brian Mulroney an exemplar. Emmett Carter, ever the master of the moment, gave one of his most poignant speeches — an Irishman's autobiographical frolic marked by a courtly modesty, an impish self-deprecation, tempered only by a light touch of the solemn, the homiletic, the old pastor's gentle warning. He loved it, and so did his listeners.

He quipped at the outset: "I have maintained from the beginning that having all three of these anniversaries fall in the same year, yea within four months of one another, constitutes one of my more successful managerial coups. Of course, I had to let my mother, my Archbishop and the Holy Father in on it, but then, getting other people to do it your way is the essence of good management."[1]

If there are echoes of G.K. Chesterton in these lines, it is not without intention. Chesterton has remained an abiding influence on Carter's imagination and prose. But Chesterton, admired as he was, would not have had so many political and social luminaries gathered to pay him honour so lavishly; they were often the principal victims of his satire and polemics. Whereas G.K.C. in his time would have avoided their company, Carter in his time has drawn it. On this May night, Carter was among friends.

Surrounded by the highest temporal and spiritual dignitaries of the land, including American Cardinals John Dearden of Detroit and Bernard Law of Boston, Carter chose mostly to reminisce and entertain. But he also took the occasion (his successor, the Archbishop Coadjutor Aloysius Ambrozic and the Apostolic Pro-Nuncio, Angelo Palmas, were present) to remind his audience that as a bishop, and a bishop who had attended the Second Vatican Council (1962–65), he knew only too well the turbulent waters of controversy and confusion that have attended the years since the Council's conclusion. He has found them exhilarating, rewarding years that allowed him to show his stuff as a combative Irishman. And the Irish spark was very much there that night. "I have several times expressed my view that the Barque of Peter is not a power boat but a sailing vessel. And we all know that in sailing we have to put our weight against the wind. I have tried to do that in the leadership required of me in the Church. That is why I have been so variously described at some moments as being progressive or liberal; at others, conservative or reactionary. My question is and always will be 'progressive' to what? What, or from what are we 'liberating'? Is there nothing we wish to conserve? As to 'reactionary', it depends on what we are reacting to. 'Mindless' is the only adjective that comes to my lips when I contemplate the indiscriminate use of these characterizations. And that has always been the fun of being a contemporary bishop. My favourite anecdote about bishops has always been the comparison to the cross-eyed javelin thrower in the Montreal Olympics. The moral is that while he didn't win any medals, he sure did keep the crowd alert."

And Carter has *always* kept the crowd alert. When he finished his speech that night, they gave him a standing ovation. The powerful paid homage to one of their own, and the powerless looked on with pride and awe. It was a triumph for the man and his church.

John Fraser, Canada's self-designated John Aubrey, the former Beijing correspondent for the *Globe and Mail* and now the distinguished editor of *Saturday Night*, wrote of Cardinal Carter in his collection of brief biographical portraits, *Telling Tales*: "His eminence is no less than his grandeur as a cardinal-archbishop. This is a man who enjoys his high office: its trappings, its power, its potential for leadership, its effect on other people. ... He also enjoys the company and hospitality of those who wield power and control vast sums of money. If it is true that it is easier for a camel to get through the eye of a needle than for a rich man to gain entrance to heaven, it is also true that if His Eminence has any say in the matter — and I do not rule it out entirely — then at the Gates of Paradise, needles will stand 60 metres high, and their eyes will be sufficiently wide, not just to allow for the passage of dromedaries, but a few Rolls-Royces as well."[2]

For many of the Cardinal's critics and admirers, Fraser's paragraph captures the essential Carter. The small band of Christian Worker protesters outside the Metro Convention Centre, and the conspicuous neglect of the gala by the left-leaning Toronto-based newspaper, *Catholic New Times*, is ample evidence that Fraser's assessment enjoys great currency.

Beneath the rich satin vermilion, however, beneath the confident demeanour of an advisor of popes, stands the Montreal lad of Irish stock and modest origins.

ONTREAL

(1912–1961)

CHAPTER ONE

Youth

Although Tom Carter had never been to Ireland in the flesh, in the spirit it was very much his home — his home and that of his youngest son, Gerald Emmett. Born in Quebec City of several generations of New World blood, Tom Carter was nurtured on the dreams of a free Catholic Ireland. Like the conquered French of Lower Canada, the Irish knew the political meaning of religious identity, an identity that could assure them some measure of autonomy, some dignity in the face of British overlordship. Utterly Catholic and utterly Irish, Tom Carter knew who he was.

Irish expatriate writer Kildare Dobbs calls Irishness "an identity with a holy land and a diaspora." But for all their wandering — physical and metaphysical — the Irish are a rooted people, rooted in memory, dream and in a less ephemeral mode, in the land. They are not recent arrivals in Canada; they are shapers of its past and future. "The Irish have been coming to Canada since the seventeenth century, not only as barefoot economic refugees but as soldiers and servants of the British Empire which was at once the oppressor of their home country and their way out to the world. At Confederation, people of Irish origin were the second-largest group in Canada after the French Canadians. They had been leaders in the struggles for religious toleration and responsible government, prominent in journalism, in politics, in the churches. The vision of a new nation in North America had been given most powerful expression in the oratory of the Irishman Thomas D'Arcy McGee. It is fair to say that without that vision, which caught the imagination of colonists scattered from the Atlantic to the Pacific, it would have been possible to see Confederation as a mere business arrangement, a matter of railway dividends, freight rates, profits and tariffs."[1]

Tom Carter, the Irish dreamer, shared in D'Arcy McGee's vision. But he also shared in that mistier, less productive feature of the diaspora Irishman: nostalgia for the Old Sod. His identity was quintessentially Irish-Canadian and he sought, with varying degrees of effectiveness, to impart this identity to his own children. With Emmett, he enjoyed signal success.

Tom took an active part in numerous Irish bodies, such as the Ancient Order of Hibernians, the Emmett Club, the United Irish Society and the St. Patrick's Society of Montreal. This last organization was founded in 1856 and enjoyed from its inception the sanction and support of the Coadjutor Bishop of Montreal and the Irish clergy of St. Patrick's Church. The preamble to its constitution ably sets out its purpose: "Whereas, it is deemed expedient to establish upon a basis, adequate to the objects thereof, an IRISH CATHOLIC NATIONAL SOCIETY in MONTREAL, which shall unite and harmonise varieties of opinion, and through which, as an organized means, the members thereof may act for charitable and patriotic purposes; and whereas, the proper objects of such a Society should be, 1. To promote HARMONY and GOOD WILL amongst Irishmen; to foster NATIONAL FEELING and LOVE OF FATHERLAND. 2. To render assistance when necessary to persons of Irish birth or descent, in the District of Montreal, and especially to Emigrants. 3. To ensure the due celebration of the FESTIVAL DAY OF THE PATRON SAINT OF IRELAND. 4. To represent, when circumstances require, the Irish interest in the City of Montreal and elsewhere, where the interference of this Society may be deemed proper."[2]

Tom Carter was a member of this Society for more than thirty years. He would brook no mockery of Irish festivities and solemnities, particularly those associated with the St. Patrick's Society. With his son Cyril there were many fierce, if not always sincere, battles over the annual St. Patrick's Day parade, although in the end Cyril always supported the parade. It was Emmett who didn't. But they all knew that Tom Carter took his Irishness seriously.

Mary Agnes Kerr took her Irishness seriously as well. Born in New York City, but brought to Quebec City at a very young age, she was eventually destined to marry Tom in Montreal and become the supreme Irish matriarch.

Tom and Minnie brought eight children into the world, although only seven would grow to maturity. In order of noble succession, they were: Margaret, Irene, Cyril, Tom, Frank, Mae, Alex and Emmett.

They were a tightly bound, combative family, in which authority, love, playfulness and obedience each played a crucial and duly-proportioned role.

Margaret, the eldest, was the closest in affection to Emmett, who was the youngest. She was, quite simply, "in a family of abrasive, opinionated people, . . . gentle, understanding and always seeking to defend, to explain, to condone."[3] Married to Wilfrid Duggan, who managed the Montreal Forum during season and worked at the Blue Bonnets racetrack during the summer, Margaret raised, virtually alone, two children of her own, Gerry and Lenore, and was instrumental in the raising of Tom and Michelle, her nephew and niece, by brothers Cyril and Tom, respectively. Mature, reliable, with an "extraordinary gift of love," and surprisingly even-tempered in a family of mercurial individuals, Margaret had a special bond with Emmett.

Increasingly over the years, particularly on matters related to the disciplining and education of her children, Margaret came to rely on the advice of her educator-brother. In the words of her son, the unpredictable and ebullient Gerry: "I think that, occasionally, just occasionally, my mother and father interfered with Emmett's bringing us up." Exaggerated, no doubt, but illustrative of the eldest child's trust in the youngest child's judgement.

One of the gestures that secured the bond over the years was the love of literature that Emmett and his sister shared, a love that found a special expression in the oral recitation of verse, mostly the verse of the English Catholic poets Francis Thompson, Gilbert Keith Chesterton and Hilaire Belloc. In no small part, Emmett's predilection for peppering literary quotations throughout his homilies, public addresses, books and correspondence was ably nurtured by Margaret's own fondness for the finely crafted and expertly delivered word. Margaret Carter Duggan's death in 1981 deprived the Cardinal of his oldest friend.

Irene, although the second child in the family, was the first to enter religious life. Tom and Minnie Carter were, in a classically Irish-Catholic manner, wholeheartedly supportive of their sons' religious vocations, but less enthusiastic about their daughters' callings. Tom, in particular, was cold to the idea. When Irene mentioned her intention to enter the Sisters of Providence at their motherhouse in Kingston, Ontario, having been influenced in that direction by Father Cotter, a Jesuit, Tom's opposition became more open. "My decision was made — I would remain at home until after Christmas, and enter on January 6. But, unexpectedly, the coveted permission was denied; I must wait until I was twenty-one, my father decreed. No intercessions on my behalf were of any avail. My Director announced that he could do no more — it seemed that I would have to wait. Knowing the attraction of the world and my own love of pleasure, I feared this delay, so made a final appeal to my father, telling him that I was convinced that if I did not enter at that time I would never enter and my vocation would be lost. Somehow, this was the telling argument. Still feeling that this was but a whim, and asking that I telephone him immediately when I realized my mistake, he reluctantly gave the permission."[4]

It was a permission he would give again and again, but Irene, whose religious name was Sister Mary Lenore, SP, was the first. She was eighteen years old, and Emmett was only four.

Mary Lenore, who, until her death in July of 1990, lived in retirement at the Kingston motherhouse where she sought admission as a teenager, had a distinguished career in church and educational leadership. For many years she was principal of a Catholic secondary school in Belleville, Ontario, and served in a leadership capacity, often in an unprecedented way, on the executive of the Ontario English Catholic Teachers Association and the Ontario Teachers' Federation. In her own order, she served on the Provincial Council and eventually, during the turbulent years following the renewal initiatives of the Second Vatican Council, she assumed responsibility as Superior-General. It was during her years as General that the Sisters of Providence opened missions in Guatemala and Peru.

Every inch the Carter, Mary Lenore deployed her energies in various directions and never hesitated to call upon the name and influence of her bishop-brothers.

Cyril was the black sheep of the family, by his own designation the BBB (the Bishops' Bad Brother). At one time he too entertained the idea of proceeding toward the priesthood while attending Montreal College (Collège de Montréal). But he abandoned the plan. He studied for a while at Loyola College, and in time earned his living as an accountant. But the joy Mary Lenore knew in her life as a religious seems to have eluded Cyril.

Not always on the easiest terms with his father, Cyril was often the favourite (before the ascendancy of Emmett) of his mother. According to his younger sister Mary: "My mother always used to have the meals right on time, everything just for Cy. And then it happened that after his marriage to Nora began to deteriorate, and the care and nurturing of their son Tom became imperilled, Cy came home and Tom was reared under the watchful and devoted eyes of my mother."

It was Cyril who would make sport of his father's Hibernian enthusiasms, but it was also Cyril who, after his father's death, maintained membership in the various associations that were his father's joy. Cyril died in 1972.

Tom, the second son, had a bit of the rebel in him as well, although he would die some thirty years younger than Cyril. He was attracted to the Christian Brothers, a teaching order that administered the parish elementary school, St. Patrick's, but he determined instead to look for his fortune out west. One day he left a cryptic note and was gone.

He would send money and gifts to his family and would return periodically, sometimes with a woman-friend. Stories of his easy ways abound. He would have fun skirting Customs regulations, bypassing admission charges at amusement parks and simply prodding the authorities. He was the card, the restless wild card, but not without heroism, as indicated by the circumstances of his death in 1947, at the young age of forty-one.

Tom's new wife, a Hungarian-American (he had been married previously and had a daughter named Peggy), was pregnant with their first child, Michelle, when Tom died on the beaches of Atlantic City. He was helping rescue a drowning girl when he had a lethal heart attack on his way back to shore. He died dramatically, a figure cast in the style of an Irish hero: gallant, reckless, spontaneous, undisciplined and capable of the grand gesture. His father, after all, would have been pleased.

Frank lived but a few months after his birth before he succumbed to pneumonia. His tragically premature death reminded the Carter parents of life's fragility and their own mortality, but with a spiritual resignation characteristic of their time and religious upbringing, they refused to be haunted by Frank's death. There were other children and there would be more children.

Mary, the third daughter, was a spirited and independent girl who knew her own mind and whose stubborn will was capable of causing parental distress. Mae, as she was called, was the first child of the second tier (the Carter children found themselves in chronology, if not in sympathy, divided into "two families": Margaret, Irene, Cyril and Tom, followed by Mary, Alex and Emmett).

Not as pious as her mother, and inclined to take charge of her own life in a way that posed some threat to feminine identity in the Carter household, Mae worked, dated and struggled to be as independent as the sometimes suffocating circumstances of an Irish-Catholic family life would allow. Though she respected and loved her mother, it was her father who commanded her true affection. She found in him — tall, strong, principled and firm — a soft heart and tolerant spirit. In a way, perhaps, she found a co-conspirator. "My mother said I had the loudest voice on the street. Everyone would congregate at our house, and my mother would complain: 'Why do they all have to come here?' It was my mother who raised us; it was she who took the active, direct role. In a way, I was afraid of my father. Until one day, when I was carrying a certain, and dangerously large, number of dish plates from the kitchen to the dining room cabinet — having ascertained that I could save considerable time by taking more than the specified number — I dropped them all and broke nearly every one. I broke into tears and panic and started to pick up the dinnerware, both the shattered ones and the few remaining intact, when I heard footsteps in the distance. I kept saying to myself: 'Dear God, let it be Mother. Please don't let it be Dad! Please don't let it be Dad!' But it was my father, and as he stood there, his shadow looming in the doorway, he asked, 'What's the matter?' When I told him what must have been obvious, he simply said, 'Hurry up and pick them all up before your mother sees it.' From that time on we became the very best of friends."

A cigarette-smoking, music-loving girl whose sisters were dutifuly employed in either the convent or the domestic network, Mae came to rely upon her younger brothers for a degree of friendship and intimacy that age and circumstances prevented with her sisters. Alex and Emmett became her buddies.

When she decided at the age of twenty-nine (appreciably older than the norm) to enter religious life, there were not a few who were surprised: her parents, a few boyfriends and several workmates. But decide she did.

The Religious of the Sacred Heart of Jesus were a more cloistered or contemplative order than the Sisters of Providence, whom Irene had joined several years earlier. Mae, like her older sister, found in her father some measure of resistance to her decision to enter religious life. This may have been because of her stubborn spirit, the late entry and the close sympathy between the man and his daughter. But, as her sister had before her, she won a reluctant benediction from him. Nevertheless, he would not accompany her to the train that brought her from Montreal to the religious congregation's novitiate, Kenwood, in Albany, New York. It was a tearful parting. With Alex and Emmett already in the seminary and his youngest daughter entering religious life, Tom Carter understood in the clearest terms the enormous hold the church had on his family. It had claimed four of his seven surviving children for service.

In deciding to become a nun, Mae was considerably affected by her younger brothers' decisions to study for the priesthood. While both Alex and Emmett wrote to her from the seminary, it is the correspondence with Emmett that she most cherishes. On one occasion he bluntly observed: "In the way of things, I miss most of all MUSIC; in the way of people, YOU."[5]

The bond between Mae and Emmett was strengthened by her occasionally reverential reliance on his counsel and priestly skills. Over the years, he gave countless conferences to members of her community and their charges in Halifax, Winnipeg, Vancouver and Montreal. Strong in mind and spirit, she was, however, in the manner of the Carter women, always prepared ultimately to defer to the men, particularly the clerics. It was the pattern, from the beginning.

Alex, three years Emmett's senior, is both most like and most unlike him. Their careers have followed relatively similar paths in the ecclesiastical world, though they are very different churchmen. Ordained by Bishop Deschamps on June 6, 1936, Alex served in a parish for just a year before being sent to Rome for graduate studies in canon law at the Angelicum. When he returned, he was appointed Vice-Chancellor of the Archdiocese of Montreal and was subsequently sent on loan to the Archdiocese of Winnipeg as Chancellor, with the assignment to make order out of a chaotic ecclesiastical administration. When he returned to Montreal he was appointed to serve both on the Marriage Tribunal and as the chaplain at St. Mary's Hospital. He then had a short stint as a pastor of a parish until being named the Coadjutor Bishop of Sault Ste. Marie by Pope Pius XII in December 1956. He became the third Bishop of the diocese in 1958.

Most everyone thought that the bishop in the family would be Emmett. And so did Emmett, Tom and Minnie's youngest child, born on the first day of March, 1912. And indeed the younger priest's time would come. But Alex would break the trail by his own strong and controversial leadership.

During his long tenure as bishop of a northern Ontario diocese, a region of the country with which he had no previous experience, Alex initiated several ecclesial and social projects that have earned him the esteem of Catholics and non-Catholics alike. For instance, he instituted the first Native peoples' diaconate program and established the Order of Women, a non-ordained body commissioned to serve the church in the Diocese of Sault Ste. Marie. His enthusiastic support for Latin American missions, and his vocal and visible identification with various progressive causes during the period after the Second Vatican Council have contributed to his national and international reputation as a genuinely liberal church leader. But unlike Emmett, Alex has never been accused of unchecked ambition.

Competitive from the beginning, but more particularly since they entered the Grand Seminary (Grand Séminaire de Montréal), during which time they were separated by only a year, the brothers struggled for supremacy in athletics, studies and social acceptance. It was playful, good-willed competition, but serious for all that. Emmett plays for keeps, even with his brother.

But in spite of the banter, rivalry and intransigence, the family has always performed a pivotal role in the life of each of the Carter members as they have fought to define themselves in relationship to it. Tom and Minnie have always ruled supreme, but they have not been without disappointment and trouble. The four who entered the professional life of the church have enjoyed a stability, success and happiness that eluded the others, but the parents are indicted by no one. The vocations of Alex, Emmett and their sisters owe much to the robust faith of their father and the common-sense devoutness of their mother, but no one was forced; all the children, in the end, chose their own paths.

Outside the immediate family there was one person in particular who had a formative influence on bringing Alex's and Emmett's clerical vocations to fruition: the indefatigable Monsignor, Gerald J. McShane, pastor of St. Patrick's Church and indisputable powerhouse of the English-speaking Catholic community in Montreal. McShane was not a patient man, but he was full of ideas and energy, in the style of the typical Boston or New York Irish pastor, and he had links with the influential civil and ecclesiastical administrations, which he used to enviable advantage. A priest of the Sulpician community (Société de St. Sulpice), a French foundation dedicated to the education of priests, McShane had a vested interest in fostering vocations. In addition, a staunch hibernophile with a superb command of French, McShane was determined to augment the negligible ranks of the English-speaking clergy in Montreal. Despite his love of things Irish, McShane was of solid Montreal pedigree and counted a mayor of the city among his ancestors.

He was a builder, a supporter of Irish causes (although less Republican in his sympathies than some would have liked) and an avid and persuasive recruiter. Alex remembers: "He would come into the classroom at St. Pat's elementary to talk, with informal authority, about the priesthood. He would talk in stirring terms about the need for priests in Montreal and the need to serve the people. After his presentation, he would stay on for about twenty minutes or so chatting with us and then would conclude by telling us that he was going over to the principal's office and that if any of the boys was interested in the priesthood he was invited to come to the office and talk with him."

McShane was not only a talker and a builder, he was also a liturgist of high style. At an early age the Carter boys were part of the deftly-orchestrated liturgies of St. Patrick's Church. Alex Carter remembers those times in St. Patrick's Church: "We were both altar boys and members of the chancel choir. Father McShane had a great love of church music and was a fine impresario or master of ceremonies. He was very exacting when it came to the rubrics, and he demanded absolute neatness in appearance. He would check our hair, fingernails and shoes. He would tolerate no sloppiness in either appearance or performance. The chancel choir boys were dressed in something approximating a little evening suit, like they wore in English public schools, such as Eton. We would process down the main aisle at the beginning of high mass, four in a row, singing and carrying ourselves with dignity, ending up assembled in the choir loft with the men's choir. McShane had very fine musicians, organists and music directors, and as a consequence, along with his flair for the majestic style, he drew large numbers to church, including many from outside St. Pat's boundaries, indeed, in those pre-ecumenical days, outside Roman Catholic boundaries. His success assured him enemies as well as admirers. But that wouldn't trouble him greatly."

As influential as McShane was in encouraging the Carter vocations — and there can be no doubt that his effect on Emmett's sense of liturgy was determinative — the prime mover behind the Carter clerical careers was Minnie. Devout and resolute, she knew what was demanded of her by her faith, tradition and sex, and she gave generously. But she was no pawn; she was the power broker in the family. She was decisive and firm, though always welcoming. One old friend of the family thinks of her as inseparable from Emmett: "Mary Carter was very Irish. She wasn't far off a hundred when she died. Three times in years before that the family had been warned her time had come, but she held on. She was never big. By the end she was only a little snip but she had all her faculties. She had piercing eyes and what seemed at first a naive view of life. She was sharp but generous, witty but kind. Father Emmett is like her in that he is always aware of who is around and what they're thinking and needing. Oh, she ruled that household from her kitchen and through the tone that she set at the table. There was always room there, and good food and talk. I never knew her husband but they said he was straight as an arrow, the man who always led the St. Patrick's Day Parade in Montreal. She loved good talk and repartee. She cared particularly for nurses. She thought they had a hard life. She knew I was lonely and hungry and she took me in, and a lot of others too. So I never really separate Father Emmett from his mother. . . ."[6]

Minnie was far from indifferent to the careers of all her children, but she took a special interest in the lives of those who had chosen to be professional religious, and especially in the lives of her priest sons. Alex Carter has no doubt about the human source of his own vocation to the priestly life: "My vocation goes right back to mother. Definitely. Mother was a very religious woman and devoted to the Church. And she had an immense devotion to Our Lord and Our Lady. She taught us our prayers and we didn't learn the basics about religion in school. We learned them before we went, right from her."

For his part, Emmett was destined from an early age to embrace the celibate life. Unlike their elder sister Mae, whose call to the sisterhood came in her late twenties and after many friendships with young men, neither Alex nor Emmett dated in any regular way. With respect to Emmett, Mae does remember an attractive young woman named Andrée Champagne, whom the Carters would see at their summer home on Fourteen Island Lake and "who had eyes for Emmett." Alex, too, recalls a young French lass, Mimi Clement: "I don't think it ever got serious," he adds. "It was just one of those crazy summer things. We all hung around together. But Mimi and Emmett were a little thicker than we were. They did a lot of what may have been flirtation between the two of them, but there was never anything very serious, to tell you the truth."

Alex explains that there were parties at the Carter home and he recalls how the brothers went out to typical adolescent male and female get-togethers. "We knew some girls, but we were never deeply involved with anybody. We knew the kids, and you had fun with them, but we were oriented towards the priesthood and that could put a damper on that sort of thing." Lifelong friend and neighbourhood chum Charles Wayland reflects on the question: "Funny, you know, I never thought of that before, but I can't recall either of them going out on a date. They always had the priesthood in mind, from the time they used to say mass at the age of twelve with the apple juice their mother used to give them instead of wine."

At the drop of a biretta, she would entertain any number of priests and seminarians with food, accommodation and commentary. Alex and Emmett could always rely on her to welcome their clerical peers, and although her hospitality was never limited to the ranks of the clergy, they were the ones who had unrivalled prominence. Still, for all her Irish reverence, she could quickly deflate the self-important and the pompous. "When Alex was named a bishop," wrote John Brehl of *The Sunday Star*, "Emmett called their mother, didn't give her the news, but told her he was bringing a distinguished visitor for dinner. When he and Alex got to her home, she said 'Where's the guest?' 'Alex is the guest,' Emmett said. 'Humph,' she sniffed. 'Some distinguished guest.' Emmett told her the news. 'Well,' she said, 'that's good.' She turned back to the stove. 'Do you want onions with your steak?' she asked."[7]

With a strong taste for the ascetic running in her veins and with a keen love for humility supporting her Irish soul, Minnie would naturally downplay what her hidden heart exalted. And she would do it again on the occasion of Emmett's own episcopal nomination. Brehl described it this way: "Emmett went to tell her that he'd been named auxiliary bishop of London, Ontario. 'That's nice,' she said. Then she pondered. Alex was in North Bay, Irene in Kingston, Mae in Vancouver. 'Does this mean you'll have to leave Montreal?' 'Well, yes, Mother.' 'That does it,' Minnie declared. 'This is the last son I am giving to the Church.' At the time, she was 83, and Emmett was 49."

If Emmett has emulated his mother's firmness of character, her wit and her steadiness of purpose (though not her piety), he has learned from his father the value of quiet fortitude and solid conviction and the role of race memory. Tom Carter knew the price of honour and paid it. Each one of the Carter children knew how much it cost their

father to establish a typographical union at the *Montreal Daily Star* —
he was fired; and each one of the Carter children knew that the tall,
bony, athletic Irish Canadian who was Tom Carter carried this very
disappointment and shame with characteristic dignity. His fight for
justice was a lonely one, for very few of his fellow workers publicly
supported his efforts to unionize. His father's isolated stance left
Emmett Carter with a permanent impression of the man's nobility.

The Carter family were, and the surviving members (including the
next generation) remain, a tightly knit unit. They were taught to make
their own fun, and they did — with sports, music, cards, vigorous
banter and spirited debate. Whether at home in downtown Montreal
or at their cottage at Fourteen Island Lake, the Carter family were
one, but not indivisible and not without strains.

Emmett learned early how to hold his own in a household full of
stubborn folk. He could charm his sisters — clad in short pants and
standing on a table, he would sing endearingly for Irene's religious
community — and he could astound them all with his academic and
physical prowess. As the youngest child, and his mother's favourite,
Emmett knew from the beginning the perks of privilege, and he
learned how to wield his power of persuasion and charm with promis-
ing efficiency.

He was destined for great things. He knew it and so did Minnie.

CHAPTER TWO

Seminarian and Newman Chaplain

For Minnie Carter's youngest, pomp and celebration were inseparable aspects of an Irish home and an Irish church, which together were to become father to the man. But neither hearth nor church could in itself guarantee the heady pilgrimage from the Montreal of Emmett Carter's youth and early manhood to the halls of honour and prestige which awaited him in Orange Ontario. Honour and prestige must be forged in the smithy of lived experience, and that experience began in earnest for Emmett in the classrooms of Montreal College and the Grand Seminary, then stretched inexorably into the educational apostolate that consumed his priesthood. Indeed, when young Emmett left father and mother for Montreal College as one of Father Gerald McShane's boys in pursuit of the priesthood, he was responding to a call destined to leave an indelible mark on the country's two largest provinces.

McShane, who was then one of the few, if not the only English-speaking Sulpician priest in Montreal, advised the Carter family that Emmett's ambition for priestly ordination could be realized in Montreal only if he were to receive a French education, and the sooner the better. Hence, Emmett began his secondary schooling at the age of thirteen in the *cours primaire complémentaire* at Montreal College as an anglophone in a French classical school system. Not knowing a word of French, he followed his schoolmates from class to class, doing his best to absorb what he could. In fact, he began his educational odyssey at Montreal College with a dozen or more English-speaking young men, though their numbers were quickly decimated, since the rigours of the challenge proved too much for most of them. But Emmett had always been a gifted student, so with the help of Bishop Lawrence Whelan, who was then a deacon at the College, and by dint of hard work and native intelligence, he was rewarded with the top prize in a compulsory province-wide French composition contest, beating out all the province's college students, both French and English. Later, he scored among the top few students in the French examinations at the University of Montreal. Indeed, Emmett's francophone companion and English tutor from the Grand Seminary, his lifelong friend Cardinal Paul Grégoire, stresses Emmett Carter's impressive academic acumen, noting in particular his remarkable achievement in placing first in the French composition contest. Emmett's academic accomplishments also continue to be sources of admiration for his grade-school and neighbourhood chum from Hôtel de Ville Avenue, Charles Wayland, who recalls how Emmett was inevitably the first to escape the confines of class detentions through virtually instant recall of poetry, whose memorization the teacher had prescribed as the price for individual liberation — this in spite of the fact that Emmett himself was likely to have been the original cause of the detention. Clearly, Emmett was a competitive lad who always loved a challenge — in the classroom, on the athletic field or wherever the opportunity presented itself. And in the years ahead challenges were to present themselves with persistent frequency.

This man, who was ultimately to become the most powerful cleric in Canada, was inheritor of a complex fabric of suppositions and personal convictions, some of which he imbibed with his mother's milk, some of which he received from his dynamic pastor, Father McShane, some of which he assimilated in the process of his formal education at Montreal College, the Grand Seminary and the University of Montreal, and some of which were shaped by his educational apostolate.

While studying in the Grand Seminary, Emmett Carter refined his already established interests and pursued new ones. As Emmett's brother Alex (now retired from his bishopric of Sault Ste. Marie) recalls, the English-speaking boys at the Grand were a group of about thirty in a throng of perhaps three hundred French-speaking seminarians. Even though seminary officials formally stressed bilingualism by twinning individuals from one language group with a linguistic mentor from the other for a twice-weekly walk around the Seminary's "mile" (in fact a half-mile of wooden pathway), it was inevitable that the English-speaking lads from Canada and the United States should become very close, and indeed, should be frequent recipients of mother Minnie Carter's boundless hospitality. "Talk about racism or segregation," says Alex. "The English boys all went about together, so we were much more involved with the Americans. We were a kind of clique with them at the seminary."

These early friendships with U.S. clerics were to be the first of many; the lesson concerning the two founding cultures was one of many still to come. So Emmett played hockey, baseball, tennis and football with his colleagues from the United States, enjoying the athletic challenge which is still a vital part of an aging heartbeat. Emmett excelled at sports, as he did at his studies. Academically, Emmett the seminarian achieved grades which friend and colleague Cardinal Paul Grégoire confirms have likely never been topped at the Grand. His older brother Alex, who was just one year ahead academically because of a two-year interlude in a commercial school, was himself an able athlete and an academic of some note, but where circumstance allowed them to compete it was usually Emmett, Alex admits, who carried off the laurels.

The Grand was pre-eminently, of course, an educational institution in the preconciliar mode. Charles Wayland recalls the Grand's reputation for culinary austerity and blames the spartan nature of the Seminary's lifestyle for Emmett's brief bout with tuberculosis. As a seminary in the traditional mode, the Grand stressed discipline, relative seclusion, spiritual formation (though Cardinal Carter tends to dwell little on this aspect, as, indeed, does his brother Alex) and theological comprehension, with a special emphasis on the teaching of the thirteenth-century philosopher-theologian, Saint Thomas Aquinas, the Angelic Doctor whom Pope Leo XIII declared Patron Saint of Catholic Schools and whose philosophy has traditionally been the backbone of priestly intellectual education.

Emmett had, of course, been introduced to Thomas Aquinas at Montreal College, especially in the two years before he obtained his baccalaureate in 1933 at the age of twenty-one. At the Grand, the teaching of Thomas Aquinas had often been a process of infusion rather than of inquiry — Emmett recalls with some delight Alex Carter's challenging a somewhat flustered instructor who was more used to lecturing than debating; for his part, in the class of one professor who was in the habit of merely "narrating on the textbook," Emmett took to reading his Aquinas in advance, and bringing his *Summa theologica* to class with him, a habit which so impressed — or intimidated — the professor that Emmett got very good marks: "The professor was intelligent enough to recognize that I knew what I was talking about." Whether it was the inspiration provided by some of the more talented instructors or his own intellectual curiosity and boundless initiative, as a young seminarian Emmett had found in the philosopher saint much to be admired. In particular, Emmett saw in Aquinas a disciplined mind, whose formal theological cut and thrust had developed an intellectual system that attracted him both for its form and for its insights — it is a system whose appeal for Carter has not diminished with the passage of time.

Aquinas's epistemology, for example, was to have an abiding influence on Carter the educator. Aquinas's theory of knowledge and understanding, which derives in part from Aristotle's observation that there is nothing in the intellect which is not first in the senses, is echoed in Canon Carter's pedagogical theory, particularly in his theory on the teaching of catechetics. Hence his stress on audio-visual teaching aids and the power of imitation, especially imitation of biblical and modern heroes with whom students might readily identify. Similarly, Aquinas's pedagogical style — the objection and response format of the *Summa theologica*, itself an imitation of the socratic method and the medieval debate form — became for Carter the pedagogical method to be adapted to the modern classroom. One should lead a student to comprehension, not smother that student with rote memorization.

But more than anything, it was Thomas Aquinas's intellectual discipline that Carter found fascinating. Aquinas's is a discipline surely to be admired, but it is a discipline which in western christian society has often been over-emphasized to the exclusion of the emotional side of human nature, a makeup which Aristotle and Aquinas defined in terms of the rational and the animal (*animal rationale*). This oversight, Carter agrees, has too often led to a lack of appreciation for the sensitive and emotive properties of humankind. Carter would not likely place the blame for this at the feet of Thomas Aquinas, however. In fact, there are not a few who lament the overemphasis on the intellectual and the underdevelopment of the emotional in the Cardinal's own makeup. Nor is it an issue of which Carter himself is unaware — he does take seriously his own psychological theory concerning self-realization and self-understanding. He recalls his own counselling as a young priest, noting that he was trained to test ideas, to be challenged by them, and he appreciates the possibility that he may have tended to the rational rather than the emotional: those who had come to him for counselling "wanted more of an emotional feel or a spiritual feel and, of course, I was probably formed the other way." One ought not, however, to overstate the case. Those of us who have heard his voice break and have seen the tears come to his eyes during discussions of the injustices done to Montreal Archbishop Joseph Charbonneau, the man whom he has admired perhaps more than any other, can attest to the existence of a genuinely sensitive side to this man who so values reason.

This elevation of the intellectual over the emotional in the writing of Thomas Aquinas also caused the Angelic Doctor to elevate the male over the female in his ordered scheme of things, this in imitation of his pagan mentor, the philosopher, Aristotle. Thomas Aquinas's adaptation of the Aristotelian principle that one should move from the known to the unknown is wholly and reasonably accepted by Emmett Carter; on the question of the known with respect to women, the models are domestic and intellectual. For her part, Minnie Carter was by no means Aquinas's stereotypical passive female, but she was before all else a wife, a mother, and a devout Roman Catholic. Emmett's early appreciation of women derives from this restricted personal, traditionally religious, and studied philosophical experience.

Given his thomistic temperament and his personal background, it is not surprising, for example, that in a 1942 address to the Ladies' Section of the Montreal Catholic Teachers' Association he should anticipate the gratuitous observation the Council Fathers at Vatican II offered in their conciliar "Message to Women." Emmett Carter observed in 1942: "Your share is to save mankind." In 1965 the Council Fathers implored: "Women of the entire universe, whether Christian or non-believing, you to whom life is entrusted at this grave moment in history, it is for you to save the peace of the world."[1] Such a view seems to originate not so much in Thomas Aquinas's writings as in the medieval and abiding Marian teachings, which depict Mary as mediator, the Mediatrix, a view likely deriving from Carter's mother's and from Sulpician devotions to Our Lady, and expressed in such obvious sources as the oft-repeated final admonition of the Ave Maria: "Pray for us sinners now and at the hour of our death." Naturally enough, therefore, Emmett Carter's early personal files do contain numerous examples of the Marian homily so characteristic of the 1940s and 1950s. The Virgin Mary, Minnie, Mae, Margaret, the

Sulpicians at the Grand and Thomas Aquinas all combined to shape Emmett Carter's enduring understanding of womanhood.

Although an enchantment with thomistic philosophy and a devotion to the Virgin Mary were thoroughly rooted in Carter's spiritual makeup by the time he was a young priest, he has never shied away from an intellectual challenge or the need to re-evaluate a philosophical concept when faced with the practical challenge of lived experience and a clear reading of the signs of the times. In a 1951 reflection on the spirituality of marriage, for example, he modified Aquinas's philosophical position that man is perfected without woman, whereas woman's perfection requires male participation. Carter does not adhere slavishly to Aquinas's every word; rather, he is wont to reshape Aquinas in light of contemporary insights. His statement, therefore, does perfectly reflect Aquinas's teachings on complementarity which have become the touchstone of contemporary Roman Catholic thinking with respect to the relative role of male and female. "Man," Emmett Carter said, "will always see the world in male fashion, woman in female. A true view of the world comprises both manners of seeing it; men and women are two complementary beings made to be identified one with the other. Man is a whole as a person, but as a male he depends upon the woman from the strict point of view of personal perfection. Man and woman mutually beg of each other the fullness of their life. For the human spirit to attain the sum total of its knowledge, it must have at its disposal a double instrument, the human body with its diversity of sex."[2] These ideas clearly inform Carter's attitudes towards women still, and are to be found at the heart of his present philosophical assumptions concerning sexuality, though he appears now to have become sensitive and sympathetic to the plight of women in the church and in society. Over the years, that phrase "beg of each other" has been amplified in the Cardinal's thinking on the testy question of the relationship between complementarity and equality.

Emmett emerged from the Grand, therefore, thoroughly grounded in the traditional teachings of his church and personally equipped to face the challenges that lay before him. On May 22, 1937, he was ordained a Roman Catholic priest in the Basilica of St. James in Montreal by Bishop Deschamps. A few days later, on May 30, 1937, he returned to the church of his youth, Father McShane's St. Patrick's, where the homilist for the occasion was, propitiously, Father J.J. Stanford, Inspector of Schools — an appropriate choice for the newly ordained priest who was destined to become the father of English-Catholic education in Quebec.

Indeed, it was only a few months after Emmett Carter's ordination to the ministerial priesthood that Archbishop Georges Gauthier summoned him from the pastoral and idyllic solitude of his little Irish parish in the Laurentians — St. Hippolyte de Kilkenny on Fourteen Island Lake — to announce an irrevocable shift in the young priest's vision of service. Emmett Carter's long-time ambitions to minister pastorally to his people as a simple Quebec curate were neither the will of his bishop nor of his God, whom Father Carter understood to be speaking through the person of his bishop. Even though he felt unworthy and ill-equipped, Emmett accepted the position of Ecclesiastical Inspector of English Schools in Montreal, a challenge which sent him scurrying to his grammar books, to his catechism and, ultimately, back to the University of Montreal where he was eventually to receive a Ph.D. in Education. In fact, but for the brief respite at St. Hippolyte de Kilkenny, the nearest Emmett Carter ever came to the pastoral care he had always assumed would be his life's work was when he was appointed chaplain to the Newman Club at McGill University in 1941.

The Newman Club on North American university campuses provides an intellectual, liturgical, spiritual and social base for Roman Catholic students enrolled in non-Catholic universities. Carter's chaplaincy, therefore, opened intellectual and pastoral avenues which were particularly appealing to him. While serving as chaplain to the Newman Club, he was able to exercise the pastoral function of priestly counselling, preaching, role modelling, premarital counselling — and the performing of weddings themselves. The limitations of space at the Newman Club meant that wedding celebrations always required the cooperation of local pastors for the use of their churches, cooperation not always eagerly granted by pastors with their own instincts for the territorial imperative. Still, the Newman Club proved to be a fulfilling and effective apostolate. Indeed, influential converts like the Russian count Robert Keyserlingk look back on the young priest's chaplaincy work with fondness.

But the appointment cost the youthful priest the friendship of his childhood mentor, Father Gerald McShane. Since the influential and ubiquitous McShane had taken the Newman Club under his wing and housed it at St. Patrick's, Carter assumes, rightly no doubt, that it was McShane who had prevailed upon Archbishop Joseph Charbonneau to offer the position to him. Emmett Carter and Gerald McShane soon had a falling out when the younger priest refused to take up a collection among the members of the Newman Club who were, after all, university students and by definition short on cash. McShane responded to such insubordination by turfing Emmett and his Club out of his hall. This forced the chaplain to find new quarters, which he did, in the Convent of the Sacred Heart, where his sister Mae was Mistress General. After the Archbishop formalized the transfer and McShane was informed by his youthful protege, McShane huffed off with a "Have it your way then," and the two rarely spoke to each other again.

Practical things also had to be done if one were to minister effectively to the intellectual youth of McGill. Emmett Carter was convinced, for example, that the wearing of a cassock on the city streets was a barrier between him and the people he was serving. As a result, he argued his case with Archbishop Charbonneau that he be allowed to abandon the cassock while outside the walls of his home. The Archbishop was reluctant to grant the request but ultimately did so — for the English priests. By the time Charbonneau's successor, Archbishop Paul-Émile Léger, inherited the bishopric, there was one rule for the English and one for the French; it was a situation which Léger did not like. Emmett advised the newly appointed archbishop that if he forced the English priests back into their cassocks, he would lose their acceptance. And so, ultimately, in a complete reversal of his original position, Léger issued an edict that *no* priest, French or English, was permitted to wear his cassock on the streets of Montreal.

Then there was the question of housing, since the Convent of the Sacred Heart could ensure only short-term accommodation at best. With the help of Archbishop Charbonneau and some of the friends whom Carter had cultivated on the McGill University campus, the Newman Club was ultimately in a position to purchase a house on McGill College Avenue. His surroundings were not as plush as those his counterpart enjoyed in Toronto, but at least the Newman Club had a home. The real pastoral work could now begin, since there were quarters for pastoral counselling, and a place to welcome the young men returning from the Second World War, eager for education and religious insight. Emmett undertook this pastoral work in addition to all the other responsibilities he had accumulated, but it gave him pastoral contact and another ear to the educational wall. It also put him in touch with other socially active religious groups, such as the Young Christian Workers, for whom, the retired bishop of Antigonish William Power recalls, Emmett Carter provided rent-free office space. The position put him into direct contact with Newman people in Ontario as well, since the national association of Newman Clubs was formed during his tenure; he served as its national chaplain on three separate occasions. Carter maintained the connection with Newman House until 1956, by which time it had all become too much, and he decided to resign.

If his experiences at the Grand had helped to form the successful Newman chaplain, they had also helped to shape Emmett Carter's sense that theology was not something merely to be contemplated, but something to be put into practice. This perception of the practical nature of theology flowed naturally from lessons learned early in life from a father more inclined to the active than the contemplative life, and it was expressly reinforced by his Sulpician instructors at the seminary. The practical sense of Sulpician spirituality, combined with the French cry of Catholic Action — *voir, juger, agir* (see, judge, act) — helped to make Emmett a no-nonsense, practical, down-to-earth man of God who is no contemplative, but who is the consummate churchman able and willing to get things done for the church he had eagerly embraced as his lifelong spouse at so early an age.

Emmett Carter is among the first to admit that seminary teaching in homiletics was and is woefully inadequate: "I have this theory," he says, "that lay people will be spared the pain of purgatory — they've served their time listening to sermons." His own skill as a homilist is legendary, however. It seems to come naturally, perhaps sharpened at a dinner table which family friend Charles Wayland has termed "a debating society".[3] Carter's sermon format is in the best tradition of the fourth-century Church Father and master of rhetoric, Augustine of Hippo, and of Alanus de Insulis, the pre-eminent twelfth-century theorist of effective homiletic form. The message was, and is, quite simple: make your presentation pleasing, and adapt your presentation to the interests of your audience.

Carter's conviction that the teaching of theology could be simultaneously enjoyable and effective was naturally fused with the exercising of his Newman chaplaincy in the catechetical sketches he called his "Screwball Letters". There is no surer sign of Emmett Carter's innate gift to sense the interest of his audience and to shape his message accordingly than the series of "Screwball Letters" which he wrote as chaplain of the Newman Club at McGill University in the early 1940s. Imitating the style, tone and form of C.S. Lewis's *Screwtape Letters*, Carter fashioned a series of catechetical lessons for the young, based on the Ten Commandments. The tone is lighthearted — naive and ironic banter between a demonic uncle named Sulphur and his inquisitive nephew, a neophyte tempter, called Screwball. The method is not only imitative, but exploratory. "The Screwball Letters" are crafted in the tradition of an author whom Emmett Carter clearly admired, but the letters are also wholly in keeping with the biographical and captivating biblical exegesis for the young which would be at the heart of his pedagogical theory. And Alanus de Insulis would have nodded approval at the absolute adaptation of material to audience in lines such as Uncle Sulphur's advice to his untutored tempter concerning the sanctity of the sabbath: "From our point of view, the best part of Sunday is Saturday-night. Your student doesn't have lectures on Sunday, and like all his kind, he can easily be persuaded that Sunday is made for the express purpose of sleeping off the effects of the night before. Sunday is made or broken on Saturday evening. Get him out at the right type of party (some of those frat parties with the lights out are perfect), with the right kind of girl . . ."[4]

Although "The Screwball Letters" are first and foremost an example of Carter's effective pedagogy, they also provide insights into the man who became Cardinal Archbishop of Toronto during the 1980s and '90s. One might note, for example, Sulphur's advice: "You see all authority holds together. Break it in one place and you break it everywhere." Words of the consummate churchman with unflinching commitment to the institutional church. And then there are the attitudes towards women, attitudes which seem to ascribe to the female sex the Eve-like characteristics so prevalent in western christian tradition. Here is Sulphur castigating his novice: "And now to come to the point, what have you done to secure the downfall of that young fool you have been assigned to damn? . . . You poor stupid dolt! Don't you realize that he would have managed that without any help from you? That girl he has been going out with is doing a far better job than you are." Or there is the advice on how to distract the young man who actually makes his way into the church: "Then when you have him well out of hearing of most of what goes on, and perhaps out of sight of it, distract him with the irrelevant things around him. Pretty girls, of course, are the best stock in trade and you won't have to work hard at it either. And from the back of the church they'll all look pretty. . . ." Not very flattering stuff, though the observations do suggest the unquestioning assimilation of a tradition which was still prevalent at the time.

In "The Screwball Letters" there are also interesting lessons concerning the relationship between politics and business, lessons in which Sulphur advises with satiric, serpentine tongue: "Above all you must teach your man that in business and politics there is an entirely different code of honour. The rule here is 'every man for himself' and a premium for strength and cleverness. For example, making big profits and paying low wages is not to be compared with vulgar stealing." Strong and courageous sentiments in Duplessis's Quebec, a society overtly built on political patronage. Sentiments Carter is still not averse to airing formally even before Toronto's corporate elite and many of his good friends.

And there is here, too, an implicit attack on sociology — one of Carter's favourite targets — and a plea for universal principles of right and wrong, of justice and injustice. Hence, Sulphur advises his bungling protege to approach the stupid dolt of a student to whom he is assigned and to "try to convince him that it is old-fashioned to talk about objective truth, or absolute principles, or certitude. All that has been debunked by the newer sciences." The measure of the satire and the nature of the psychological approach are relatively transparent, but the tone and the tack are as effective as C.S. Lewis's. In "The Screwball Letters" we have at work a fine teacher, an effective writer, a traditional churchman, an individual with modern attitudes towards the expression of doctrine and its applicability to social situations.

Even as a young man, Emmett Carter exhibited an interesting combination of traditionalism and liberalism. He has always felt that "the thomistic structure is irreplaceable," but he was also ready to convert Sigmund Freud for the modern christian. As for Emmett Carter's oratorical talents, one writer observed of him upon his leaving Quebec: "Noted for his flashing wit, sharp humour and catalogue memory, Bishop Emmett is regarded as one of the most eloquent speakers in Quebec, and his Irish ancestry is abundantly evident throughout all his discourses."[5]

The keen intellect, quick wit, outspoken manner and spontaneous sense for the dramatic that came naturally to Emmett would continue to prove effective tools in his various ministerial positions. Public signs of Carter's inherited affection for the blarney appear as early as March 17, 1941, in an item entitled "Irish Humour is Analyzed" in the *Montreal Star*. The title for the young priest's St. Patrick's Day address to the Xavier Guild was "Smiling Irish Eyes", an address in which he spoke of laughter at the expense of others, laughter at one's own expense and laughter in the face of stress. Interesting analysis this, one which was put to the test in a series of letters to the editor of *The Montreal Beacon* at about the same time. Carter's *Beacon* letter is fashioned with a rapier-like wit, which Thomas Aquinas would have admired. That letter opens with a light-hearted *ad ridendum* argument, banter intended to disarm the opposition, and it then develops a series of thomistic distinctions and subdistinctions. Replying to a correspondent who had misinterpreted his lamentations over the inadequacy of speech training available for those aspiring to the priesthood, Father Carter begins his rebuttal: "A letter of mine commenting on your now famous — or infamous — editorial on Speech seems to have aroused considerable animation not to say condemnation. I only hope that the circulation of your paper has been stimulated as much as that of your readers. Joking aside. . . ." Emmett Carter loves to play with the double meanings buried in words, and he is not above poking fun at himself as a lead-in to a serious discussion. It is a knack he still possesses, one much envied by his brother, Alex, and one typical of the skilled orator wanting to put his audience at ease. It is a characteristic reminiscent, for example, of Carter's opening quip in an address he gave at the University of Waterloo while accepting an honorary degree at the May 25, 1989, convocation. Struggling through a serious bout of influenza and much slowed by the effects of a stroke, the Cardinal walked slowly into Convocation Hall and equally slowly to the microphone. His opening jibe, "I used to be the quickest gun in the west," was the tell-tale sign of a man whose body is letting him down, but whose mind is as fleet as it was in 1941. With that, he immediately took command of his audience and never relinquished his hold. By poking fun at himself, he de-fused what must have been, for him at least, a stressful situation.

The responsibilities attached to the Newman appointment were only a small part of Carter's Montreal professional life, which grew more active as his energy and his ability attracted the attention, confidence and gratitude of his superiors. Archbishop Joseph Charbonneau, for example, named him assistant director of the English section of Catholic Action in 1943, and director of the newly formed English-speaking Secretariat of Catholic Action in 1944; in 1948, the Archbishop recognized the exceptional talent exhibited by his energetic young priest, appointing him to the prestigious Montreal Catholic School Commission, a position Carter was to hold for most of his time in Montreal.

Ecclesiastical and civil honours were to follow as naturally and as lavishly as the numerous ecclesiastical and civil postings entrusted to the youthful Carter. On January 30, 1953, Paul-Émile Léger, who was now a cardinal archbishop, announced Emmett Carter's elevation to the position of Canon of the Basilica of Our Lady of the World in Montreal, and he was invested as such in the following February; in the same year he was honoured by the provincial government with the Medal of the Order of Scholastic Merit of the Province of Quebec; and in 1958 he received the Department of Education's most distinguished award, Commander of Scholastic Merit of the Province of Quebec. And, finally, there came the short-lived appointment as Rector of St. Lawrence College in Ste. Foy, Quebec City, where he was to be director of a fledgling high school in need of a gifted and steady steersman. It was an appointment destined to last only a few months, since Rome had other plans for a man of Emmett Carter's ability.

CHAPTER THREE

Educator and Theorist: Carter the Writer

Carter's principal early contribution to his church and to Quebec society was in the field of education. It was an apostolate which began shortly after Carter left the seminary, when Archbishop Georges Gauthier summoned his newly ordained priest to inform him that he was about to become Ecclesiastical Inspector of Montreal's English-language schools. In retrospect, one might cynically label the appointment clericalism, since the posting was to a senior administrative position and the appointee was, by his own admission, wholly unqualified to assume such a post. "I didn't know the front door from the back door. I really began on a very pragmatic basis. I learned the programme and how things should be in the schools. To some degree that meant that I had to learn my way by going into classes and seeing what was going on. It really was an inductive process. And when I saw the problems, then I started to work on the solution on the higher levels, such as the foundation of the teachers' college and the foundation of the Thomas More Institute. So that you went from the known to the unknown, if you want to put it in that theoretical way."

There is no doubt, however, that Father Emmett Carter was the right man for the job at hand. With enthusiasm, dedication and innate ability, the young priest set out to learn his job and earn his stripes. He began by studying basic grammar, by reviewing the teaching of catechetics and by returning to school. When he had finished, the teaching scene in English Quebec was altered forever, and the teaching of catechetics had assumed an entirely new shape. Cardinal Carter cannot and does not take sole credit for all of this, but at the same time, he was clearly the principal actor on Quebec's English-speaking educational stage during the 1940s and 1950s.

Talking with characteristic candour, Canon Emmett Carter pointed out to a Montreal journalist that his youth and clerical status were, in fact, assets rather than liabilities in his ability to achieve what he had for Montreal's English-speaking Roman Catholics. In an interview shortly before leaving Montreal, Carter said: "I was able to do all this for a great many reasons . . . none of which I can claim as individual triumphs or tribute to my then untutored abilities. I was 25 when ordained and immediately plunged into the problems of education with the brashness of the young. I had no fear of loss of security, but enjoyed the independence of being a man of the cloth, aware that the worst that could happen to me would be a transfer to a parish or some other duties with the Church. Unlike others who might have tried to accomplish these things, I was not dependent for my job or security on education officials."[1]

When Father Emmett assumed his responsibilities as inspector of schools in 1937, no formal program was provided in Quebec for the training of teachers, the textbooks English-speaking students were using were rather literal translations of the French texts being studied by the French-speaking majority, and there were no standardized high school examinations, hence no university entrance equivalents. Emmett Carter and a group of dedicated English-speaking Quebec Catholics embarked on a course of action designed to set matters right.

Carter recalls the seriousness of the situation, noting that there were no Normal Schools for the English, only for the French. "And I could see," he reflects, "that these kids were coming out of high school and immediately passing a little examination which could have been passed in something like grade nine. And they were getting the [teacher's] certificate for that. So I made that my major project, and I gathered men around me — I say men accurately and purposely because women were not very strong at that time in terms of the power structure in Montreal Catholic schools. There was Jim Lyng and Michael McManus and Ed Wescott, who was the provincial inspector of schools, and one or two others. They used to meet in my office. It was almost clandestine in a way, because we were really plotting to rebuild the system. So I became sort of a stalking horse for the operation."

As Canon Carter explained in his *The Catholic Public Schools of Quebec*,[2] the distinction concerning separate schooling in Quebec was traditionally not along linguistic but religious lines, with the two governing bodies being a Protestant and a Catholic Committee, the latter consisting of the bishops with dioceses centred in the Province of Quebec, plus an equal number of lay Catholics. In order to effect change, therefore, Carter and his group did need the cooperation of the archbishop of Montreal and the predominantly French-speaking Catholic Committee. And so it was with the complete cooperation of Archbishop Gauthier and of the essentially French-speaking Catholic Committee of the Council of Education that provision was made in 1939 for an English-speaking section of the previously all-French-speaking Jacques Cartier Normal School.

So, with Carter barely two years into his term as inspector, Gauthier appointed him English-speaking Director of the École Normal Jacques Cartier, which was then located in Lafontaine Park. He was joined by Professors E.J. McCracken and E.-St.-J. Gough. "We got a couple of classrooms, and I was given a room. In fact, I took my meals there, and I lived at the school." Carter's "room" was a rather spartan garret, which has assumed its own legendary proportions, Alex being fond of recounting his brother's exploits as he scattered the rats from the kitchen, frightening them off with a piece of coal so he could approach the refrigerator for a midnight snack. It became his base, nonetheless, and he set out from there to visit all of the high schools in the area to explain to the fourth-year students the plans he was developing for a teachers' college.

In this circumstance, as in so many others, Emmett Carter showed himself to be a practical man of action. In order to make his rounds, for purposes of planning and of inspection, for example, he clearly needed a car at a time when clerics, as a matter of ecclesiastical discipline, were not permitted to own cars. Recognizing what was reasonable in the situation, Father Carter bought his car, parked it at the bottom of the hill leading to Archbishop Gauthier's palace and set out to explain his need to his superior. "Almost the first thing he said to me was 'You'll have to get a car.' I said, 'I've got one. It's at the bottom of the hill.' 'Good,' he said. I had a sort of principle in dealing with bishops: I didn't ask for permission, but I let them know what I was doing. I still am the same way as far as Rome is concerned."

The first class to graduate from the two-year teachers' program numbered eight students, a small but influential cohort. The press coverage of the event registers Father Emmett Carter's note of satisfaction: "Their numbers are not very great, but the extent of their influence may be judged by the fact that already they are entrusted

with the teaching of over 300 children in Montreal schools." Jacques
Cartier admitted only male students, however, since the education of
prospective women teachers was entrusted to the communities of
teaching sisters. When, in 1952, an arrangement was made to involve
mutual cooperation, the student population swelled to 51 and the
stage was set for the provincial Council to establish a wholly integrated English-Catholic teachers' college, which it did on June 6,
1955, following the earlier recommendation of the Catholic Committee. The new college was named St. Joseph's, and it was so
successful that by the time Carter left Quebec in 1961, its annual
student population numbered over seven hundred; in fact, St.
Joseph's was then in the process of establishing satellite colleges in
Quebec City and Cross Point, Gaspé. Moreover, it was the only
English-language Catholic institution in Quebec awarding Bachelor
of Education degrees, a right which Carter had negotiated through
the University of Montreal. It is a tribute to Carter's organizational
skills that he was later invited to breathe life into the newly formed St.
Lawrence College in the Quebec City suburb of Ste. Foy.

The final chapter in the history of St. Joseph's was written when
the college was ultimately absorbed into the Faculty of Education at
McGill University after Carter had left for London, and the essential
work which inspired its inception had been formally assured a continuing existence.

The founding of St. Joseph's was not the only important step taken
by Emmett Carter and his dedicated band of English educational
visionaries. In 1937 the textbooks used by English-speaking Catholic
students in Quebec were often awkward translations of French texts
and reflected French cultural aspirations and assumptions. Early
efforts to correct the situation were formally rejected by the government of Quebec in 1938. Nonetheless, the group of educators per-
severed. By 1950 an entirely new program of studies for English-
speaking students, complete with their own textbooks, was in place.
As part of this drive at professionalization and accreditation, the
English-Catholic group had arranged for the establishing of standardized high school examinations by 1940, a standardization which was
monitored and perfected in succeeding years; at the same time, the
group approached McGill University for entrance equivalency and
were granted a five-year trial in 1940. The result was that Carter and
his band of enthusiasts succeeded in redesigning Roman Catholic

education for the English-speaking minority in Montreal over the short span of some fifteen years.[3]

During the same time period, Carter was involved in founding the Thomas More Institute for Adult Education in Montreal. The Institute grew out of the intellectual curiosity of a group of Montreal English Catholics — mostly of professional status and graduates of the Jesuits' Loyola College — who wondered if some structured form of post-baccalaureate education wasn't possible in Montreal. Acting on the invitation of several laypeople, Emmett Carter, Jesuit priest R. Eric O'Connor and Charlotte Tansey decided to seize the moment, and the Institute was born, albeit in modest surroundings at Montreal's D'Arcy McGee High School. At the outset, the curriculum was centred on the concept of the Great Books of the Western World as an organizational principle. In addition to the lectures which Carter himself provided over the years on thomistic thought, medieval philosophy and psychology, and classical and modern religious literature, Eric O'Connor taught mathematics, and other instructors were enticed to join the ranks as guest lecturers. Among them were the eminent transcendental-thomist, the Canadian Jesuit Bernard Lonergan, and Thomas Francoeur, an instructor of pedagogy from St. Joseph's Teacher's College.

When the University of Montreal agreed to accept the Institute's courses as university credits (this even though the university was not actually equipped to deal with English-language courses at the Institute's level), its success was assured, and its first graduates received their diplomas on May 17, 1948. So it was that Carter became the cofounder and the first president of The Thomas More Institute for Adult Education, the only permanent adult education institution in Canada at the time. When it was set up in 1946 it registered 90 students, but by January of 1963 their numbers had grown to almost 1,200. The Institute still stands as a monument to Carter's talents and his energy.

Given Carter's accumulating teaching and administrative experiences, his 1948 appointment to the Catholic School Commission of Montreal was a natural progression in a catapulting career in education. As an appointee of the Archbishop of Montreal, Father Carter was joining an educational administration that was hardly an example of responsible government in its strictest sense. For years, Quebec had been blatantly administered under a system of patronage which

Maurice Duplessis had perfected, though he had hardly invented it. It was a system which is meticulously detailed in Conrad Black's biographical tour de force, *Duplessis*. Emmett Carter describes the system in candid detail: "It has been pointed out that by Catholic tradition and historical experience the French Canadian is warned away from excessive state control. This remains true, but it is not without interest to note that psychologically, and perhaps racially, he tends a little to gravitate to autocracy. His attitude on democracy is not entirely that of his English-language compatriots. He is more obsequious to established power and by a psychological reversal more inclined to wield it despotically when he has attained it."[4] And the administration of education was not immune to this method of administering democratic power, nor had the church escaped entirely from its tentacles.

When Emmett was appointed to the Montreal Catholic School Commission, it consisted of seven members, four appointed by the Lieutenant Governor in Council — that is, Carter suggests, by Maurice Duplessis — and three by the archbishop of Montreal. By legislative stipulation, one of the four members appointed by the Lieutenant Governor in Council had to be English-speaking; for his part — "Charbonneau being Charbonneau," Carter insists — Archbishop Joseph Charbonneau reciprocated by appointing two French-speaking canons and one anglophone, who, in 1948, was Father Emmett Carter. However, the board was wholly appointed and, Carter asserts, it "was obviously structured for control by Duplessis." By way of demonstration, the Cardinal recalls how during the process of reviewing construction tenders for new schools he used to amuse himself by predicting to the clerical appointee seated beside him, "Well it's got to be so and so because all the others have their contracts." This was how the system worked. In the words of Carter: "I remember one time a contractor came in. He had got on with a little bit of help from his friends, and when he tendered he had the lowest tender. But when we examined it, we found out he had forgotten the windows. And they let him off the hook. They could have, and should have, stuck him for it, but they just let him withdraw his tender. So he came second. And it was funny, since it looked very honest because of the open tender — what with the board meetings and all the ceremony. They split the envelopes open to see what the tenders were. The representatives would all be there, but it was only people who had been approved in advance by Duplessis. We understood very well. There were three priests on the Commission and we knew we were there to accept the terms. We were not to interfere with the administration from that point of view, the political patronage we would call it today. And they, on the other hand, respected us when it came to questions of pedagogy, religion and the like. So it was all a bit of a saw off. We were all very happy with it."

Given the structure of things, however, the bishops of Quebec were also in a position to exercise no little influence. It was the Archbishop of Montreal, for example, who would give his personal approval to Carter's request for any given textbook; legally, the decision was made by the Catholic Commission, but the ground needed to be prepared in advance with the Archbishop. For their part, the actual discharging of the bishops' control of the hospitals and social services depended very much on their personal relationship with Duplessis. "I'm not excusing anybody. Maybe they should have fought him better than they did. But I could understand their position. Duplessis was ruthless when it came to handing out patronage. I have literally seen places where you can be driving on a road and the pavement comes to an end and then you're on gravel for the next five or ten miles, and then you're back on pavement. I remember hearing Duplessis himself saying, 'He wants a bridge? Let him make sure that his constituency votes for the Union Nationale next time.' I never did anything to help Duplessis, but at least we were on good terms. I'd let him tell his jokes, and we got along fine. And I was on good terms with the Superintendent of Education, Desaulniers. It was really through my friendship with Duplessis that I got the Normal School." Effective testing grounds for the educational debates and political manoeuvring that lay ahead in Orange Ontario.

Carter was also on the receiving end of manipulated interference. He recalls that a Doctor Ray Carson was appointed to the Montreal School Commission in an effort to cut Carter down to size. The move was engineered by some who felt the Canon was garnering too much power on the educational scene in Montreal. After a series of unpleasant exchanges and discourteous encounters, Dr. Carson made it clear that he was not going to support the slate of representatives being proposed by Carter. When the encounter had abated and the vote was taken, the dentist stood alone, soon to vanish into political oblivion. Carter recalls the anecdotal aftermath: "I was called in by Duplessis a little later. I knew very well it wasn't Duplessis's idea to summon me for an explanation; it was Eugene Ducet's, the president

of the Commission and a very good friend of mine. So I went down to
Quebec City and I was received by Duplessis in his office. Duplessis
said, 'I want you to know something. I think if Dr. Carson walked into
this office, I wouldn't know who he was. I don't know him at all.' And
then he told me who was behind it, thought I would not want to reveal
that individual's identity. The whole thing was definitely a cabal in
Montreal who obviously thought I had too much power." Carter
concludes the story by recollecting how a friend had gone to Dr.
Carson to have some work done on his teeth, and Carson had marvelled to him, "God, that guy Carter, has he got power!"

Emmett Carter had obviously earned his stripes as an educational
innovator in Montreal, and as a visible testimony to Canon Carter's
stature within Quebec, Omer-Jules Desaulniers, the Superintendent
of Education for the Province of Quebec, provided a preface to *The
Catholic Public Schools of Quebec* (1957), which he had encouraged
the Canon to write. The book not only contains a practical and useful
history of education in Quebec, but also provides a succinct summary
of Carter's developing educational philosophy — and incidentally of
his political and social sympathies. Throughout his text Carter lav-
ishes praise on the cooperative understanding he and his English-
speaking colleagues had received from the French-speaking majority,
though he also hinted that this might not always be so. Carter
observed that "the laudatory things the truth obliges us to say of the
French Canadian majority will not sit well with all. Nor is this a static
matter. Because we have enjoyed the sympathetic cooperation of the
authorities over the last twenty years does not mean that we shall
always do so."

The sensitivity which Carter expresses towards the French of
Quebec does not extend to relationships between the sexes. Quite
understandably, and quite appropriately, especially so in Catholic
Quebec before the Quiet Revolution, he uses Pope Pius XI's 1930
encyclical letter on the education of the young, *Divini illius magistri*,
as the basis for his own Catholic theory of education. Nonetheless,
Carter quietly amends the papal insistence that the church fills the
primary role as educator, suggesting instead (as post-conciliar educational theory would do beginning in 1965) that it is the Catholic and
Quebec position that "the right of the parent to exercise full responsibility over his children is perhaps the first and most dynamic

principle." On the other hand, Carter adopted without question the uncritical and unnuanced thomism which informed Pius XI's thinking, even when that thomism was no longer literally appropriate. Obviously, he was not alone in embracing the teachings of Pius XI and of Thomas Aquinas, but insofar as those teachings shaped his assumptions about maleness and femaleness and insofar as they may well affect his thinking even today, his acceptance of these attitudes is of some importance in appreciating the complexity of Cardinal Carter.

In his summary conclusion concerning the role of the family in education, for example, Canon Carter quotes Pius XI at some length, noting, in part, that "The Angelic Doctor, with his wonted clearness of thought and precision of style, says: 'The father according to the flesh has in a particular way a share in that principle which in a manner universal is found in God. . . . The father is the principle of generation, of education and discipline, and of everything that bears upon the perfecting of human life.' . . . That this right [of the family with respect to education] is inviolable St. Thomas proves as follows: 'The child is naturally something of the father . . . so by natural right the child, before reaching the use of reason, is under the father's care. . . .' "

Similarly, in introducing the question of the role of the state in education, Carter refers to papal authority influenced by the teachings of Thomas Aquinas. In this case, he repeats Pope Pius XI's reference to Pope Leo XIII: "The children are something of the father, and as it were an extension of the person of the father; and, to be perfectly accurate, they enter into and become part of the civil society, not directly by themselves, but through the family in which they were born." Aquinas's reflection of the male and female roles in the divinely ordained chain of being becomes Pope Leo XIII's, Pope Pius XI's and Gerald Emmett Carter's. It was the temper of the times.

And then, with a bewildering leap into the future characteristic of Emmett Carter's studied complexity, the final chapter of *The Catholic Public Schools of Quebec* sketches a thoroughly sensitive, biblically rooted, and psychologically insightful analysis of "A Catholic Philosophy of Education". It is in many ways an inspired and even impassioned chapter curiously succeeding an exposition of thoroughly outdated thomistic anthropology and an extended exposition of captivating but somewhat straightforward educational history. The contradictions are in many ways the measure of the man, a man who defies labels, a man who holds doggedly to matters of ecclesiastical tradition but who courageously explores the realms of possibilities in areas uncharted.

At the heart of the thesis is the anthropological definition which some twenty years later was to captivate the theological imagination of Pope John Paul II: for Canon Carter the divine intention, "Let Us make man to our own image and likeness," elevates the human being and makes of humankind a part of the Masterplan, "part of an intelligent and loving design, and his end is not for this world." From this it follows, with syllogistic certitude, that the intelligence of an educator's charges is a sacred responsibility and a sacred property. Proper teaching, therefore, respects the intelligence of the individual, challenges that intelligence and does not attempt to inform through dogged repetition and mere memorization in a mindless act of assimilation. Rather, "Every child must learn for himself. And that is why, no matter how great the truth with which we are dealing, we must respect always the individuality of the human mind." The theory which spawns this particular thesis is not only based on the book of Genesis, but also owes much to Carter's study of Thomas Aquinas and modern psychology. Carter explains in the precision of thomistic language: "[T]he assimilation must come through the self-operation of the individual involved. Therefore we may stimulate the intellect, we may propound the truth to it, but we can never make the act by which the intellect actually moves to assimilate this truth to make it its own. Therefore, in the whole realm of knowledge and teaching, the greatest skill is to arouse the interest of the child." As a result, he continues, "we must avoid the ready-made solution. In the schools of philosophy which dot the Catholic world there is a procedure which is difficult to justify in terms of this philosophy of education. It is what may be described as the 'thesis technique.' . . . It is as though we are told: 'Here is the thesis. The truth has been found for you. There is no need for you to look any further; simply understand what these other people have thought, and you will have wisdom.' "

Carter suggests instead that instructors should use the technique Thomas Aquinas employed in the structure of his *Summa theologica*. Challenge the opposition. Present objections. Then offer one's own informed insights, one's own opinion on the topic, showing only then where the opposition has erred. Indeed, the intellectual cut and thrust so favoured by Thomas Aquinas has a particular attraction for Emmett Carter. There is no prize for intellectual sloth, no merit in a truth insufficiently tried. And, as Augustine has pointed out, true insight and full human satisfaction can only be properly valued with a challenge met and overcome. It is a thesis Gerald Emmett Cardinal Carter has lived all his life. Gainsay who dare. In the maze of opinion which surrounds the Cardinal, there seems to be absolute unanimity on only one issue: he does not suffer fools gladly.

What is true of the intellectual life is equally true of the moral life. In prophetic anticipation of the teachings of Vatican II, Carter "subscribe[s], without hesitation, to the idea that man must meet the challenge of his own individuality and of his own life, and by his own actions achieve happiness." The educator's task, therefore, is to point the way, to show encouragement and to support with love. It is not enough to inculcate conditioned responses of virtuous behaviour; one must understand the principle behind the behaviour, embrace that principle and then act willingly. As a result, proper education begins with respect, with an appreciation for the fact that the child "is an individual human being, a real, complete, loving, thinking, feeling son or daughter of the Almighty and also of his human parents."

Such a system of education relies totally on the person of the instructor. Indeed, the teacher is clearly more important than the knowledge that individual possesses. The ideal teacher is a role model, an example of good living. And so, by definition, the "teacher who loves children and desires to awaken in them the appreciation of virtue, love of truth, and awareness of the problems of life, with a desire to arrive at something of a personal solution, is the teacher who will make the greatest contribution." This is Carter at his best. The Carter who combines biblical lessons on love, psychological lessons on human understanding and theological lessons on the power of example, the Carter who eschews the language of scholastic sophistication and speaks plainly with the heart of the seasoned christian educator.

It is this Carter who argues the progressive theses of both *Psychology and the Cross*[5] and *The Modern Challenge to Religious Education*,[6] who advances his case with scholarly conviction, but who fashions his presentation in clear, nonspecialist prose sensitive to the educational diversity of his audience.

Psychology and the Cross, published in 1959, is a reworked version of the thesis he submitted to the University of Montreal in 1947 in partial fulfillment of the requirements for his Ph.D. in Education.

Entitled "The Psychological Import of Religious Education", the doctoral dissertation received a good bit of attention in the Catholic press of the time both because of the reputation of its author and, more importantly, because of its rather daring fusion of psychology and religion. Eighteen years after Canon Carter had defended his thesis, the Council Fathers gathered in Rome for the closing session of Vatican II issued a landmark statement on the church in the modern world, *Gaudium et spes*, in which Rome formally embraced the social sciences, literature and the arts in its ongoing analysis of the human condition, but in 1947 when Canon Carter was working through his thesis, and in 1959 when he saw it through the popular press, he was walking in undeveloped territory.

So controversial was the Carter thesis that *Psychology and the Cross* was greeted with rejection, delay and near oblivion as it made its uncertain path through the publishing industry. Macmillan of Canada, for example, informed him that their Religion Department had concluded that "[t]here is little doubt that it could be sold but it would surely have a rough time in the hands of Catholic educators in America."[7] The editors went on to explain that not only did Macmillan fear that such a book could not survive in the lucrative United States market, but that there was even some question about its orthodoxy: "Some of the viewpoints are quite progressive, and although I would be in personal agreement, it is doubtful that the Office of the Censor in this diocese would be in accord. Of course, such a matter could easily be handled by getting an Imprimatur elsewhere." Despite protestations of personal agreement, nonetheless, the Religion Department concluded "that the Catholic review media would give the book a hard time. In view of this feeling, we will not want to go into the matter further in respect to revision for publication." In his response to the manager of Macmillan of Canada's School Book Department, Carter terms such opinions "amazing", adding: "I know that certain areas of the Church in the United States tend to be ultraconservative, but I cannot believe that there would be any question of the orthodoxy of what I have written."[8] Such an assessment must have been a particularly bitter potion for a man who had spearheaded the introduction of proper English-language textbooks into Quebec and whose vision of church had been from the beginning a call to fidelity on issues touching on matters of religious orthodoxy. It was indeed a lesson not soon forgotten: the opening words of his *Modern Challenge to Religious Education* note that "One of the most astounding things about the Church in North America is its traditionalism."[9] There must also have been no little satisfaction in his ability to confirm with relish as late as 1987, that the *Modern Challenge to Religious Education* had sold briskly in the textbook markets of the United States and that "it was used very widely in the teachers' colleges in the United States, very widely."

Encouraged by friends such as the noted psychiatrist Karl Stern, whom he had helped to convert to Catholicism, Carter saw his text through to its final publication, some twelve years after its original submission to the University of Montreal, and some five years after the rejections suffered at the hands of Macmillan of Canada. In fact, Macmillan's assessment of the media reception which awaited *Psychology and the Cross* was certainly not realized in Canada, although a quick glance at the headline to the review that appeared in the February 21, 1959, edition of *The Canadian Register* seems to validate the view of Macmillan's Religion Department: the introductory banner "How Far Can Faith Be Furthered by Fraud?" contained a typographical error, in which "Fraud" appeared as "Freud". A verbal gaffe sure to tickle a Celtic sense of humour — once the original panic had subsided! In the review itself, J.G. Shaw praised the book both for its content and for its style.

Despite its jarring introduction, *The Canadian Register*'s typographical error does provide the unintentional service of getting immediately to the heart of the matter. Beginning once more with the anthropological statement from Genesis 1:26, "Let us make man in our own likeness and image", Carter finds in this text an invitation to psychological speculation, to the discovery of the Spirit, and in so doing he turns to a science (psychology), which had been seen as incompatible with religion, and a psychiatrist (Sigmund Freud), who had been seen as antagonistic toward religion. Noting that the times in which Freud lived had assumed that religion and science were in a death struggle, Carter argues for a reading of the new times, for the unity of truth and for the utility of Freud's theory of the unconscious in the process of self-knowledge. In any event, Carter suggests that he is merely taking up the challenge of Pope Pius XII that scholars turn to modern sciences like psychology in their quest for truth. To all of which Carter adds: "[We] do firmly believe that there is no reason why the cross cannot be set upon psychology at the meeting of the ways. . . ."

Developing the emphasis in his first book on the importance of self-knowledge and self-realization as elements of personal growth to be facilitated by a teacher who is sensitive to the individual's *potential* for self-realization, Carter wrote that everyone must arrive at the point where one can "judge himself by himself, not by comparison with others, because his worth is an absolute thing, not relative." Accordingly, one should expect our youth to yearn for independence, and by way of corollary, "One of the greatest disabilities of our Catholic school systems, and of some of our clergy-lay relationships, has been the failure to understand these urges of self-assertion and proper independence." These are insightful and brave words, enshrining as they do not only the christian sense of the participation in the divine, but also the Catholic social teaching of subsidiarity — of shared responsibility to be assumed at the lowest, most immediate level of operation — Catholic social theory spawned in the 1930s, forcefully reinforced in the 1960s, and central to the varied teachings flowing from Vatican II. Indeed, there is here a reasoned sense of subsidiarity and of lay–cleric relationships which is well ahead of its time.

Also flowing from this thesis of the sanctity of self-realization is Carter's insistence that rote memorization is, in itself, a bankrupt and psychologically inappropriate form of education. Students must be challenged intellectually: "We must make our students intellectually independent and capable of conducting their own research." Sentiments like these are not to be found in Pope Pius XI's 1930 document of education, which Carter had drawn upon in his *The Catholic Public Schools of Quebec*; they are, however, at the heart of the teaching on individual conscience and Catholic education which was to flow from Vatican II. Individuals, Carter argues, must be made to accept responsibility for their actions, and that is most effectively done by mature persons capable of reasoned acceptance of right and wrong.

Carter then applies this idea convincingly to cleric–lay relationships, though at times the enunciation of that thesis can sound condescending to an educated and actively committed laity. He suggests, for example, that when one gives those involved in church activities the authority to make organizational decisions because it is ego building, "Errors will be made, of course. But errors in matters like this may even be beneficial in a way. They are at least proof that the young or the lay are doing things by themselves." There is here a hint of "father knows best". Carter the Bishop, or Carter the Cardinal Archbishop, would not as glibly slip into the condescending tone.

Nonetheless, the comment does underline the human difficulty inherent in the exercise of subsidiarity (the doctrine of allocating power to the lowest competent authority), especially when power is in the hands of someone as thoroughly competent as Gerald Emmett Cardinal Carter. All his training, all his instincts are clearly directing him to share power, and he does, though some would call his ultimate exercise of authority "shared subsidiarity". Others suggest that the principle is a fine one, and should be more visible in ecclesiastical behaviour.

Carter goes some way to explain the widespread problem of clerical power sharing, though the Canon does overlook the difficulties this presents for the overachiever like himself who shares power with an individual whose accomplishments are more run-of-the-mill. He reasons: "To give responsibility means to relinquish authority to some degree. Authority in Catholic circles is for the most part in the hands of religious (priests, brothers, nuns). Religious are formally dedicated to a life of chastity. Now there are three fundamental human drives: (a) the preservation of self, (b) the propagation of the species, (c) the will to power. Celibacy involves the repression of the second of these. What is more natural than to expect that this repression will take the form of a transfer of drive at least in some degree and that the will to power will be proportionately strengthened? Besides, parenthood is the normal means of satisfaction for the drive to power. Since this is impossible for the celibate, he tends to concentrate on the power given him by his position. Religious are notoriously jealous of their rights, privileges, and prerogatives." As a result, the natural impulse, he suggests, is for the clergy to surround themselves with yes-men, a phenomenon for which, he adds, they have an international reputation. It is a practice he has frequently and consistently lamented. It is, ironically, an accusation not infrequently levelled at the Cardinal Archbishop of Toronto himself, an accusation he dismisses with the observation that only an insecure prelate would appoint such people. And no one has suggested that Cardinal Carter is unsure of himself.

To his theory of self-realization, Carter adds the christian recognition that we are all flawed, all imperfect as human beings. As a result, we should accept our infirmities, note that Christ ministered to the poor, the weak, the infirm, and that there is value in every human ego. In such humility one will find truth, and in truth one will find peace. Such is applied christian psychology. The impulse to *un*bridled independence, however, is an evil resulting from our flawed human nature, from the original sin of Adam and Eve. Carter introduced this theme in "The Screwball Letters" and explored it further in *The Catholic Public Schools of Quebec*. One needs enough independence to satisfy one's need for self-assertion, but to overstep the bounds and ignore the appropriate obedience owed to proper authority is an act of human pride. In *The Catholic Public Schools of Quebec*, Canon Carter addressed the question of motivation and independence, noting that "The term *blind obedience* is one which has very often been misused. It is acceptable in the sense that we can obey where authority rests. But there is nothing really blind about this. We obey authority because we believe that all authority comes from God." From both the theological and the psychological perspective, therefore, the will to unbridled independence is a sinful act; it is motivated by a pride which ignores the flawed character of human nature and which demands perfection in a state which is essentially imperfect. Therefore, Carter reasons, the psychiatrist owes his profession "to Adam and original sin."

Having provided his introductory analysis of the misuse of authority and the drive for independence, Carter returned to his thesis of cleric–lay relationships, arguing for the empowering of a passive laity relegated to an inferior role in the church by centuries of doctrine inappropriately applied. "The idea that the Church and the hierarchy are synonymous and that the laity are a kind of inert mass to be pushed and kicked or flattered and cajoled through the Pearly Gates took hold of the minds of Catholic people everywhere. Such terminology as 'hearing Mass' betrayed the general mentality." To document the orthodoxy of what appears to be a radical point of view, and anxious to remain in consort with Rome even while pursuing revolutionary paths, he characteristically quotes Pope Pius XI on the role of the laity, as well as several of the theologians who were to be influential mentors for the Council Fathers when discussing such issues some five years later.

Psychology and the Cross reinforces other christian and Catholic values as instruments of psychological well-being: concepts of love (christian love) and community (communicated through the Trinity and the mystical body), concepts which clearly bear heavily on the manner and purpose of Catholic education as Carter and Vatican II were to discuss the matters. According to Carter's fusion of religion and psychology, communal solidarity provides an expression of the superego, which limits one's impulse for unrestrained power as expressed by the id. Fear is an expression of Freud's killing of the father, of a society which has rejected the care of the Father, though the cure for such fear, he suggests, can lie in the virtue of confidence and can be alleviated through the psychological power of the sacrament of penance.

In *Psychology and the Cross*, therefore, one finds the sensitive instructor, the pastoral priest, even the learned thomist, combining his experience as priest, teacher, Inspector of Schools and chaplain for the Newman Club to offer a useful synthesis of his experiences in Montreal. There was one final chapter, however, to be written from the lived point of view of Carter's experiences during the twenty-five years which took him from ordination to episcopacy. As Ecclesiastical Inspector for the English Schools of Montreal, Carter had witnessed his share of dull religion classes, and his instincts as teacher, his studies in psychology, his pastoral passion for the dissemination of the message of salvation to be found in the christian gospel — the kerygmatic message — all of these things told him that something had to be done. As he had commented thirteen years before in his *Lumen Vitae* monograph, "The Training of Teachers of Religion", "the religion period has been known in many cases as the dullest, the most uninteresting and the most dreaded."[10]

Curiously enough, such does not seem to have been his own experience as a student, though his recollection of his catechetical training with the Christian Brothers at St. Patrick's School seems to be limited to an incident with his good friend Charles Wayland. As Cardinal Carter tells the story, and as Charles Wayland confirms with Nordic bemusement, Brother Jerome's catechism class consumed the last half hour before lunch, but since the Brother did not have a watch, he often wandered past the allotted time and reported late for the reflective meal with the Brothers, for which he was reprimanded by his Brother Superior. To solve his problem he appointed Charles Wayland the keeper of the watch. The arrangement worked fine until several days later when the Brother got himself wound into his lesson and ran overtime, at which point Charles Wayland interrupted to point out that fact to Brother Jerome. "And he comes down and slugs him and says, 'Who are you to tell me what time it is?' So that's all I remember about my catechetical formation."

At Montreal College, however, Emmett Carter remembers his catechism as being upbeat, positive, challenging and personal. The experience he drew on for his catechetical theory was therefore garnered while he executed his responsibilities as Ecclesiastical Inspector. The experience was obviously shared with his sister Irene, Sister Mary Lenore, who was herself an educator of some note and a recipient of the coronation medal from Queen Elizabeth II in recognition of her educational accomplishments. She recalls complaining to her brother that "just memorizing things didn't convey the spirit of religion. I think you needed something more gripping. Just memorizing Butler's Catechism without understanding too well just what the meaning was certainly wasn't my idea of teaching." In spite of the similarity between her views and her brother's, she disclaims having any influence on his thinking: "I think he's one who formulates his own thinking."

The young ecclesiastical inspector seems to have had some assistance in formulating his opinions, nonetheless. He recalls one instance where a teacher organized a circle of boys and shot questions at them as he walked the circle. The students shot the answers back. And when the event was over, the teacher beamed to Father Carter, " 'How was that? Not bad, eh?' He thought he was great. I thought it was dreadful, absolutely dreadful."

In his 1946 *Lumen Vitae* article, Carter outlined the heart of his thinking with respect to the teaching of religion; namely, Christ taught by example, in parables, and so should the effective teacher; the human intelligence is not a filing cabinet, so the essence of good teaching lies in the stimulation of the intellect to seek understanding; formulae are deadly teaching tools, illustrations lively ones; memorization must be preceded by comprehension; the purpose of religion class is to promote sound behaviour, not to transmit sterile information.

Although he also provides a wealth of historical information, it is essentially these principles augmented by the psychological insights which inform *Psychology and the Cross* that are developed in impressive detail in Canon Carter's *The Modern Challenge to Religious Education*. It is a book which enjoyed no little success not only because it was adopted as a standard text in many teachers' colleges in the United States, but also because its insights were much admired by catechists with international reputations, such as Jesuit priest Johannes Hofinger who insisted that "Canon Carter's book, first of its kind composed by an American author, is the book to use as a manual for training catechists."[11] Calling Canon Carter's work "revolutionary", Hofinger says that drawing on his wide personal experience, and reacting to the pastoral traditionalism of North America, Canon Carter produced "*the* catechetical manual of our times for America." It was no doubt accolades such as these which prompted Jesuit Father Walter Abbott to invite Carter to write the introductory segment for the educational document in Abbott's influential edition, *The Documents of Vatican II.*

Given the reputation as an educator which Emmett Carter had earned during his years in Montreal, and given the educational experience he had accumulated during that period of his life, it is instructive to note that former students at St. Joseph's have been eager to tell their stories. Ron Locas, a teacher and graduate of St. Joseph's Teachers' College, who was a student there during Emmett's final days at the school, remembers standing outside Thomas Francoeur's classroom to eavesdrop on lectures in which he was not enrolled but which he found stimulating. Emmett, he says, was a natural teacher, who inspired him to read beyond the text and instilled in him the sense that learning was "something to be enjoyed". This was no common feat under the circumstances. During the time that Locas attended the College, Carter taught large numbers of students in a gymnasium which served as a lecture hall and was shouldering all the administrative burdens associated with the principal's office.

In Emmett Carter, Locas also found no average priest. "He had something that was different from most priests. I think most priests take themselves somehow very seriously. He seemed to have been very, very much down to earth, very practical, and yet at the same time a hard worker and a person who accomplishes — a goal-oriented person." One comment revealing Emmett Carter's practical and pastoral sides stayed especially strong in Locas's memory. During a traditional year-end party for graduating students, which Carter was hosting at Fourteen Island Lake, Emmett commented to Ron and his wife that one had to be heroic to be married these days. It was a question which Locas related to questions of birth control and "all that it required of a Catholic." The observation "stuck with me," says Locas.

Another St. Joseph's graduate, Madeline Reiter, recalls Emmett Carter as a friendly and demanding principal. "He knew all the students by name, even though there were a lot of us at the time. If you missed his class, he would stop you in the hall and ask where you were — there were seventy students in the gymnasium where he taught.

He had a terrific memory. He walked the halls with a twinkle in his eye and said hello to everyone by name." Reiter also remembers Emmett as a wit and a ham, pointing to an instructional mock court scene in which she was to play the role of a floozy and he a judge. When Madeline Reiter (nee Karfisel) mustered a nervous, lascivious wink and flutter, she was interrupted by an "Excuse me, Miss Carwhistle", and the nickname stayed with her for two years at St. Joseph's. "He loved to act, and he was a wonderful public speaker — he still is."

Despite his amiable nature, everyone knew that Emmett was in charge. There were, for example, the post-Christmas interviews when those students who were not performing to standard were summoned to the principal's office one by one, never to be seen again. Meanwhile, the others huddled on tenterhooks, waiting for the alphabetical selection to pass them by. And then there was the trip that Emmett and Alex took to Rome for an audience with Pope John XXIII. Reiter notes that while Emmett was away, St. Joseph's was a completely different place: the quality of the teaching deteriorated noticeably, classes often failed to begin on time, others were even cancelled. "No one had to tell us he was coming back. Everyone knew before he arrived. Everything changed." Apparently oblivious to the transformation his return had effected at St. Joseph's, Carter returned from Rome bursting with enthusiasm for the humility of John XXIII, a pope who, Carter told the St. Joseph's student body, refused to accept the usual obeisance that had become customary protocol. Pope John XXIII, Carter assured his students, would transform the church.

Carter's parting words as he left for Quebec City to assume his final Quebec posting at St. Lawrence College returned to an organizational motif which appeared in several of his speeches and forms the heart of his philosophy as a man of the church: quoting Augustine of Hippo, he advised his audience, *In necessariis unitas, in dubiis libertas, in omnibus caritas* — "In the fundamental issues, unity; in matters of opinion, freedom; in all things, charity."[12] To Augustine's dicta, Carter adds his own personal reflection, "If I am anything, anything worthwhile that is, I am a man of the Church." A man of the church from a family which gave four of its children to the church; a man conservative in ecclesiastical matters, like his childhood mentor, Father Gerald McShane; a churchman whose sense of unity was born of an admiration for the ordered and combative intelligence of his scholastic mentor, Thomas Aquinas; a man liberal in social matters, like his father, Thomas Joseph Carter; a man whose educational experience and familial convictions had taught him the sanctity of the individual and the essence of love.

When Canon Carter was appointed as Auxiliary Bishop of London, Ontario, on December 5, 1961, his reputation as an educator was thoroughly established and his educational objectives in Quebec were apparently achieved. Challenge seen, challenge met: *voir, juger, agir*, see, judge, act. He was only forty-nine, and he was ready for new challenges.

PART II

LONDON

(1961–1978)

CHAPTER FOUR

Emmett Carter and Vatican II

In the spring of 1961, when Canon Carter accepted the invitation of Maurice Roy, Archbishop of Quebec City and Primate of Canada, to take charge of St. Lawrence College in Ste. Foy, neither he nor his superiors could have known the short duration of his appointment. Carter's reputation as an administrator and an educator was by this time extradiocesan if not extraprovincial, and when Roy sought the intervention of Cardinal Léger to persuade Carter to assume the rectorship, he knew what he was getting. And so did Carter.

When Carter was summoned by Léger to be informed of Roy's direct request for his services, Carter responded: "Your Eminence, if you and Roy think I should go to China, I am ready to go to China. There is no problem." The perfect answer from the perfect churchman.

And so Carter set about arranging this move, which was incorrectly characterized by his detractors as a bumping upstairs. Rolling stones do gather a certain amount of animosity. He travelled to Quebec City frequently, getting matters in order for the reception of students in the fall, hiring a staff, preparing curricular details and seeing to his living quarters. His Montreal commitments were still many, and he came "home" every weekend to honour them. But these awkward circumstances were short-lived.

At the end of November 1961, barely a few months into his new responsibilities, Carter was putting the final touches to an address he was to give to the nurses of the Ottawa General Hospital. He came up to Montreal on the Sunday evening, where he received a phone call from Roy. The Archbishop had never phoned him at home; something was in the air. Roy inquired as to Carter's plans for Monday. Was he coming in? Carter told Roy of his Ottawa commitment and assured him that he would be back at St. Lawrence on Monday night. Roy seemed amused that Carter was going to Ottawa and dropped the matter. But Carter knew that this was untypical of the man; he simply never interfered or phoned for a casual chat.

When Carter arrived at the hospital on Monday morning, he was approached by a rather befuddled Sister Superior, who informed him that the Pope's representative to Canada, the Apostolic Delegate, Sebastiano Baggio, had hurt himself and had arrived for physiotherapy. In addition, and somewhat mysteriously, Baggio had requested an interview with the Canon. Carter went to his room and found the Delegate dressed in a hospital gown, not quite the resplendent robes he was accustomed to, and heard the unexpected news: the Holy Father had named Gerald Emmett Carter Titular Bishop of Altiburo and Auxiliary to Bishop John C. Cody, Bishop of London, Ontario.

St. Lawrence College would be looking for a new rector.

Almost immediately the congratulations started pouring in, a veritable torrent. Some of the notes and letters were standard fare, but many were also genuine expressions of real pleasure in the appointment. George Bernard Flahiff, the former Superior General of the Congregation of St. Basil and an accomplished scholar, wrote to him from the Chancery Office in Winnipeg, to which city he had been recently appointed as Archbishop: "Nothing as good as this has happened in a long time. Thank God indeed for this appointment. I know how pleased the members of the hierarchy are and the large sections of the laity and the clergy who know you and your work."[1] To help defray episcopal expenses, he included a gift of $100.

In terms similarly welcoming, Philip Francis Pocock, Coadjutor Archbishop of Toronto, wrote from the Pontifical Canadian College in Rome: "Your experience in the educational field will be invaluable to us, and of course to all of Canada. You have an abundance of whatever it takes to be a bishop."[2] Pocock provided $500 for the outfitting. Toronto is more flush than Winnipeg.

The appointment of a Montreal lad to an Ontario bishopric was not new. Brother Alex was already Bishop of Sault Ste. Marie. Nor was the naming of a Quebecker to the See of London new. When the diocese was founded in 1856, its first Bishop, Pierre-Adolphe Pinsonnault, was chosen from the ranks of the Montreal Catholic School Commission. Carter, it would appear, was not to set a precedent with his appointment to London. But those who knew him then, in the late fall of 1961, knew that in the years to come there would be many a precedent-setting initiative.

Every Roman Catholic bishop has his own coat of arms and, not surprisingly, Carter's betrays nothing of an intellectual or spiritual timidity. The charges and tinctures reflect the overriding dedication to education that has marked Carter's church career, and the chief symbol is the flame of knowledge. The flame burns around the cross, the centre of christian education. The motto, *Pax et Lux* (Peace and Light), has the same basic origin as the motto of the Thomas More Institute, and the red field, the symbol of charity, recalls the work of the Newman Club ministry, with the white (argent) cross on the red field alluding to the Sovereign Order of the Knights of Malta, to which Carter was chaplain. The coat of arms, a tradition dating back to the medieval period, is completed by the star, symbolizing the Virgin Mary who guides us to her son — the right touch, given his Irish roots and traditional Marian piety. Even the date of his episcopal consecration has a Marian significance: it took place on the Feast of her Purification, which celebrates her presentation of Jesus at the Temple in Jerusalem, forty days after giving birth.

Carter was consecrated Bishop on February 2, 1962, in Montreal's Notre Dame, the largest and oldest basilica in the city. He had chosen Léger as his consecrator, with homilies by Roy and Pocock in French and English, respectively. It was a fully regal ceremony, as Emmett would want it. The procession alone had about it the air of a medieval pageant, with Knights of Malta, torch-bearers, stool-bearers, faldstool-bearers, provincials and generals of religious orders, honorary and titular canons, monsignori of every rank — cameraii secreti, domestic prelates, protonotaries apostolic — bishops, archbishops, crozier and mitre bearers, consecrators, chaplains, familiares, gremial bearer, and the Lord Cardinal of Montreal. And overseeing it all from a seat in the front pew was ninety-one-year-old Minnie Carter. With the second son elevated now to the episcopal dignity, what would Tom think?

The consecration ceremony was in every sense a triumph, even triumphalistic, and Carter revelled in the ceremony's ecclesiastical majesty. Eleven years later he revelled still, adamant that human need demands the retention of the high style. "Where have we gone under the guise of eliminating triumphalism? I am all in favour of deposing worldly trappings and outmoded conventions, some of them inherited from the princes of this world who 'lord it over their subjects!' But does it mean that we bishops may not stand tall lest we are accused of arrogance? . . . Human beings have need of symbol and cere-mony. . . . The ceremony of the consecration of a bishop is a triumph. It represents the victory of our Catholic faith and the teaching of Jesus over centuries of unbelief and hostility. It should be presented as a triumph and this does *not* mean being triumphalistic."[3]

After the consecration, Judge Paul C. Casey presided over a testi-monial dinner at the Windsor Hotel, with the main address by the Bishop of Pittsburgh, John J. Wright. Wright's address was both witty and serious, a judicious blend of the playful and the exhortative. He began his address by referring to Emmett Carter's See of Altiburo — if a bishop is an auxiliary, his See will be titular; that is, identified with some ancient and no longer functional See — and he stressed how this now defunct African See of Altiburo was at one time at the very centre of an emerging christendom. Although in time it became an eccle-siastical ghost town, in its day it played a prominent role in combating heresy. The implications are clear: Would the new Titular Bishop of Altiburo find himself girded for battle, like his predecessors, on the modern terrain of heresy?

The urbane and apologetical Wright pushed even further: "Neo-humanism and agnosticism are rampant in Europe and Asia. These and other 'isms' could leap the ocean and we could become involved in some apostasy. . . . The Sees in which you have your being are active and dynamic, but those that are defunct remind us that we must fully shoulder our responsibilities and make our Catholicity more manifest in the life of the Church. There is current talk today of leftist and rightist Catholics. . . . There are factionalisms, narrow na-tionalisms, racisms — and there is lack of charity. The Catholic Church never became a denomination. It is not one of the sects among the divided denominations of Christendom. Holy, Roman, and Apostolic, the Catholic Church remains also one and undivided. If I have any word of admonition to leave with you it is that you guard yourselves against this advancing sectarian and denominational spirit. We must each be as Catholic as the Church."[4]

These words ably reveal the highly partisan character of the pre-Second Vatican Council church. There is no ecumenical sensitivity to be found in Wright's words, no conciliatory tone, no pacific strat-egies. The words and the intelligence behind them are fierce and aggressive. Wright was destined for greater things than the pastorship of Pittsburgh. Carter chose wisely.

Carter would remain as Auxiliary Bishop for two years, resident in Windsor, Ontario, and technically pastor of the city's St. Clare's Church, until John Christopher Cody, the aging and ailing Bishop of London, died on December 5, 1963. Known as a bishop who would answer his own doorbell, Cody was a courteous and kind man, and an able administrator. The Catholics of his diocese mused aloud, and with a little anxiety, about his successor.

No auxiliary has the right of succession; only a coadjutor has that right. Carter was not necessarily the heir apparent, but on February 22, 1964, he was named the eighth Bishop to the See of London, and on March 12, he was duly installed as such in a ceremony almost as grand as his consecration.

St. Peter's Basilica in London was packed with dignitaries from the different constituencies that comprise the diocese and with representatives from other christian denominations, other faiths, the business community, the university and the political sector. Carter covered all the bases. He even arranged that Paul Martin, Minister of External Affairs in the Lester Pearson government, would read the address on behalf of the laity. As it happened, Martin couldn't be present because of an unexpected meeting of the United Nations Security Council in New York, but Carter's conviction that one should go to the top, make the most in a public statement or gesture, was not lost on the congregation. This new Bishop not only had style, but was a shrewd embodiment of the new thinking coming from Rome. He would be, in the generous words of the Cardinal Archbishop of Toronto, James Charles McGuigan, "the greatest bishop of all time".

Some might have seen the partial power failure that plunged the basilica into semi-darkness up to the very moment of his induction to the episcopal throne as an omen of a particularly unsettling kind. It was not divine displeasure that caused the outage — it was an improvident fuse. For Carter, it proved the only "power failure" of a long episcopal career.

Carter understands power and its demands. In a letter to Claude Ryan when Ryan accepted the candidacy for the leadership of the Liberal Party of Quebec, Carter observed: "And now, for a long time, you are going to pay the price! It will not be all bad. Public acclaim and the spotlight are heady compensation for any man who is normal. But . . . I doubt that you will appreciate your every word and your every action being under such scrutiny. And, above all, under such contradictory and sometimes ridiculous interpretations. But service to our fellowmen has never been easy and, after all, we walk in the footsteps of One who went the whole route."[5]

Within a short time of his arrival in the London diocese he made the acquaintance of its social, religious, corporate and political leaders. It was Montreal revisited, the same kinds of contacts cultivated, the same strategies employed. Soon after his installation, he would number among his friends the editor of the *London Free Press*, the president of London Life and the enterprising and influential car dealer and power broker, Joe McManus. He knew in London what he had learned in Montreal and what he would bring to Toronto: "People are jealous who don't move in the circles of power, and highly critical of those, like myself, who do. I don't know how a bishop can go into a diocese and say I am not going to talk to anybody who's got more than 45 cents in his pocket. I just can't get my mind around that kind of simplistic approach. When you are dealing with lawyers, when you are dealing with physicians, you have to be able to name people who are going to open doors for you, who are going to help you in whatever cause you are engaged. I had a big problem with my secondary schools in London and so I turned to people who are good financiers to provide me with suggestions and support. And so I contacted a good friend of mine, Jack Adams, then President of the Chartered Accountants of Canada. What was I supposed to do? Go and ask the rag picker how I was to raise the necessary funds to save the high schools?"

The pragmatic approach Carter takes to the administration of a diocese allows him the kind of latitude his more ideologically motivated critics deplore. In dealing with the power brokers of society, Carter seeks for common ground, for the things that unite rather than for those which perpetuate division. He could not have found a body of more influential men who could provide him with *both* temporal and spiritual understanding and support than the venerable association known as the Sovereign and Military Order of St. John of Jerusalem of Rhodes and of Malta. It was an association he made early and values still.

The Order emerged in 1099 and has a long, bloody and heroic history that is full of drama and vision. One can easily see how it would appeal to Carter's romantic imagination. As Knight and sometime President of the University of Windsor, Dr. Francis J. Leddy observed in his address, "May There Be No Dust Upon Our Banner": "Religious orders have come and gone, charitable foundations have crumbled, innumerable military and political powers have risen and fallen, but the Order of Malta is still with us after nine centuries."[6]

The Canadian Association is of relatively recent vintage. In 1950, seven Montrealers were granted individual admission to the Order so that they might plan such a Canadian Association, an Association which, in due course, received appropriate recognition from the Grand Magistracy in Rome and was legally incorporated on January 27, 1953.[7] The Knights attract members of the judiciary, the military, the academy, the sciences, the medical and engineering professions and have drawn upon the highest orders in church and state, including cardinals, cabinet ministers, and governors general. Carter had no difficulty identifying with a society like this, in which power rubs shoulders with power.

Count Robert Keyserlingk, one of the organization's founding fathers, was instrumental in bringing Carter into direct association with the Knights. Converted to Catholicism by the Canon, Keyserlingk was an emigré Russian aristocrat who had done distinguished service as a correspondent-editor with United Press and as publisher of the Canadian Catholic newspaper *The Ensign*. Keyserlingk was schooled in the ways of power in both church and state. "Carter is not a worldly prelate, but he is able to cope with the world very dexterously, because he understands that to court power, in the non-pejorative sense of court, is to have a well-developed sense of the relative nature of power, and to know, just simply to know, who can do something and who cannot."

For Keyserlingk, Carter's notion of power is realistic and pragmatic without being all-consuming. It is power oriented to a greater end, power with a spiritual purpose. The Knights are the perfect exemplars of the self-emptying character of power.

But Carter's interest in the Knights can also be discovered in his love of ritual, formal ceremony and dress — the things he shared with his former pastor, Father Gerald McShane. A Conventual Chaplain ad Honorem with the Knights, Carter assumed his exalted status with predictable dignity and did not see the Knights' concern for protocol as mere trifling. In a letter to a fellow chaplain concerning an impending investiture, he revealed the seriousness he has always attached to right form: "At the time of my appointment I received from the Grand Magistracy the description of the proper dress of the Conventual Chaplains. As no doubt you know, it consists of the red-sleeved rochet and the short red cape. When in Rome one of the Knights made me a

present of the cape and I propose to wear this dress at the investiture.
. . . Actually, the proper type of cape is one made of silk which is
usually reserved to Roman Counts and Assistants at the Pontifical
Throne, but the cape which I have is the type which usually is worn by
Bishops. . . ."[8]

But it isn't just the Order's attention to fine form, its monarchical
trappings and its solemnly inculcated respect for history that appeal to
Carter.

The Order perdures, like the Church of Rome. Carter likes that, he
likes the Order's chivalric past, its protective role in the history of
christendom. To this Montreal-bred child with an Irish imagination,
the stories of the Order's valour have great appeal, the greatest of
which are the exploits surrounding the four-month-long Great Siege
of 1565: "The Turks were ready to break through into the Western
Mediterranean, and thereafter to attack Europe directly. Malta appeared to be a minor nuisance in the way, to be brushed casually aside.
The fortifications were not ample, and Knights were few in numbers.
Yet the stakes were high, and as the siege continued, reports were
anxiously awaited as far away as England, for it was gradually realized
that the future of Christendom was in the balance, and that all the
odds were against the Knights who were vastly outnumbered. Yet,
with incredible tenacity and unbreakable morale they resisted fero-
cious attacks and endured horrible hardships, until the Turks finally
abandoned their efforts to batter them into submission. Throughout
Europe the church bells rang at the good news, so contrary to any
reasonable hope. In Protestant England Queen Elizabeth directed the
Archbishop of Canterbury to prepare a form of Thanksgiving to be
read in all churches three times a week for three weeks! When the
Grand Master's tombstone described him a few years later as the
'Shield of Europe' it was recording the universal opinion."[9]

The Great Siege enjoys the same historical importance as other
like events: Leonidas and his three hundred Spartans defending the
pass at Thermopylae against the hordes of Persian soldiery in 480
B.C.; Charles "The Hammer" Martel defeating the Moslem armies in
eighth-century France; John of Austria leading the Holy League
against the Turkish navy in the decisive victory of Lepanto in 1571.
The last of these great battles is particularly appropriate, given that
G.K. Chesterton's well-known narrative poem, "Lepanto", was committed to memory by a younger Carter and pleasurably recalled for
family entertainment whenever the occasion warranted.

Canon Carter's personal fidelity to the Holy See was strengthened by his membership in an Order whose collective fidelity is legendary. In a spirited, one might even say war-like, address given in Ottawa before the Papal Pro-Nuncio to Canada, the Grand Chancellor of the Order, the Bailiff-President and scores of Knights and their wives, Bishop Carter exhorted his fellow Knights to heed the See of Peter and spurn the several factions dividing the church. His address had about it the deadly earnest of a general's briefing, save that the enemy was not from without.

"My brethren, let us recall that the division in Christendom which began in the 16th century and which has lasted to our day and which causes us so much grief and sorrow, was caused not so much by who was right and who was wrong as by the acerbity of the dispute and the enduring hatred it engendered. Are we not in the same danger? Allow me to be Paulinian with you and to paraphrase the great Apostle. We are saying today, 'I am of Suenens [the progressive Cardinal Archbishop of Malines-Brussels], I am of Paul [the beleaguered Pope Paul VI], I am of Alfrink [the very progressive Cardinal Archbishop of Utrecht].' — 'The *Twin Circle* [a reactionary U.S. Catholic publication] has the answer,' 'the *National Catholic Reporter* '[an independent U.S. Catholic weekly of liberal view], is my bible' — or — ' I am an intellectual, I read *Commonweal* [the prestigious, New York–based intellectual magazine].' And may I say to you in the terms of Paul, 'Were you baptized in Suenens? Did Paul die for you? Is Alfrink the prophet?' — 'Are the writers of any magazine inspired? Has the Church declared that its magisterium is now vested in the columnists or the authors of the latest popular book debunking the Church?' "[10]

Again and again over the years Carter was to admonish the dividers in the church, the dissidents, and celebrate the fealty of the Knights, the defenders of her unity.

Carter has progressed through the ranks of the Order in a manner commensurate with his rise in the church, and he has remained loyal to the Order's goals. And he has not been lacking in criticism when faced with spiritual languour, confusion of purpose, questionable quality of candidates or even points of "mild" personal pique. When President Leddy recommended to the Grand Magistracy in 1979 that Carter's rank be upgraded from Conventual Chaplain ad Honorem to Conventual Chaplain, Grand Cross, ad Honorem, Carter wrote to Leddy acknowledging his "amused curiosity": "I qualify it as surprising not so much in its essence but because I really had not anticipated it. I will confess to a certain amused curiosity as to why I had not arrived at that exalted rank in view of the fact that a number of other prelates who were much later on the Malta scene had received the Grand Cross. I refer, for example, to Archbishop Plourde, Archbishop Gregoire, etc."[11]

The "amused curiosity" was not lost on Leddy. Just a few months later, following close upon Carter's elevation to the College of Cardinals in June 1979, Leddy wrote to the honours-conscious prelate, informing him that he was to be raised to the dignity and rank of Bailiff Grand Cross of Honour and Devotion. Carter responded: "Your Excellency and Dear Francis: The formality is because I must acknowledge with appreciation your diligence in having conferred upon me what seems to be the traditional rank for Cardinals within the Order. As you say, it is somewhat hard on the respiratory system to keep up with these progressions. But I presume that we have now reached a point of rest, even if not, hopefully, of requiem. Speaking of that, I would imagine that the next promotion would be to the ranks of those in shining armour who stand around the Throne. Always with the presumption that some of the Knights of Malta make it."

From Conventual Chaplain to Bailiff Grand Cross. Even though the tone of his correspondence with Leddy is good-humoured and gracious, the correspondence does make it clear that Carter values his membership in the Order greatly. The Order has provided him with connections, helped secure important friendships and provided a measure of personal satisfaction. After all, to be found in the ranks of the Knights is no less a dignitary than the former Papal Representative to Canada, Sebastiano Baggio, the Cardinal Patronus of the Order.

If the new Bishop of London displayed a keen nose for sniffing out the powerful, he acquired it earlier, much earlier, when he was a new priest. He knew from the beginning of his acquaintance with Archbishop Sebastiano Baggio that this was a man to know better. It helps, of course, that he truly admires the affable churchman-diplomat, and that their ecclesiology (their view of the church) is compatible. Baggio has long been a powerful man and Carter has benefited from his power: "I proposed Carter to the Holy See when it was clear that Bishop Cody needed assistance. . . . and although I had no direct part in Carter's appointment to Toronto, I *suggested* his name here in Rome."

Baggio took instruction in English from the Montreal educator, and his friendship with the Canon was greatly strengthened by the enthusiastic approval of Carter's administrative and research skills expressed by Baggio's secretary, Monsignor Paul Marcinkus. Marcinkus, the controversial future Director of the Instituto per le Opere di Religione (the Vatican Bank), recommended Carter to Baggio for the specific task of preparing a report for the Spanish Embassy on the various educational aspects involving bishops, religious orders and the provinces in Canada.[12]

Carter certainly supported the investiture of Baggio as a Knight of Malta while he was still Apostolic Delegate to Canada, and their mutual involvement in the affairs of the Order has been constant.

Carter has faithfully cultivated his friendship with the Vatican diplomat throughout Baggio's long and varied career in church administration. After Baggio left Canada for a posting as Apostolic Nuncio to Brazil, Carter maintained contact. He genuinely cared for Baggio, Baggio's sister (with whom he lives), and the numerous projects for the poor in which Baggio was privately and officially engaged.

Carter's interest in Baggio wasn't limited to philanthropic efforts. He knew of Baggio's love of *objets d'art*, antiques and precious jewels. He provided him with an ancient Coptic ring, a gift from a Melkite bishop, which Baggio promptly had assessed in Paris for authenticity and value. The verdict was positive. Baggio approved. Carter smiled. The ring graces Baggio's finger to this day, a sign of office and valued friendship.

Their friendship rests, however, on more than an exchange of gifts and preferment; it rests on shared perspectives. When Baggio was named a Cardinal and subsequently assigned to a pastoral appointment as Archbishop of Cagliari, Sardinia, by Pope Paul VI — a new departure for a career diplomat — Carter wrote to him reminding him of the essentially "conservative" nature of their episcopal responsibilities: "I was again admiring the profundity of your motto 'Operando Custodire.' When you chose it, you could not possibly have anticipated the movement of the Church, but now I doubt if a better motto is available anywhere. This is indeed our task to maintain those great and stable essentials which must not be sacrificed to the passing whim of the moment and yet not to be afraid to work God's vineyard for the fullest produce. It is not easy to strike this balance, but it is surely the ideal after which we all have to strive."[13]

Carter saw in the Archbishop of Cagliari a model leader in the post-conciliar tumult. But there were other opinions, many unflattering. "Baggio is outstanding in that it is said that he has not opened a serious work of theology in the last twenty years."[14]

Baggio's reputation as a theological conservative is tied to many things, principal of which were his efforts to control the Puebla agenda (the 1979 Mexico meeting of the Latin American Episcopal Conference, or CELAM). Baggio was concerned that the radical initiatives that emerged from the 1968 Medellín CELAM meeting in Colombia, with the Roman Catholic Church's commitment to social justice and its concomitant support for the new "liberation theologies" being born in strife-ridden Latin America, not be repeated at Puebla. The Conference should concentrate on ecclesiastical matters and not dabble in politics and economics. The marxist taint of Medellín would be eradicated. However, Baggio's plans to control the agenda had been undertaken during the last months of the pontificate of Pope Paul VI, and when Paul died in 1978, the Conference was postponed until 1979 when Pope John Paul II, against the advice of Baggio, attended in person. The efforts of Baggio and other conservative prelates, including Alfonso Lopez Trujillo, then Auxiliary Bishop of Bogota, to contain the potential damage of Puebla, or correct the "excesses" of Medellín, were signally unsuccessful.

Baggio's years as a nuncio in Latin America did not make him any better disposed to the indigenous theological and pastoral trends that sought a critical incorporation of marxist concepts and analytical criteria into a christian critique of society, an incorporation that set out to eliminate the prevailing ideological biases. Baggio's scepticism about the validity of any such politico-religious marriage was reinforced under the fire of experience — literally. Baggio was forced to beat a hasty retreat from Latin America's religious and political turmoil — taking leave of his nunciature through a second-storey window.

Baggio's reputation as a conservative was unmistakably secured through his appointment as Cardinal Prefect of the Sacred Congregation for Bishops, which ranks as the second most powerful congregation or curial department in Rome, next to the "Supreme Congregation" (the Congregation for the Doctrine of the Faith, the former Holy Office of the Inquisition). It is this body which recommends to the pope candidates for the episcopate, promotions of bishops to archbishops, the filling of vacant sees, etc. The significance of the appointment was not lost on the Bishop of London. Only someone enjoying the highest confidence of the pontiff would be so appointed. Carter acted quickly.

On the very day that he read of Baggio's promotion in the *London Free Press* — February, 28, 1973 — Carter wrote to his friend offering his solicitude and keeping ever before the eyes of the Cardinal Prefect the name of this Upper Canadian churchman: "I cannot hide my satisfaction that you, of all men, will head this particular congregation. . . . I can think of no one who would have a better touch and a surer sense of the centre of this highly delicate mechanism than yourself. You initiated the warm relationships between the bishops of Canada and the delegates and nuncios which prevail to this day, and I am sure that you will have not lost your skill in the interim."[15]

But the Prefect of the Sacred Congregation for Bishops was not the only highly placed Vatican prelate Carter knew and cultivated from his days as a canon. His friend John Wright, the former Bishop of Pittsburgh who had spoken at the dinner honouring Carter's consecration as bishop in 1962, was Cardinal Prefect of the Sacred Congregation for the Clergy which, like Baggio's, is a powerful body.

Wright was a witty and ebullient man, with a fierce intellect and unqualified loyalty to the Holy See. British Vaticanologist and papal biographer Peter Hebblethwaite tartly observes that he was "known in the 1960s as 'the egg-head bishop', largely on the grounds that a bishop who read books at that date was an odd man out."[16]

Wright had a thoroughly cosmopolitan education, studying in Italy in the 1930s during the heyday of Italian fascism, doing pastoral work in prewar France and completing his doctoral dissertation during the Nazi occupation of Rome. Not inappropriately, his dissertation was entitled "National Patriotism in Papal Teaching".

Prior to the Second Vatican Council, Wright enjoyed a reputation as the leading American Catholic bishop in the emerging ecumenical era. He had noted that the ecumenical age is a "time of moral testing for Catholics," but cautioned in a manner suggestive of his Windsor Hotel tribute to Carter that "the current ecumenical movement . . . raises serious *doctrinal* problems for Catholics. These center around the necessity of keeping the ancient faith uncompromised by any equivocation and undiluted by any false irenicism."[17]

At the time of the Council (1962 to 1965), Wright was considered a progressive, and on some issues he definitely was, but the future curial cardinal deplored the mounting influence of the *periti*, or theological experts. He was not one to trifle with the magisterium or teaching authority of the church: there must be no parallel magisterium — the theologians alongside the hierarchy — but just the bishops in concert with the pope. He wrote to Carter in December 1963 expressing his concerns, and Carter sympathized, observing that even though bishops can debate vigorously among themselves, and not without enjoyment, "the moment a bishop dares to question a dictum of any of our *periti*, there ensues an emotional scene of the first magnitude." [18]

Carter also shared Wright's institutional loyalty, his outspokenness and his concern for the transmission of Catholic values. Wright, in fact, admired Carter the educator so much that he succeeded, in his capacity as Chancellor of Duquesne University in Pittsburgh, in arranging for Carter's first honorary doctorate. Although they met only infrequently, they corresponded regularly. Carter's salutations were often jocular — Eminent John, Gaunt John of Pitt (Wright was unabashedly corpulent) — and the letters often invoke, with a dash of irreverence, the name and towering presence of Minnie Carter.

When Wright was raised to the cardinalate in the consistory of 1969, Carter wrote to him: "Perhaps now that you have scaled the Olympian heights you will once again smile down on your old friend and admirer. Sincerely delighted."[19]

He needn't have worried. Wright never forgot him. In fact, Carter could speak to Wright with a candour and an almost combative tone that he never used with Baggio. With Baggio there is often a muted tone of deference. Not so with Wright. He would be more argumentative, although ultimately conciliatory. After all, Wright was a Cardinal Prefect. The best illustration of Carter's two-pronged approach to Wright can be found in his correspondence over the vexatious issue of mandatory clerical celibacy. As the prelate in charge of the Congregation for Clergy, Wright had more than a passing interest in retaining the discipline, and Carter, who was not one of the delegates to the 1971 Synod of Bishops in Rome where the issue would be raised, was adamant that a full airing of the matter occur, precisely in order that the status quo be vindicated. Carter wrote: "First of all, I am totally convinced that it is wrong and mischievous to avoid the debate. [It should be remembered that Pope Paul VI had removed discussion of the celibacy issue from the Council sessions and decided that it, along with the birth control issue, would be addressed by the pontiff alone.] As long as the debate is avoided, then those who wish to chip away at the issue will have a free hand. . . . We should debate celibacy and we should debate it in full scale and before the world. I do not know what your opinion of the issue is but I have not the least hesitation in saying that the hierarchies of the world will support celibacy to the hilt. The bishops of Canada have had the doubtful distinction of being called 'the Dutch of North America' by one of your more 'extinguished' confreres. We are nothing of the kind. . . . I am convinced that once the debate is on the table and once the issue of celibacy is clearly stated, we will stand foursquare behind the issue of celibacy."[20]

This strongly articulated position was at variance with that taken by brother Alex and a sizeable percentage of the Canadian hierarchy. The Canadian delegation to the 1971 Synod of Bishops in Rome did not appear to represent Emmett's position. "This presentation of Canada as epitomizing the progressive factor at the Synod was not accidental. The Canadian delegation had carried the battle for reform in a number of important areas. Most Reverend Alexander Carter, Bishop of Sault Ste. Marie, was, with Leo Cardinal Suenens of Belgium, one of the most urgent in recommending a change in church law with regard to priestly celibacy. The Synod said a massive no. But significantly the vote on a recommendation to permit the ordination of married men while counting 107 nays, also counted the startling number of 87 yeas, which is considered to have left the door open for papal initiatives toward the ordination of men already married in cases of serious shortages of priests."[21] Wright was not edified. Neither was Emmett. The tally of Canadian votes at the Synod was actually only four.

Between 1962 and 1965 the Second Vatican Council took place, an ecclesial event of the greatest moment convoked by Pope John XXIII to create a comprehensive renewal in the church. Carter, though only recently a bishop, witnessed church politics and the operations of divine grace in the raw, and had many opportunities to work closely with Baggio, Wright and other influential figures. He witnessed the eleventh-hour effort by the conservative and leonine Alfredo Cardinal Ottaviani to contain the damage wrought by a Council unprepared to affirm that membership in the Roman Catholic Church was absolutely necessary for salvation. He witnessed the brilliant rebuttal of Ottaviani by Bishop De Smedt of Bruges who denounced the three sinful attitudes to be found in the church: triumphalism, clericalism, juridicism. And he could not help but be affected by the debates and politics of composition.

Right from the beginning, Carter was concerned about the quality and accessibility of the press, both secular and religious. In a letter to Pocock back in Toronto, he urged the Canadian bishops to make a strong representation to the Holy See to make sure that the people at the head of their communications be truly aware of the importance and techniques of modern public relations. He worried that a poorly managed press bureau could misrepresent or blur the important achievement of the Council and the presentation of a new and more intelligible image of the church to the world.[22]

Carter's concern over communications has been a constant in his teaching and practice as a churchman, although it is a concern marked by ambivalence, and it was to surface with particular force during his tenure as Archbishop of Toronto. His conviction, however, that the church *must* work with the press to ensure an honest and objective assessment of its work has never wavered. He abominates the Roman penchant for secrecy.

William Power, Bishop Emeritus of Antigonish, Nova Scotia, remembers that the recently annointed Carter was drawn to important prelates at the Council: "I would say that he distinguished himself not so much in terms of public utterances as in the people he associated with, the strong voices of the Council, Suenens, Léger, Marcos McGrath of Panama City, etc. Those kind of people."

Although he was invited to write the introduction to the decree on education for the definitive Walter Abbott edition of the Council documents, he was basically disappointed in the decree, as he was in several others, including, predictably, the decree on communications. They were harmless, unexciting things. This was not, however, the case with the central documents, the dogmatic and pastoral constitutions, and the highly important declaration on religious liberty, *Dignitatis humanae*.

This document fired the imaginations of the Fathers and the non–Catholic Observers in a way that few had before. It celebrated the inviolable right to religious liberty on the part of all, and in no small measure implied a repudiation — indirect, of course — of nineteenth-century papal teaching. Carter prepared his own intervention [Vatican parlance for a submission], but the occasion to present it never materialized. It is unfortunate that it did not, because in its succinct and passionate way the intervention is Carter at his most theologically astute. He applauds the document for calling the political authorities to honest account, and then proceeds further to argue for ecclesiastical accountability, for ecclesiastical justice. "And so we must admit the need, within the Church, for an emancipation from needless restraints and coercion which is consonant with the changing state of subjects in the Church and with the changing human condition itself. We need not be surprised that there can be in the Church men who might exercise authority in an unenlightened way, so that the best interests of the People of God are not achieved. We could cite cases in which persons subject to ecclesiastical authority were not treated as persons with rights and dignity of their own. So it is that I submit we must include in this document a statement that the Church herself is ready to reform in this matter of undue restraint and coercion. . . . we should add a statement concerning the meaning of true Christian freedom . . . in order to prevent any misunderstanding which might do harm to the People of God."[23]

Carter's contact with Rome was not limited to his personal relationship with Baggio, Marcinkus and Wright, and his attendance at the Council sessions. No sooner had the Council concluded in 1965 than he was chosen as a member of the newly created body, the Consilium for the Implementation of the Constitution on the Sacred Liturgy (Consilium Ad Exsequendam Constitutionem De Sacra Liturgia).

The Consilium had the onerous task of overseeing the implementation of the new Council's liturgy constitution throughout the world. As the liturgy or public worship of the church affects ordinary Catholics in a way the more abstruse deliberations in theology and canon law do not, it is far from surprising that liturgical change occasioned strong emotional response. In some circles, like the Latin Mass Society, it still does. To alter a ritual and to tamper with a "sacred" language by bringing the vernacular into the sanctuary, is explosive stuff, more explosive than the Council Fathers ever anticipated. Carter observed: "In the late, and for some, much lamented days of the Latin, totally Rome-controlled and rigidly inflexible liturgy, there was no confusion. Some say that there wasn't much liturgy either, but that is an issue I would like to avoid, at least for now, while I try to shed some light. There was one language, one set of rubrics without

options, and one central control of all editing and publishing. The
break in this monolithic structure appeared to be in a single act, but it
was really a multiple fissure. The apparently single change was the
introduction of the vernacular or popular language to the Mass and its
universal use in the rites of the sacraments. Many of us sitting in our
places at Vatican II saw only the first aspect. We saw it and we rejoiced
because it was indeed high time, but we did not see 'the many a weary
mile' of adaptation and adjustment that we would have to face as we
bid adieu to auld lange syne."[24] Carter came to know, personally, the
exorbitant cost of that "weary mile".

He met numerous bishops and liturgical experts while sitting on
the Consilium, and he quickly developed the smarts he needed to
explain Rome to Canada and Canada to Rome. He never missed an
opportunity.

When the much esteemed Governor General Georges Vanier died
in 1967, Carter wrote to Father A. Bugnini, Secretary of the Consilium, lauding Vanier as the leading citizen and most distinguished
Catholic in the nation. Then he quickly got down to business: "Ottawa is one of the dioceses authorized to conduct the experiment [on
the new Funeral Rite] and the family had immediately requested the
use of white vestments, etc. As a result, we had a most spectacular
opportunity of experimenting with the Funeral Rite as drawn up by
the Consilium. Moreover, the Canadian Broadcasting Corporation
put most of the ceremony on film. I may report immediately that the
Rite drew extraordinarily favourable comment right across the country. The comparison between this Rite and the Funeral Rite used at
President Kennedy's Funeral was much discussed. May I say in
passing that Vice-President Humphrey of the United States was
present, along with all the outstanding ambassadors and dignitaries of
Canada and most of the world. In every discussion which we have
heard the reformed Rite was chosen as far preferable."[25]

Carter went even further in his desire for the full adoption of the
reformed Rite by offering to bring a copy of the CBC film for a private
showing for Pope Paul VI, who had known Vanier personally. At the
same time, while far from shy in representing Canada's wishes to
Rome, he was zealous in transmitting Rome's instructions and cau-
tions to Canada.

In a report he prepared for the Canadian episcopate in his dual
capacity as a member of the Consilium and Chairman of Canada's
Episcopal Commission on Liturgy (English Sector), he wrote: "The

present state of unauthorized experimentation is damaging the whole cause. It is causing dismay in Rome, particularly in the mind of the Holy Father, and it is introducing changes which will not be permanent and, therefore, which can only sow confusion and disarray in the minds of all. We respectfully suggest that the Bishops of Canada should insist upon compliance with the basic rubrics until the matter has been properly worked out, at which moment we will all happily transfer to some other condition of affairs which at least will have the merit of having been examined carefully and exhaustively."[26] Although Carter can be very critical of Rome, he remains devoted not only to the exercise of authority, but also to the ways of obedience.

In 1970 the Consilium was dissolved and in its place emerged the Sacred Congregation for Divine Worship. Carter was elected to the Congregation. Clearly, his work on the Consilium had met with papal approval.

But the most troublesome and challenging task Carter faced was associated with the work of the International Commission on English in the Liturgy (ICEL), a commission on which he would serve as vice-chairman and then as chairman. Composed of eleven English-using countries (Australia, Canada, England-Wales, India, Ireland, New Zealand, Pakistan, the Philippines, Scotland, South Africa and the United States), its job was to translate the reformed texts of the liturgy into English. Easier said than done. Carter encountered Roman interference and British intransigence. He also encountered a solid dose of bureaucratic inefficiency, compounded by the fact that, although the chairman of ICEL might reside in Edinburgh or London, the Secretariate was permanently situated in Washington. Communication problems were gargantuan.

But the greatest problem for ICEL was interference from various curial mandarins. In fact, a considerably distraught chairman, the Archbishop of Edinburgh, Gordon J. Gray, wrote directly to the Pope protesting the dire consequences for ICEL should its work be undermined. It had approved a translation of the canon of the mass for universal usage in the English-speaking world, only to find that various experts in Rome were now raising substantive objections to the texts. Gray wrote with episcopal restraint: "To many Catholics and non-Catholics the impression will be given that more than 600 English speaking Bishops and their *periti*, spread all over the world, who in close collaboration have studied and approved the version, have failed to find in it deficiencies and errors that, according to reports, have been noted in Rome. It will appear that the English speaking Bishops and *periti* have been lacking in liturgical expertise."[27]

Carter wrote to Gray instantly, supporting the thrust of his letter and its tone. He deplored unauthorized Roman interference and noted "the necessity of open discussion with the Holy Office, which may have changed its name but does not appear to have changed its spots."[28] Bold words, but characteristic of Carter's no-nonsense approach to the Roman departments or dicasteries when they exceeded their rightful authority. And he would be bolder still when he himself became chairman of ICEL in 1971.

There could be no better training course for survival in the convoluted tactics of Rome than the chairmanship of ICEL. Containing the centralizing trends of Rome was only one of Carter's headaches. The various constituencies of ICEL were warring with each other, and he had to keep unauthorized experimenters in line.

But Rome was the delicate act. First of all, Carter was deeply troubled by the direction the Congregation for Divine Worship was beginning to take under the leadership of the Australian James Cardinal Knox in 1974 following its absorption of the Congregation for Sacraments. With stunning directness he reminded the Cardinal Prefect of the old procedures of the Consilium and the success the implementation of the Constitution on the Liturgy enjoyed through the Consilium's effective decentralizing initiatives, which consisted in emphasizing local authority and diminishing the "Romanità of the whole process."[29]

A couple of months later he would have cause to be more direct still. This time the matter at issue revolved around a procedural ploy that undermined the "principle of subsidiarity" and Carter was furious. But his prose was polite and temperate: "No one, and I least of all, questions the right of the Holy See to regulate the universal concerns of the liturgy or even those matters which would concern multi-national hierarchies. But it seems to me that the principle of subsidiarity has, at least in recent years, been strictly respected by the Roman authorities. I understand the principle of subsidiarity to mean that when a legitimate authority is already in the field, a superior authority does not intervene. In the case which we are presently considering, the representatives of ICEL were being consulted in regard to the question of the ICET [International Consultation on English Texts] texts and, in effect, a ballot was in their hands. You have decided to go over their jurisdiction to the Presidents of the Conferences. That you have every right to do so is self-evident. But I am wondering if it constitutes respect of the principle of subsidiarity and if you will not reduce the role of those bishops who have served so well in ICEL to a point where outstanding members of the hierarchies will hardly wish to serve on such a Committee. . . . [A]s long as ICEL is vested in representatives of the national hierarchies appointed by those hierarchies, I find it difficult to postulate that policy-decisions will be taken by other bodies."[30]

Carter is firm on the principle of subsidiarity, but he is firmer still on the matter of the will of a majority being subverted by a disaffected minority. Frustrated by the unhelpful attitude he detected in the English and Welsh hierarchy over various ICEL translations, and their obstinate refusal to abide by any consensus save their own, Carter dispatched an angry letter to Knox when he discovered how the English had politicked in Rome with some success on the matter of the Form of Confirmation. "Like my predecessor, Cardinal Gray, I have devoted most of my efforts as Chairman of that International Commission to healing breaches. I fear that this latest development will not be productive in this direction and, indeed, may open up some new wounds. Our democratic countries are rather sensitive to a minority imposing its views on the majority even if they succeed in doing it through authoritative channels. . . . In a word, Your Eminence, I am not at all happy with this development and I feel it is my duty to express my opinion to you. . . . I have always considered that the greatest service is to express a loyal dissent when such is indicated."[31]

His years on the Consilium, the Congregation for Divine Worship and ICEL taught Carter a great deal about Roman machinations, lobbying and constructive conciliation. He learned how to speak his mind in a way that was forthright when necessary, accommodating when appropriate, and always polite. He could apply his Roman experience to the temporal order, and he did that, most adroitly, in the area of Catholic education in the province of Ontario.

CHAPTER FIVE

Reshaping Catholic Education in Ontario

Carter's training in the arena of Roman politics and the international machinations of Roman decision making, coming on the heels of his apprenticeship in Duplessis's Quebec, were clearly instrumental in making Gerald Emmett Carter a shaper and reshaper of educational politics in Ontario.

Though influenced greatly by the Roman Catholic school system in Quebec, the educational scene in Ontario had a history and shape all its own. As Carter demonstrated in *The Catholic Public Schools of Quebec*, the Roman Catholic and Protestant schools in Quebec had developed along unambiguously religious but laudably cooperative lines; in Ontario, on the other hand, the educational rights which Section 93 of the British North America Act had guaranteed the Roman Catholic or Protestant religious minority had not been extended as generously or as willingly. It is a history recalled successively by Ontario's Premier John Robarts in 1963 when extending funding to the separate school system and by his successor, William Davis, when he rose in the Legislature in 1971 to explain his government's decision not to provide *"full* funding" for Ontario's Roman Catholic Separate Schools.

While introducing the Ontario Foundation Tax Plan, 1964, Premier John Robarts had explained to the House on February 21, 1963, that Section 93 of the British North America Act, together with The Separate School Act of 1863, entrenched "any legal right or privilege with respect to denominational schools as such existed on July 1, 1867 . . . . This fact can only be changed by an amendment to The British North America Act, which is completely impracticable. Even if such a change were desired by the Roman Catholic minority in Ontario, for example, or by the Protestant majority, for that matter, the fact that the enactment affects minority rights of other groups in different ways in other provinces would make any constitutional change a practical impossibility."[1] As a newcomer to the Ontario scene, Carter, who had been dubbed "Mr. Education" in Quebec, faced a formidable task, but he brought with him impeccable credentials, and he had already attracted influential friends in Ontario. In the long run, they were to stand him and Catholic education in good stead.

John C. Cody had taken care to court the influential members of his diocese. In addition to institutionalizing the periodic levees hosted for London's elite, Cody had been quick to cultivate the friendship of those who might help him perform his episcopal duties more effectively. One such friend was John Robarts, a citizen of London, past Minister of Education in Ontario's Conservative government, and the Premier of the province. It was a happy acquaintance, which extended to Cody's Auxiliary Bishop virtually coincident with the latter's arrival in London. Indeed, the Carter–Robarts friendship was destined to become a lifelong one, and it extended well beyond the formalities of professional protocol. Emmett Carter was, in fact, most likely the last person to speak to John Robarts before his suicide.

In reply to John Robarts' congratulatory letter on the occasion of Carter's accession to the episcopal throne in the diocese of London, Carter addressed the Premier in tones of praise and respect which were to characterize their personal and professional associations: "A man of your qualities of statesmanship recognizes the intermingling of the temporal and the spiritual, and the importance of mutual respect and support."[2] Similar expressions of affection, admiration and support were exchanged with the Who's Who of Ontario and Canada as tributes to the new bishop hurried through Her Majesty's Mail. Future prime minister John Turner wrote a letter that is ironical in light of later political events, but which shows the extent to which Carter cultivated friendships in high places. "I miss seeing you and talking with you . . .," Turner wrote. "There is probably one big difference between us. I have no desire for any larger field than I have now whereas your talents are fitted for greater things."[3] Governor General Georges Vanier wrote: "Please remember that when you come to Ottawa we shall always be pleased to see you." And in his responses to the greetings of the great, we see some classic Carter. This is his answer to Prime Minister Lester B. Pearson's congratulations: "Although we in Canada enjoy a happy State-Church rela-

School Days: A young lad
prepares to leave his home
on Prince Arthur Street.
Later, the young
seminarian poses near his
parents' house on Jeanne
Mance Street, 1937.

Emmett and Alex with a
boy's best friend, at Lac
Paquin, 1925.

Carter has always loved out-of-doors activities. At Fourteen Island Lake: Mae (with dog), Aunt Alice, Emmett, Uncle Pat, Alex, 1925.

. . . And has had a bit of the showman in him. Emmett (at far right) in a school drama, circa 1925.

The Carter siblings' lives have been closely intertwined. (Top)
Emmett and his three sisters: Margaret, Irene, Mary.

Family get-together: Emmett, Tom, Alex; Minnie seated (centre)
and sister Margaret Duggan (far right) with niece Lenore Duggan,
cousin Ray Linagh, and nephew Gerry Duggan, 1943.

Emmett poses with his mentor, Father Gerald McShane, and a classmate, Father John Brennan.

Mom and Dad Carters' 50th Wedding Anniversary in 1945, with Emmett (far left) and sister Mary Lenore beside Alex. PETER TANSEY, MONTREAL

Emmett receiving his doctorate from the Université de Montréal, 1947, and (below), the investiture of Canon Carter by Paul-Émile Cardinal Léger in 1953.

Pope John XXIII with the Carter brothers in Rome, 1959, at Alex's *ad limina* visit, a once-every-five-years reporting to the pontiff.

The Canadian Association of the Knights of Malta. SIMA/INT'L PRESS SERVICE

Chaplains of the Knights of Malta, 1961. At far left, Count Robert Keyserlingk beside Canon Emmett Carter. Third from right is Sebastiano "the Bishop maker" Baggio, beside Quintin J. Gwyn, one of the Canadian Association's founders. Far right: Monsignor Olivier Murault, a Director of the University of Montreal. SIMA, MONTREAL

Carter the Educator: at St. Benedict School, Sarnia, in 1977; and with fellow commentators Richard Alway, Betty Kennedy, Bill Walker, and communications director Brad Massman, after the election of John Paul II in 1978. DIOCESE OF LONDON; PAUL SMITH PHOTOGRAPHY

tionship, based mostly on both parties minding their own business, it is inevitable that since we both have to deal with human beings our interests meet and merge."[4]

More greetings with varying degrees of cordiality and conviviality flowed in from large numbers of prominent citizens. From Michael Patrick, mayor of Windsor, came a warm testimonial which captures the sentiments of many: "Your friendliness, your charm and your innate graciousness impressed all those with whom you came in contact, and from every facet of our community the reaction to your personality, your abilities and your versatility could be summed up in one little three-word phrase 'I like him.' "[5]

Emmett was also quick to become friends with then Education Minister and future premier of Ontario, William Davis. Like his friendship with John Robarts, this relationship was born in the halls of power but flourished in the privacy of the sitting room — it remains to this day a friendship based on mutual respect and the natural attraction of kindred spirits. William Davis recalls his early acquaintance with Emmett, and with Alex, during the bishops' regular Easter meetings that took place in Toronto at the same time as the annual sessions of the Ontario Separate School Trustees' Association. "My initial impressions of Cardinal Carter have remained consistent throughout the entire period that I have known him. And that is so apart from whether one agreed or disagreed with the other's point of view on issues. He has one of the finest minds I have ever been exposed to. I want to stress that this takes nothing away from the intellectual capacities of the other bishops, but it is fair to say that Cardinal Carter and his brother were really very articulate and logical in their discussions."

Appropriately, therefore, as soon as Emmett Carter settled into the Diocese of London, his fellow Ontario bishops appointed him to their Education Committee, and it was he who drafted the position paper that was to serve as the argumentative basis for the most significant step to be taken by Roman Catholic education in Ontario since the turn of the century — the extension of the provisions of Section 93 to include funding for grades nine and ten. By 1962 the school system was burgeoning, but the religious communities of women and men who had traditionally staffed the Catholic schools were in the early stages of the contemporary decimation of their ranks. In Quebec, Duplessis had depended on the free or nearly-free services of the religious men and women working in the province's schools and hospitals to provide the indirect funds for his social programs; and in Ontario, too, the religious congregations had offered a source of cheap labour. The lay instructors who would now have to take their places could hardly be expected to assume their teaching roles without benefit of a professional salary. Ontario's Catholic schools were not only at a crossroads, they were in crisis. Without the new sources of funding provided by the Ontario Foundation Tax Plan, 1964, their very survival was in serious doubt.

Regulation 16/64, which legitimized the Ontario Tax Foundation Plan, 1964, established an equalization formula for the distribution of corporation taxes, a formula which John Robarts introduced by arguing that it was the fairest means for assessing both public and separate school entitlement from residential and farm assessment. According to the provision, both the public and separate schools would receive revenue from corporate assessments in the same ratio that they had previously received them from residential and farm assessment. The measure provided a large step towards solving the troublesome issue of corporate tax assessment, though history has proven William Davis correct when he predicted at the time that this was not the final resolution many had hoped it to be. Nevertheless, it did provide massive new support for Roman Catholic schools, and though he was hardly the lone player in a drama which had in fact begun before his transfer to Ontario, Emmett Carter had performed the crucial function of drafting the bishops' position.

William Davis notes that the initiative which was to culminate in the Ontario Foundation Tax Plan, 1964, had actually begun under the premiership of Leslie Frost, and that John Robarts was obviously sympathetic. "I sensed then a very genuine expression of appreciation on the bishops' part for what the government had done, appreciation on Carter's part too. This did not alter Carter's ultimate objective for the extension [of full funding to all grades] of the Separate School System." As a prelude to the final scene in this educational drama, John Wintermeyer, leader of the Opposition Liberals, and Donald MacDonald, leader of the Ontario New Democratic Party, rose to applaud the government's sense of justice and equity.

Looking back on the event, Carter recalls his relationship with John Robarts and the importance of Regulation 16/64. "When Robarts became premier, he and I were quite friendly. He was a Londoner, of course, so we had a very good rapport. I talked a lot with Robarts. In fact, I was quite instrumental in our getting the Robarts

Plan [Regulation 16/64] into law, which was in many ways almost as important as this recent funding arrangement. It's never been presented as being historically very important, but we were really going down the drain."

As a result of their experiences in Rome during the Second Vatican Council, which was in full swing during the funding debate, the bishops had learned the value of collegiality, of working and planning together. So they formed committees, and they appointed Carter secretary of the Commission on Education. Carter recalls the several very intense meetings and his writing the brief, "though I don't think I signed it because in those days auxiliary bishops didn't sign everything. But I did write it. It was right in Pocock's house, here on Beaumont Drive, downstairs in the present library that we met: Pocock, Robarts, myself, and I think that Bishop Ryan [of Hamilton] was there too, and Robarts' financial and educational assistant, Dr. R.W.B. Jackson. We presented our case — the total exclusion we had from most sources of finance. There was assessment on companies — industrial, commercial, and so on — none of which was going to the Catholics, except in cases where you had a totally owned group which could vote their corporate taxes to the separate schools. And there were very few of those. And then we didn't get anything else, except for the private taxes from municipal assessment. Nothing else, really. And there were no equalizing grants. So we presented our case to Robarts, who seemed quite taken aback by it. And this fellow, Jackson, was very helpful. Robarts admitted he hadn't realized things were as bad as they were, and he went out to study the matter. I think we met three times down there in the basement. Then, finally, Robarts came up with the equalization plan, though we've never got up to full equalization."

Because Emmett Carter was the Auxiliary Bishop of London at the time, it was his superior, Bishop Cody, who took the appropriate initiative in formally signalling his gratitude for the crucial role played by Premier and fellow Londoner, John Robarts. In a letter dated April 13, 1963, bearing the salutation "Dear Friend", Cody wrote to Robarts, expressing his gratitude and sounding at times like his auxiliary, Gerald Emmett. Cody was grateful, but he wanted to see the Regulation in action. He also wondered out loud about the training of Catholic teachers, and added: "In regard to our High Schools, at least implicitly guaranteed by the British North America Act, I cannot understand why it would be impossible for Ontario to provide High Schools for her Catholic minority when Quebec has always found the means of providing High Schools for her Protestant minority . . . ." Cody was not satisfied, and neither was Carter. There would be further volleys. Cody continued: "It took a long time to persuade the majority of our fellow citizens that we would never surrender our elementary schools but in the atmosphere of today and taking into account our numerical strength, it will not take us long to vindicate our rights in the field of secondary education. Without High Schools our system of education would not be pedagogically sound because abnormally truncated. Political expediency will soon be on our side." Cody was right, but that lay more than two decades in the future.

By 1969 the bishops were again agitating for full funding, and the Roman Catholic population was mobilized in a campaign of letter writing and political protest. Newspapers bristled with letters to the editor for and against the extension of funding to the Roman Catholic separate schools, and Emmett Carter's name began to appear as a *leitmotif* in many of them. The political activity culminated in the Bishops' Brief, which deplored the situation and insisted on the urgency of full funding; the issue had become such a political hot potato that William Davis recalls his predecessor, John Robarts, commenting to him as he assumed the Premier's responsibilities: "I left you with two problems — Spadina and the Bishops' Brief."[6]

Government studies documented the purported fiscal strides resulting from the 1964 Regulation, but the figures were not enough. Newspapers in the London diocese carried Carter's warnings that several of their high schools were in jeopardy.

William Davis huddled with his caucus, and on August 31, 1971, he explained his decision to the House. The Premier recounted the history of the problem in tones similar to his predecessor's in February 1963, but unlike his predecessor, he concluded that to extend public funding, throughout the secondary system in this instance, "would fragment the present system beyond recognition and repair, and do so to the disadvantage of all those who have come to want for their children a public school system free of a denominational or sectarian character. . . . We would inevitably be obliged to proceed throughout all our educational institutions to fragment and divide both our young people and our resources, from kindergarten through post-graduate university studies. . . . To accept such a philosophy [as extension and full funding], and to foster it, the government would be obliged to create an entire educational system which would be, at the very least, a dual one, comprising a system for Roman Catholic students, and a further system for the Protestant students, another for the Jewish students, and possibly still others representing the various denominations of Protestant and other faiths."[7] These were prophetic words, and they would gain the Conservative Party a staggering majority in the October 21, 1971, provincial election. For his part, Carter had urged his people not to characterize the funding question as a political issue — his was a pro-democracy stance, and not the last of its sort on which he was to take a firm stand.[8] Despite the setback, at no time did Carter question Davis's motives, accepting the fact that the position had been taken not on the basis of partisan political assessment but on what Davis genuinely believed to be right at that moment in time.

The government's decision triggered a round of belt-tightening financial studies and overtures to various public boards, thereby pushing Emmett Carter into trying to rally his troops by accusing separate school supporters of apathy. The gravity of the financial situation also virtually compelled Carter to urge his teachers to accept lower salaries, an ironic and bitter twist in light of Carter's vigorous efforts to professionalize the teaching profession in Quebec and gain for them a wage appropriate to their professional status. Mustering his best rhetorical style and swallowing hard on the thoughts of battles fought and won in Montreal, Carter addressed a gathering of teachers at Brennan High School in Windsor in June 1975, where he bemoaned the "decline of dedication to superior values on the part of some teachers." He advised them that the local board could not match their demands for wage parity with the public system. Carter pleaded not for starvation wages, but for moderation. It cannot have been his happiest hour. Many of the Catholic high schools in his diocese were in serious trouble. St. Patrick's in Sarnia, F.J. Brennan in Windsor, St. Anne's in Tecumseh and Catholic Central in London had all been forced into deficit financing, and cures could not be found for all.

More and more, Carter's presentations were to educational audiences, and more and more his talks dealt with educational themes. In his September 11, 1971, address to the Brennan High School teachers, he picked up on what were becoming frequent and familiar themes; in fact, he delivered the identical speech to the teachers of Kent County on the following October 5. Facing the government decision head on, Carter argued that one might pretend that there is such a thing as a neutral school, but "teachers are *never* neutral." As a result, the Roman Catholic separate school must be staffed by committed professionals intent on passing to the younger generation both the values and the faith commitment which is at the heart of the Catholic heritage. Education, Carter insisted, is not a matter of disseminating information, of transmitting facts, but of stimulating intellectual development. Moreover, children "do not grow in sections"; therefore, education is properly a fusion of school, home and church, all committed to the ideals embodied in the Catholic tradition.

Carter echoed his thesis to the Conference of Catholic Teachers in Chatham in February 1974, to an Ontario English Catholic Teachers Association audience in March 1974 and again to the Canadian Catholic Trustees Association in Toronto in May 1974. But he began to add a further dimension to his theme; namely, personalism in a pluralist society. According to the philosophy of pluralism adopted by the Second Vatican Council, everyone has a right to one's opinion and a right to express that opinion; in addition, everyone has the right to pursue legitimate objectives, even when those objectives differ from majority opinion. This, he explained, is pluralism. On the other hand, according to the personalist philosophy espoused by the Council, everyone "has a duty to have convictions and to recognize that his convictions invariably influence others."[9] By definition, then, there can be no such thing as a neutral teacher; for a teacher there can be no such thing as a private life; indeed, "to accept a position in a Catholic School is to accept a public and religious trust."

For Emmett Carter the survival of the Catholic school system is no narrow sectarian issue; it is a matter of moral consequence with international ramifications. In an October 29, 1973, celebration of Quebec educationalist John McIlhone, Carter insisted that "The Catholic school is one of the last remaining supports of Christian teaching and moral values in the world. This is not some supercilious assumption of superiority. This is hard and sad fact." "How," Carter wondered, "can Christian values triumph in the present world when they have been abandoned in the educative system?" In a society which espouses secular humanism, how is a student to learn christian values if there is no parent, no school, no teacher presenting a christian personalist perspective and inspiring the young with the witness of christian values?

Given the need for appropriate witness and the concomitant need to teach the christian message, Carter grew more and more alarmed during his London tenure about what he saw as irresponsible dissent in the church. Speaking to Sarnia's separate school teachers in May 1975, he insisted that "[t]he Catholic Faith has *never* consisted in a consensus," but worried aggressively about what had happened to the Roman Catholic message. "Your publications are quoting the far-out theologians — including positions diametrically opposed to the magisterium — the *ONLY* official teaching organism of the Church on: the indissolubility of marriage, on sexual morality, on a host of subjects, as if it were a concerted action of your leadership to affirm that the age-old traditions of the Church are superseded by the new Morality. And you, individually and collectively, must be held responsible for what your organization is doing and teaching. Many teachers are themselves playing down the difficult aspects of our religion. I know that the catechetical program may be partly to blame, but these programs are only instruments . . . . Your attitudes far outweigh any book." These were difficult issues, indeed, and Carter faced them head on, using as his tools his convictions concerning the personal role of the teacher, the authority of his office and his unshakeable belief that there must be unity in essential matters. The ideas and convictions Carter had developed during his Montreal ministry were on the line, and he was expressing them with a mounting sense of urgency. For Carter the educationalist and the man of the church, the development years had been replaced by the survival years.

As Auxiliary Bishop and then Bishop of London, Carter assumed greatly expanded obligations in the educational arena. He became the principal teaching authority in his diocese and a member of the collective Ontario and national episcopal bodies assigned to oversee church teaching in Canada; and as Bishop, Carter became one of the elect to whom Rome might turn for consultative purposes. Thus, he had access to the ultimate teaching authority of the church. As he reminded the Knights of Malta in an October 1973 address, teaching authority rests not with the theologians, not the clergy, not the laity, "not even the media, but [with] the successors of the apostles. Keep your eyes on the bishops of the Church, and if there is any doubt *turn to look to Peter for guidance.*"

On the level of theory, Carter had, of course, been well versed. As a Canadian bishop attending the Second Vatican Council, he was particularly well placed to influence and assess Rome's contemporary pedagogical directions. The Council document on education, *Gravissimum educationis*, is generally seen as one of the weakest of the many statements to emanate from the deliberations of Vatican II, even though it was strides ahead of the most influential papal document on education to precede it, Pius XI's 1929 *Divini illius magistri*. Carter fully agreed with this assessment, even though *Gravissimum educationis* formally embraced most of the educational and interpersonal theory he had long been advocating himself. Carter explains: "I suppose if you weren't from a free country you might find it very exciting: that way you were saying something that needed to be said. But I found that it was so obviously deja vu that the points the document was making were accepted and taken for granted, that it didn't speak to me, or make me want to shout 'This thing is marvellous.' I would have liked to have seen an appeal, morally, to the concept of conscience and individual freedom in education stated better than it was. The appeal to the judgement of the individual as well as a psychological approach to the Christian person. I would also have liked to have seen the opening of a discussion of relationships between those in authority, teachers and students, and so on. And in those days, of course, we had not raised the feminism of today. I think that if we were to write that document today, we would want to talk about equality and difference. I think that would have been a marvellous chapter. Equality, difference, and the two sexes. But we were published before our time."

Although these final observations have as their source the Roman and thomistic thesis of complementarity which posits divinely imbedded and quite distinct methods of learning and social roles characteristic of male and female, Emmett Carter's own thinking with respect to the nature of womanhood was clearly evolving with the times. He was beginning to more beynd the more simplistic and traditional views of Pius XI, which he had accepted without criticism in the writing of his *Catholic Public Schools of Quebec*. Indeed, the Carter of the 1970s would surely reject the assertion made as a young man concerning the education of women when he had argued that "to meet modern conditions women must be trained in the skills which she will use as a woman such as the care of children and the making of a home."[10] Although these ideas are thoroughly consistent with those of Pius XI, Carter's call for a conciliar statement on equality and difference implies an openness to investigation and an openness to contemporary insights. He was beginning to distance himself from Pius XI's unflinching celebration of the "trusting obedience which the woman owes to man" and that Pope's blunt rejection of woman's aspirations as "false liberty and unnatural equality."[11]

In his introduction to *Gravissimum educationis*, Carter makes the apparently contradictory observation that the conciliar document "cannot fail to bring some clarification, if only to establish that the Church has not changed its traditional positions."[12] This, despite the fact that Pius XI's germinal encyclical on education had posited the natural superiority of the father in the domestic society and hence the father as the primary teaching authority in the household, had rejected as an occasion of sin any serious efforts at sex education, had ignored the role of individual conscience or personal development in education, and had not given prominence to the social dimension of education in any serious way.

Gravissimum educationis may in fact be stating ancient Catholic principles on freedom of conscience, but they are not principles to be found in papal educational theory; rather, they are principles which form a *leitmotif* throughout the documents of Vatican II, particularly the document on religious freedom (*Dignitatis humanae*), the pastoral constitution on the church in the modern world (*Gaudium et spes*) and the decree on ecumenism (*Unitatis redintegratio*).

Gravissimum educationis talks of the inalienable right to an education, a right springing from the dignity of the human person, of the need for the individual to pursue "authentic freedom" through education and of the parents' natural pre-eminent responsibilities in educating their children. It also underlines the importance of "positive and prudent sex education."

The Vatican II document plays a variation on a recurring conciliar theme by arguing that "children and young people have a right to be encouraged to weigh moral values with an upright conscience, and to embrace them by personal choice." In addition, the properly educated individual, the Council Fathers argued, should be eager to promote "that Christian transformation of the world by which natural values, viewed in the full perspective of humanity as redeemed by Christ, may contribute to the good of society as a whole."[13] The tone and even the topics are so far removed from Pius XI that *Gravissimum educationis* is a breath of fresh air; the document is also so close to Emmett Carter's own thinking that for him it is apparently a matter of deja vu despite his celebration of Pius XI throughout *The Catholic Public Schools of Quebec*. One is reminded of Canon Carter's testimonial dinner as he prepared to leave for Quebec City and St. Lawrence College in 1961 when he argued: "Either we grow, either we search, either we develop the truth which is given to us or we decline."

If the theory and nature of the church's teaching had progressed rather dramatically during the forty-plus years after Pius XI's encyclical letter on education, so had her approach to catechetics and the catechism; that is, to the basic means by which the faith is to be taught. This, of course, is an area in which Gerald Emmett Carter had earned an international reputation, and during his tenure in London it became a matter of serious concern for the Canadian bishops collectively. Indeed, Carter's role in the development of what was tagged the Canadian Catechism is pinpointed by many as one area where he has been found seriously wanting.

Thomas Francoeur, professor of religious studies, philosophy and counselling in the Faculty of Education at McGill University in Montreal, recalls that even when he was a student of Carter at St. Joseph's Teachers' College in Montreal, the revised Baltimore Catechism was still in use, and it was Carter who had experimented with the Schorsch series as an alternative to rote memorization, experimenting further with *Our Life with God* from William H. Sadlier Publishers in New York. Carter, however, was still not completely satisfied with either series and began actively to plan his own catechism in cooperation with Thomas Francoeur. It was a project which Carter mentioned in his correspondence to renowned U.S. catechist Alexander Schorsch and Schorsch's colleague, Sister Dolores, as early as 1953. The project actually was started and Francoeur still has segments of it stacked away, but the undertaking never reached completion, in part because of the introduction of the Viens vers le Père catechism in Quebec.

The history of the Viens vers le Père, its pedagogical value, its ultimate translation and adaptation into the Come to the Father series in English Canada, and its unofficial transition to the "Canadian Catechism" Carter himself traces in a *Catholic Register* article dated October 15, 1977. The thrust of the new catechism appealed to his own theoretical approach to education. He termed it radical, since Viens vers le Père replaced the traditional a priori approach of doctrinal assertion and theological analysis with an approach rooted in childhood experience, from which gospel meanings were extracted and their application to real-life situations discussed. The method was consistent with Carter's own pedagogical convictions.

Since Carter had published his highly successful *The Modern Challenge to Religious Education* with William H. Sadlier, and since that book had become a standard text both in the United States and Canada (including, of course, St. Joseph's Teachers' College), the political and practical decision to back the Come to the Father series, which would be published under the auspices of the Quebec Assembly of Bishops, had to be a particularly difficult one for him. Sadlier, in fact, was a potential publisher of the Carter–Francoeur catechism while it was still a live project, so that Carter was faced with the prospect either of turning his back on an established working relationship with a reputable publisher with demonstrated marketing skills, or, conversely, of rejecting a Canadian catechetical package which he found personally attractive. In the end, the pedagogical superiority of Come to the Father won the day, though the decision was not an entirely happy one. The enormous success of the translation was soon a cause of no little friction between the English and French bishops, simply because the English translation of the French original had been such a lucrative undertaking for the English bishops. In addition, the use of any translated work tended to negate Carter's own efforts to replace English translations of French textbooks in the early 1940s in Quebec; his decision to back a translation must have seemed like a betrayal of earlier principles. And, finally, there were the problems with the product. Students were simply not learning the articles of their faith.

James Hayes, the Archbishop of Halifax, looks back on this period in the history of the Canadian catechism and gives Emmett Carter full marks: "He had that whole religious education background, and he was a strong supporter of the English, not translation really but adaptation, of the Canadian catechism, Come to the Father. Then we got into struggles about ownership and revenue and so on. He really handled that very adroitly and with great courage and strength. I think that was one enterprise of his that really impressed me."

Nonetheless, Carter's support for the project was eventually to sour. Indeed, several bishops and many educators close to the scene have wondered about Carter's sudden abandoning of the Come to the Father series. According to Francoeur, Carter had understood its shortcomings well enough from the beginning; he and Carter had discussed the strengths and weaknesses almost from the time it was introduced. In fact, in a November 1972 talk at the Catechetical Institute in Harrow, England, Carter had given his own warnings about diluting doctrine for the sake of clarity and simplification, observing that there was a need to introduce basic terminology into the teaching of the faith.

By 1974 the series was coming under continuing fire. Parents complained that their children did not know the basic elements of their faith, personal friends like Count Robert Keyserlingk added their voices to that chorus, and critical articles began to appear in print, such as the historical critique which Sister Mary Jackson prepared for *Our Family* in June 1974. These expressions of opinion were followed by a detailed and damning critique by Father Anthony Durand, who had been an instructor of thomistic philosophy at St. Peter's Seminary in London, an instructor whose reputation amongst his students was not altogether enviable but whose intelligence, forthrightness and theological conservatism appealed to Carter. They corresponded often, and Durand became a source of theological advice for his bishop. For his part, Carter placed so much confidence in Durand's judgement, that he forwarded to John Cardinal Wright, Prefect of the Sacred Congregation for the Clergy, Durand's defence of clerical celibacy, noting that he "may be a little on the conservative side but that, as you will easily concede, is hardly much of a liability particularly since his devotion to the Church is the truly traditional one which allows for no substitute for respect for authority. Hence, his conservatism truly conserves including the Holy Father and the hierarchy."[14] Carter's characterizing Durand as being "a little on the conservative side" is, by most accounts, a case of gross understatement, and demonstrates Carter's own predilections for conservative theology, respect for authority and commitment to the hierarchical model of church. Durand was clearly an influential man in the Bishop's life, and he may well have provided the final blow to the Come to the Father series as far as Carter is concerned.

In November 1974 Carter had written to the Bishop of Calgary, Paul J. O'Byrne, explaining to him that Pope Paul VI was expecting great things from Canada's bishops. He recounts a conversation with the Pope, in which Pope Paul is reported to have challenged the Canadians: "Canada is a remarkably equipped country to serve the Church with an outstanding catechism. You have the experts, you have the ability, you have the doctrinal orthodoxy which will be a model to all . . . . I order you to produce a masterpiece."[15]

By July 2, 1975, Carter was writing to O'Byrne to express his concern for Come to the Father in light of the advice he had received from one Anthony Durand, concerning whom Carter writes: "I consider him one of the brightest of the priests who ever taught at St. Peter's Seminary." On July 15, 1975, O'Byrne replied, acknowledging Durand's objections, and recognizing Carter's "deepening concern for what appears to be a growing risk over the Canadian catechism." For Carter, there was no turning back.

During his address at the testimonial dinner held in his honour before he left for St. Lawrence College in Quebec City in 1961, Carter had suggested that "If God had wanted everything stereotyped and decided ahead of time, He would have given the faith to robots or to IBM machines." Come to the Father reflected that position, but it had created problems. Carter, Schorsch and Hofinger had all agreed that there was a place for memorization, or at least for virtual word-for-word recall; the question was one of timing, degree and technique. With Come to the Father, Carter argued, "the transition from a doctrinal orientation to a psychological one has not been without errors and omissions. In my personal opinion, these have been disastrous."[16] In the eyes of others, like Halifax's James Hayes, the failure was not so much in the instrument itself as in the demands it placed on its users. The philosophy of Come to the Father was premised on the active collaboration of school, home and church — an appropriate, though overly idealistic approach to the educational process.

In the long run and on the level of pedagogy, Carter was reduced to the role of critic in an area where he ought to have supplied leadership, though friends like Thomas Francoeur are quick to point out that Carter had enough on his plate, and there were plenty of capable catechists who had been trained to serve the bishops on their catechetical commission. Carter had, in fact, taken another bold step to ensure a supply of well-trained teachers of catechism. In 1965 he inaugurated Divine Word, a catechetical centre conceived on the model of Lumen Vitae in Brussels, Belgium. It was an imaginative undertaking, with its own integrated curriculum, which was intended to attract prospective teachers of catechetics of various levels of academic preparedness, both pre- and post-baccalaureate. Unfortunately, Carter's fellow bishops greeted the institution with general scepticism, though the experiment might well have worked had it

been blessed with more inspired leadership. One of Carter's weaknesses, Francoeur suggests, is an inability to judge character, and in
this case, the weakness was fatal. For his own part, Francoeur reflects
with some sense of guilt his unwillingness to assume the director's
post after giving Carter and Divine Word one year of his teaching
career after taking a year-long study period at Lumen Vitae — it was a
post for which he says he had no aptitude. Carter's vision was right,
despite the criticism, Francoeur insists, adding that there is still a
place for Divine Word, and a place for it in London.

During Emmett Carter's tenure in London, there were two synods of
bishops held in Rome, to which he and several of his fellow bishops
were sent as Canadian delegates. In 1974 the bishops of the world and
other high-ranking clerics gathered at the Vatican to compare notes
and to advise the pope on questions of evangelization; they gathered
again in 1977 to take up the challenge presented by the problem of
modern catechetics. The 1977 session was tailor-made for Carter. By
way of preparation, and in keeping with his philosophy of consultative
decision making, he surveyed the youth of London diocese. Carter
mailed some thirty thousand questionnaires, and received in response
approximately two thousand letters. He took some justified pride in
this initiative, explaining to a youth rally convened in 1977: "The
gentle breeze. The gentle breeze was whispering that I should not go
to Rome without consulting the youth of my diocese." Though he
and Chicago-based priest, novelist and sociologist Andrew Greeley
exchanged curt and far from cordial correspondence concerning the
scientific nature of Carter's methodology, Carter found the exercise
confirming, if not illuminating. In response to questions about relationship with parents, the identification of modern heroes and the
like, not only was he confirmed in his own convictions about the
secularization of society, the breakdown of child-parent relationships
and the overpowering influence of television in the lives of the young,
but he also received many a sincere cry from the heart, since a good
number of the letters were confessional in nature.

    When the Canadian delegation left for Rome, they were accom-
panied by several experts in the area of catechetics, including Thomas
Francoeur, whom Carter had invited as an advisor. Despite the
detailed advance work of the delegation and the expertise they had
available to them, the end result of the synod was not particularly

impressive. Carter made an intervention which centred on the use of the media as a catechetical tool, the need for an ecumenical approach to the teaching of the christian message and the need for teacher and student to view learning as a lifelong undertaking. Then (no doubt influenced by the Catholic call to action which was part of his youth in Quebec), he concluded with exhortations to see, judge and act: "We must be concerned with a constant striving to integrate our teaching and our celebrations with a clear involvement in action; a deep understanding of its nature followed by concrete practice."[17]

It is a call to Catholic action which echoes Canadian statements at all of the Roman synods to date, but the challenge of catechetical teaching and the problems of Canada's youth have still not been met. The Come to the Father series has been replaced by an incomplete and ever-evolving approach to catechetics; in fact, the 1985 Extraordinary Synod in Rome agreed to work on an international catechism as a national benchmark for orthodoxy, but its initial appearance has been greeted with a storm of controversy. Over the years the Canadian delegation has expended considerable energy discussing the role and problems which the young experience in the church as well as in society, but with respect to Canada's young people, Carter laments: "God help us. No, I don't think we have answered them."

As Bishop of London, Carter had to assume responsibility for the diocese's two post-secondary institutions, St. Peter's Seminary and King's College. When Carter arrived in London, King's College bore the name Christ the King College and was a legal division of St. Peter's Seminary. St. Peter's Seminary, in turn, was affiliated with the University of Western Ontario. Carter felt an immediate attraction to the seminary, and tended to keep his distance from King's, leaving its administration for the most part in the hands of those duly appointed to its stewardship.

In some ways, St. Peter's Seminary provided Carter with an opportunity to relive his youth at the Grand Seminary. Resurrectionist Father Bob Liddy, now a rector of a seminary himself, but in the early 1960s a student at a house of studies immediately adjacent to and virtually part of St. Peter's, has fond recollections of Carter enjoying leisurely games of pool with the diocesan seminarians and mingling freely with them. Father Joe Snyder, Carter's long-time Chancellor in London and still his travelling companion, reminisces about their daily tennis matches at the seminary, which continued until Snyder's appointment as pastor to Pius X Parish in London shortly before Carter's move to Toronto.

St. Peter's provided Carter with the opportunity to retain his youthful vigour through his fifties and most of his sixties. It also provided a therapeutic outlet for a man driven to long hours of work, and it gave him the opportunity to relax with the diocese's future priests at a level on which he could feel completely comfortable.

St. Peter's was also an institution of higher learning, however, and by all accounts it had grown tired with the years. Its faculty needed to be reinvigorated — several really preferred parish work to the academic life — and St. Peter's had few instructors who had absorbed the spirit or the letter of Vatican II. Complaints from various quarters crossed Carter's desk. Morale was not good. Carter set out immediately to put matters right, searching for a new rector and a better-trained professoriate, sending instructors to Rome or Washington's Catholic University for further study. "The big problem was that my dear predecessor had neglected St. Peter's. Nobody went away to study. I felt that I had planted the best seed I could find; I always had somebody preparing to teach at St. Peter's."

In the meantime Christ the King College was not without its own academic and personnel difficulties, but Carter was content to leave these problems to the College's administration.[18] His successor, Bishop John Sherlock, has taken the same approach and Carter has continued it in his relationship with the University of St. Michael's College in Toronto. Both men have drawn distinctions between academic freedom in a university college and fidelity to the teaching church required of the magisterium in a seminary; neither is anxious to become embroiled in matters of university discipline except in cases of serious breech of fidelity to Catholic teaching insofar as they relate to theological matters. In fact, Carter insists that he diminished the role of the bishop with respect to King's College during his tenure in London. Nonetheless, although Carter says he had an arm's-length relationship with King's, he was drawn into the College's internal affairs willy-nilly.

Christ the King College was established as an all-male post-secondary institution; its counterpart for women was Brescia College. Brescia is an Ursuline-run facility on the south end of the campus of the University of Western Ontario, whereas King's is several blocks east of the main campus. As a result, the question of female visiting rights at Christ the King arose on several occasions, and in 1967 the students approached Carter to petition his support in the face of Principal Eugene La Rocque's opposition. What the students were agitating for, according to College historian Patrick Phelan, were visitation rights on Sundays from two to five in the afternoon. According to Carter, afternoon visitations would hardly have been a matter of concern, but the students were actually looking for hours of visitation that would have extended well into the night. The principal, the board, and the bishop stood firm, and the issue was lost. Carter pointed out that London is a relatively small city, that many of the students came from agricultural backgrounds and that their parents were entrusting their youngsters to those responsible for the College. "They didn't expect us to say it's all right for them to have girls in their rooms all night." To this day, Carter insists he'd have closed the College down rather than be part of its moral decline. Only a year later, however, and faced with serious financial problems, earlier promises made to the Ursuline Sisters notwithstanding, King's declared itself coeducational and admitted its first women.

Carter's second involvement in King's was self-initiated and occurred in response to a persistent series of decisions and omissions affecting the Catholic character of the college. As Patrick Phelan sketches the events, they begin in 1965 with La Rocque's determination to alter the College's name to King's from Christ the King, a change which Carter suggests his predecessor would have opposed vigorously. The College was faced with serious financial problems and had to attract more students. The administration felt that a less denominational name would be helpful — and Phelan believes that was a successful move from the point of view of enrolment. Still, the financial problems persisted, and La Rocque's successor, Owen Carrigan, inherited a college with an identity crisis and financial difficulties, both of which he addressed, but in the process he paid scant attention to the institution's Catholic nature. The process of professionalization centred more on academic qualifications than religious convictions, and symbolically, the Chapel was "relegated to a basement seminar room and all visible signs of the institution's Catholicity . . . [were] removed."[19] Moreover, Phelan also noted that a 1969 Commission of Inquiry into the Catholic nature of higher education in Canada had remarked that there was "considerable confusion at present concerning the identity of King's as a Catholic College." As a result, Phelan argued that "[w]ith the exception of his involvement in

the College over the open house issue, Bishop Carter's 1975 intervention in the internal affairs of King's was a marked departure from past
practice." In fact, John Sherlock reflects that "it is under him, not
under Bishop Cody who established King's, but under Carter that
King's has developed an amazing degree of autonomy, of participatory democracy both in its boards and various councils." As a
result, Sherlock suggests, he has been able to keep his distance and let
those on the scene deal with the College's own legitimate business —
though Sherlock, too, says that he talks to the College's principals
frequently about the issue of Catholicity.

The Commission of Inquiry was appointed by Carter on March 7,
1974, and consisted of E.C. Keane, pastor of Holy Name of Mary
Church in Windsor; E.R. Malley, a Basilian priest and Dean of Arts at
the University of Windsor; and John W. McAuliffe, Vice-President of
the University of Windsor. Nine months later the Commissioners
presented a forthright, balanced and temperate report. They concluded that "there is a tendency at King's College to de-emphasize its
Catholic character" in its public relations, recruitment and even in
the literature produced by its Department of Religious Studies. On
questions of personnel, the Commission underlined the need for a
core of committed Catholic instructors and called for a senior administration of dedicated Catholics so that there might be a pervasive
Catholic atmosphere at King's. Not surprisingly, the Commission
also advocated a more visible chaplaincy. With respect to the bishop,
the Commission concluded: "While it is not the position of the
Commission that the Bishop should be actively involved in the
operation of the College, it is the feeling of the Commission that his
presence, even for such a limited time as an informal lunch with the
faculty, would do much to bring home to the King's community that
it is an extremely important part of the Diocese of London. The
Commission knows that the personal attributes of the incumbent
Ordinary will permit him to do just that."[20]

The report of the Commission was obviously upsetting to some of
the faculty who felt that their livelihood and their sense of professionalism were threatened. Indeed, so strong was the aversion of some
to the very existence of the Commission that on the occasion of
Cardinal Carter's receiving of an honorary doctorate from the University of Waterloo, UW sociologist Ken Westhues wrote a letter of
protest to the University's *Gazette*, denouncing the University's decision by arguing in part that "[a]s Bishop of London in the early 1970s,

he terrorized the faculty at Western Ontario's Catholic affiliate with his 'Commission of Inquiry into the Catholic Character of King's College.' "[21] Others, including Carter's successor, John Sherlock, contend that Carter understands very well the distinction between academic freedom in a university and fidelity to the magisterium necessary in seminary instruction. Sherlock insists that King's even gained in autonomy under Carter. Thomas Francoeur recalls Carter's words concerning the episcopal criticism of his founding of Divine Word: "If they don't criticise you, you'll know you're not doing anything."

For Carter's part, when pressed to discuss the underlying purpose of the Commission of Inquiry, he says he does not in fact remember "doing anything"; the Commission was obviously not high on his agenda. In a 1975 homily delivered at King's, however, Carter reflected on the name and mission of the College, addressed the issue of secularization and reminded his audience of the central importance of the person of Christ the King. He also preached a homily at the 1976 graduation exercises for King's students, during which he argued that "in this difficult world we must learn to live with other opinions." In an open society one must expect dissent, but "[d]issent does not change the basic facts."

Both in Montreal and in London, Carter had argued vigorously for education as a means of personal human development, as a challenge to ask the right questions and formulate the appropriate answers personally. "No man," Carter assured a gathering of teachers, "ever lost his faith by using his reason."[22] Faith, reason, responsible dissent: three elements which must interact maturely in the process of conscientious decision making. This interplay between conscience, dissent, and Gerald Emmett Carter's unwavering dedication to unity in essentials (*in necessariis, unitas*) is nowhere more important in Carter's life than it is in helping to shape the reaction of Canada's bishops to Pope Paul VI's landmark encyclical letter on human life, *Humanae vitae*.

CHAPTER SIX

Humanae vitae *and the Struggle over Personal Conscience*

When *Humanae vitae* appeared in 1968, reaffirming Catholicism's traditional ban on artificial means of contraception, Carter says "it was one of the most crucial moments of my life as a bishop."

Although Pius XII had addressed birth control issues in a number of his allocutions in the 1950s, the last detailed papal document was *Casti connubii*, issued by his predecessor, Pius XI, in 1930. This encyclical was occasioned by the Anglican Church's Lambeth Conference of the same year, which decided that contraception could be permitted in certain circumstances, although it was never the normal or preferred course. *Casti connubii* was, in contrast, blunt and categorical, condemning contraception "as an offense against the law of God and of nature." T.S. Eliot summed up the difference between the Roman and the Anglican approaches in a way wholly appropriate to its time: "To put it frankly, but I hope not offensively, the Roman view in general seems to me to be that a principle must be affirmed without exception; and that thereafter exceptions can be dealt with, without modifying the principle. The view natural to the English mind, I believe, is rather that a principle must be framed in such a way as to include all allowable exceptions. It follows inevitably that the Roman Church must profess to be fixed, while the Anglican Church must profess to take account of changed conditions."[1]

But Rome's position appeared increasingly less fixed, despite papal utterances to the contrary. Pope John XXIII established a six-man commission to advise him on the birth control question. It consisted of the French Jesuit sociologist Stanislaus de Lestapis; British neurologist John Marshall; the Belgian Jesuit demographer Clement Mertens; Swiss Dominican and Vatican observer at the United Nations in Geneva, Henri de Riedmatten; Belgian physician Pierre Van Rossum; and Louvain professor Jacques Mertens de Wilmars.

Before they could meet, John died, but his successor, rather than disbanding the Johannine commission, greatly augmented it. It became known as the Pontifical Commission on Population, Family and Birth and was broadly representative of the Catholic world: it included lay and clerical members, ethicists, psychiatrists, gynecologists, theologians, philosophers, lawyers and population experts. The church seemed to be poised for a change.

And people did expect a change, or at least some clarification. Research on oral contraceptives and rising disagreement among moral theologians on the morality of artifical contraception contributed to Catholic confusion. Catholic physicians and lawyers were no longer of one mind. Rome had to do something.

Lawyer and eventual Ontario Supreme Court Justice John O'Driscoll made a statement typical of an increasingly restive Canadian laity when he reminded the hierarchy that "as a layman I feel that . . . an immediate and definitive statement should be made so that those in the married state will know right from wrong. I feel that such a statement should issue only after a full discussion with Catholic laymen living in the married state; it should not be a document on marriage issued by celibates."[2]

The pressure on Rome mounted throughout the 1960s, and when the Report of the Pontifical Commission was clandestinely published in 1967 by *The Tablet* of London and the *National Catholic Reporter* of Kansas City, revealing that the majority opinion of the Pope's own high-level consultative body recommended a change in the church's teaching on contraception, expectations reached a pitch. The report was unambiguous in its respect for the church's long tradition regarding conjugal relations and the transmission of life, but it was also unambiguous in its argument in favour of a rightful evolution of that teaching: "The large amount of knowledge and facts which throw light on today's world suggest that it is not to contradict the genuine sense of this tradition and the purpose of the previous doctrinal condemnations if we speak of the regulation of conception by using means, human and decent, ordered to favoring fecundity in the totality of married life and toward the realization of the authentic values of a fruitful matrimonial community. The reasons in favor of this affirmation are of several kinds: social changes in matrimony and the family, especially in the role of the woman; lowering of the infant mortality rate; new bodies of knowledge in biology, psychology, sexuality and demography; a changed estimation of the value and meaning of human sexuality and of conjugal relations; most of all, a better grasp of the duty of man to humanize and to bring to greater perfection for the life of man what is given in nature. Then must be considered the sense of the faithful: according to it, condemnation of a couple to a long and often heroic abstinence as the means to regulate conception, cannot be founded on the truth .... The doctrine on marriage and its essential values remains the same and whole, but it is now applied differently out of a deeper understanding."[3]

Pope Paul was unpersuaded. When he issued *Humanae vitae*, the Roman Catholic Church went into a state of crisis. Emmett Carter would later observe that "the tragedy of *Humanae vitae* was not that the pope spoke alone, but that, apparently, he thought he had to."[4]

When Carter received news of the encyclical's release, he was with his brother Alex and three other bishops: Plourde of Ottawa; Gérard-Marie Coderre, Bishop of Saint-Jean Longueuil; and Pocock of Toronto. They were at a meeting in Plourde's chalet just north of Ottawa when the papal nuncio, Archbishop Emmanuele Clarizio, arrived with suitable gravity of purpose and demeanour, although, as Carter recalls, he introduced them to the most controversial papal document of the century "in a way that was funny. He said, 'I am very sorry but here is the pope's statement.' He had, of course, already examined the pertinent parts. So, we promptly dropped everything else we were doing and pored over the encyclical. It was with a certain sense of dismay that we read the vital passages in it. He had clearly taken a position that was contrary to the majority position of his own Commission. We felt that this was going to be a major problem."

Indeed they did have a major problem on their hands. Article 14 of the encyclical categorically condemned "any action, which either before, at the moment of, or after sexual intercourse, is specifically intended to prevent procreation — whether as an end or as a means." The document went on to argue that by retaining the ban on all means of artifical contraception the church was upholding the integrity of sexual love and resisting the "general lowering of moral standards." In Article 18, the church was portrayed in heroic terms as engaged in no less vital a task than the "creation of a truly human civilization." The church, it said, "urges man not to betray his personal responsibilities by putting all his faith in technical expedients. In this way [the church] defends the dignity of husband and wife."

The moral and theological argumentation of *Humanae vitae*, specifically in the light of the unofficially released Final Report of the Pontifical Commission, was far from persuasive for the majority of Catholic people, lay and cleric alike. In fact, *Humanae vitae* ushered in a whole new set of problems for the post-Vatican II church. The Mill Hill missionary and demographer Father Arthur McCormack observed in an article in *The Tablet* that although the Pope was convinced that papal authority and the very credibility of the church were on the line in 1968, "nothing has done more harm than *Humanae vitae* to that authority, which reached its lowest ebb as the protest mounted and the motivation for the encyclical became clear. Few documents in the course of the long and turbulent history of the Catholic church have caused such widespread and immediate consternation and opposition."[5]

Popular and critical attention soon moved from the controverted debates about sexual morality and natural law to an examination of the legitimate role and exercise of papal authority. Priests throughout the world wrote letters of dissent to secular and religious publications, acting out of their conviction that quiet submission to a teaching they considered in error did violence to their spiritual integrity. But the price of public dissent was high. Brocard Sewell, a British Carmelite friar and literary biographer, signed his name to a letter of dissent submitted to *The Times*, and was publicly censured as a result. In *The Vatican Oracle*, a work he concluded in 1970 while teaching at St. Francis Xavier University in Nova Scotia, he spoke for many a suspended cleric when he said that "while not presuming to judge the consciences of others, those priests who made some kind of public protest did so lest, by seeming to support the teaching of the encyclical, they should incur the judgement that awaits those who knowingly impose on others burdens from which they are free themselves, and which they do nothing to help others to bear. In so doing it was not in their minds to make any criticism of their fellow-clergy who conscientiously accepted the teaching of *Humanae vitae*."[6]

Tortured by the irony that through his efforts to affirm the authority of the church by disallowing any possibility of deviation from previous papal teaching, he had seriously undermined that authority, Pope Paul chose the road of gentle correction rather than blatant repudiation when it came to rebellious clerics and uncomprehending or unreceptive laypeople. While some hierarchs, like Cardinal O'Boyle of Washington and Bishop McNulty of Buffalo, were severe in meting out disciplinary penalties to recalcitrant priests (some of McNulty's priests sought exile in Pocock's Toronto, including Tom Dailey, a prominent and respected moral theologian), the Pope did not indulge in such summary condemnations and suspensions himself. "While he seemed to feel a mystical need to uphold the Church's pro-natalist position," wrote one observer in later years, "he did little to curb the conferences of bishops who interpreted the pastoral teaching of the encyclical broadly, telling their people that the pope proposed a high ideal; but that if, in conscience, they could not live up to that ideal, they should not consider themselves in sin."[7]

One of these conferences of bishops was the Canadian Catholic Conference, composed of bishops who were often compared to the avant-garde Dutch bishops, and their Winnipeg Statement in the fall of 1968 was widely recognized as one of the boldest in the Catholic world.

From the very moment that Clarizio arrived at the doors of Plourde's chalet, Carter and the others knew that they would have to issue a statement that, in Emmett's words, would give them some manoeuvring room in dealing with the people of Canada. And so to Winnipeg from September 23 to 27, the city chosen that year to host the Canadian bishops' annual assembly (the Archdiocese of St. Boniface was holding anniversary celebrations). But it wasn't the anniversary celebrations that dominated the meeting.

The President of the Conference in that fateful year was Alexander Carter, and sitting on the Theological Commission was the man who, during Emmett Carter's Toronto years, would often function as his *bête noir* — the Bishop of Victoria, British Columbia, Remi De Roo. Trained at Rome's Angelicum University, De Roo had demonstrated competence in systematic theology, but the Theological Commission was going to have to rely on the professional assistance of numerous experts to draft the particular episcopal statement required by *Humanae vitae*. The Winnipeg *periti* included the Jesuit moralist Edward Sheridan; Father Ora McManus, Chairman of the Western Canadian Conference of Priests; Father André Naud, President of the Canadian Institute of Theology; Mr. Bernard Daly, the Director of the Family Life Bureau (English) of the Canadian Catholic Conference; and Father Charles St. Onge, the French Director of the Family Life Bureau. It did not appear on the face of it that Emmett Carter would have a role to play in Winnipeg, but such was not to be the case.

Returning to his room for a nightcap after a dinner with Alex, he discovered a note from Pocock imploring him to join his brother bishops of the Theological Commission immediately. He went down to the room where they were closeted, and found Emmett Doyle (Bishop of Nelson, B.C.) banging on a typewriter and surrounded by the Theological Commission. He was working on the draft of a declaration for the Conference and they were a little panicky. It was late Wednesday evening and their deadline was noon on Friday. They were totally at a loss; they hadn't even got past the first paragraph. Carter relates the story: "So Pocock says, 'Well, we thought you could help us put this thing together.' I demurred at first, but I eventually relented, told them that I wouldn't type anything. They agreed. The system I worked out proved satisfactory: I would take notes point by point, and while they were making up their minds as to what it was that should be included in the next paragraph, I would go into an adjacent room and compose in paragraph form the points they had made to date. When I came back into their room, I would pick up where I left off after we examined the paragraph I had just composed."

In addition to this rather rough drafting procedure, they had to consult with their *periti* and translators and they ended up working well into the morning hours. At about 3:00 A.M. Carter dispatched them to bed and promised them a statement that they could either approve or send back for revisions by the next morning. At about 5:00 A.M. he slipped the completed draft under the secretariat's door for typing and went to bed himself.

It is not surprising that Pocock should have asked Carter for his help; Winnipeg's Archbishop Flahiff had requested as early as 1964 that Carter prepare (*sub secreto*) the Canadian response to a questionnaire issued by the Holy See, which had been designed to test the waters regarding contemporary attitudes and expectations about birth regulation in the Catholic world. His report (April 11, 1964) does not make light of the contemporary unhappiness over the official position and the turmoil compounded by Roman indecision. It was characteristically forthright. Something had to be done, something "sympathetic and comprehensible." *Humanae vitae* wasn't what he had had in mind. And so he accepted Pocock's invitation.

The draft was thoroughly debated on Thursday, and that evening proved to be a replay of the previous night's activities. Carter was up all night again, and when he took his corrected draft down to the secretariat his room was rifled, but because he hadn't made a carbon copy of his draft the morass of notes and files clearly flummoxed the would-be thief, and nothing of consequence was stolen. It was a measure of the interest, not to say the desperation, inspired by the Winnipeg proceedings.

On Friday morning the debate continued. Archbishop Joseph Wilhelm of Kingston and Bishop Joseph Ryan of Hamilton provided what little opposition there was. That afternoon, as scheduled, the Canadian Catholic hierarchy issued its pastoral statement on *Humanae vitae*. Carter felt that his efforts as editor/amanuensis ("It was my authorship but not my substance.") and the intention of the Canadian bishops were fully realized: "Our statement was definitely meant to indicate to the people of Canada that if they found, as we anticipated, and God knows history has proven us to be correct, that they couldn't follow the directives of the encyclical, then they were not to consider themselves as cut off from the church. We were trying to create a situation wherein Catholics would not feel that they were alienated from the church although on the issue of birth control they could not follow the teaching of the pope." Carter believed that they had succeeded, and thereby avoided the strife that some nations, especially the United States, experienced.

Emmett's labours, to a considerable extent, went unnoticed in Winnipeg. Alex, by contrast, was more visible. As President of the CCC and Chairman of the Plenary Assembly, he was the one who had to rule Kingston's Wilhelm out of order when he attempted to scuttle the statement, and he was the one saddled with the unhappy task of providing the nuncio with a copy of the finalized and approved Winnipeg Statement for His Holiness. Along with De Roo and Archbishop Baudoux of St. Boniface, Alex handled the press conference that launched their document. "Each insisted that the bishops had not intended to make a doctrinal statement, but that they had attempted to help the People of God in Canada to face the agonizing situation in which they found themselves after the encyclical. . . . The bishops had rejected *simpliste* attitudes either ignoring the encyclical or regarding it as a legalistic document, and they had, above all, rejected the 'contraceptive attitude' within marriage."[8]

The Statement acknowledges, from the very beginning, Canadian episcopal solidarity with the pontiff and proceeds to outline the role of the christian conscience and the divine law in a way wholly consonant with the best of the Catholic tradition. The Statement is respectful of official church teaching but recognizes the pastoral necessity that must sometimes mollify abstract moral principles in the light of concrete human behaviour. It concludes by pledging loyalty to the institutional church, yet acknowledging the very status of that church as a pilgrim, a people in process. "We stand in union with the Bishop of Rome, the successor of Peter, the sign and contributing cause of our unity with Christ and with one another. But this very union postulates such a love of the Church that we can do no less than to place all of our love and all of our intelligence at its service. If this sometimes means that in our desire to make the Church more intelligible and more beautiful we must, as pilgrims do, falter in the way or differ as to the way, no one should conclude that our common faith is lost or our loving purpose blunted. The great Cardinal Newman once wrote: 'Lead kindly light amidst the encircling gloom.' We believe that the Kindly Light will lead us to a greater understanding of the ways of God and the love of men."

Alex Carter was informed by Clarizio that Pope Paul said of the Canadian Statement, "*L'accettiamo con soddisfazione*" (We accept it with satisfaction). Similarly, when Emmett had occasion to be in Rome on Consilium business shortly after the Statement appeared, he was cautioned by Cardinal Gray that some of it was "strong meat, my Lord," although Carter reports that when he met Pope Paul the pontiff assured him that he had no objection to the Statement.

Carter must have been puzzled, if not a little pained, by the strikingly different direction his friend John Wright chose to take on the issue. Pittsburgh and London did not see eye to eye on this one.

If Carter moved carefully, choosing nuance over exhortation, demonstrating the need for universal consultation and the reasonable application of the principle of collegiality, it is because that was his preferred way of operating. He courted Rome's attention; he had no desire to emulate its procedures. The Roman mentality was irksome, a puzzle, a thing to be avoided. But not so with Wright. He argued, in sharp contrast to the conciliatory and progressive Statement of the Canadians, that what "Pope Paul has done, what he had to do, is recall to a generation that does not like the word the fact that sin exists; that artificial contraception is objectively sinful; that those who impose it, foster it, counsel it, whether they be governments, experts, or — God forgive them! — spiritual directors, impose, foster and counsel objective sin, just as they would if they taught racism, hatred, fraud, injustice or impiety."[9] Wright was never inclined to ambiguity.

Carter, who chose to accentuate the positive rather than the negative and to respect the individual's personal obligations of conscience,
Carter, Gaunt John's old friend, could not have been impressed by
this legalistic rebuke of error. It conveyed little in the way of compassion. The statement that Wright chose to issue did not represent him
at his best. Within a year, Wright was named a Cardinal.

Carter has never been partial to ambiguity either, and when various
readings of the Winnipeg Statement called into question the Canadian bishops' loyalty to the Holy See and the universal magisterium,
he appreciated the necessity of releasing a "clarifying statement." He
wrote this one entirely himself, though the bishops saw it before it
went out. "It was not one of the 'ethical statements' as was issued in
1983 with no consultation. They'd all seen it and they'd all had the
chance to talk about it. There was no hidden ballplay; I wrote it." It
was released following the plenary assembly of the Canadian bishops
in Ottawa on April 18, 1969.

But it did not appease critic Anne Roche Muggeridge, a formidable
polemicist with a taste for apocalyptic prose and easy judgements.
Muggeridge excoriated the Winnipeg prelates and their *periti* in a
way that still smarts. For her, the Winnipeg Statement illustrated the
triumph in Canada of that spirit of Vatican II which, in her estimation, disguises the Protestantizing tendencies of the liberal theologians and their witless dupes, the *episkopoi*, the shepherds of the
church. In *Gates of Hell: The Struggle for the Catholic Church* she
moves in for the kill: "The bishops had spent the two months between
the publication of the encyclical and their Winnipeg meeting (according to the *Western Catholic Reporter* and Douglas Roche) listening: to
the Catholic Physicians' Guild of Manitoba, to 351 members of the
Western Canadian Conference of Priests, to fifteen directors of departments within the Canadian Catholic Conference, to eighty-two
Catholics in Dialogue [a group of academics originating at the Basilian Fathers' St. Michael's College, University of Toronto, with leadership by such liberal notables as Gregory Baum and Leslie Dewart],
to the 'all-important Canadian Institute of Theology', and to fifty-
eight of the 'Cream of Antigonish' [dissenting Catholic priests and lay
academics attached to St. Francis Xavier University], all of whom
disagreed violently with the encyclical. This listening apparently left
them no choice, for as the *Western Catholic Reporter* remarked, 'with
the integrity of so many of the protesters irreproachable, the progressive bishops were able to discern the Holy Spirit speaking to them

through the people.' That sentence is the most perfect definition of the liberal elitist 'spirit of Vatican II' mentality ever written."[10]

The very integrity of the Catholic Church itself, argues Muggeridge, was thus sundered by its own chief protectors. Eager to pacify a disaffected and highly vocal Catholic laity infected by a doctrinally spineless liberalism, and eager to accommodate the new darlings of the post-conciliar era, the *periti*, the bishops so qualified *Humanae vitae* that its punch was reduced to a gentle slap. Some leadership, she said. And the Carter brothers, she contended, were in the forefront of this betrayal. They had capitulated to the clever stratagems of the *periti* and they had outmanoeuvred the bishops who opposed them. That was her line; the Carters vigorously disputed it.

Convinced of the scandalous liberalism of Alexander Carter and ever fearful of the wily Emmett, Muggeridge persists in seeing the Winnipeg Statement as the product of a cabal of theologians and obliging bishops determined to undo the perceived damage of *Humanae vitae* and pledged to continue the Protestantizing of the Roman Church in Canada. In her 1986 book, *The Desolate City: The Catholic Church in Ruins*, Muggeridge recalls that from the very "beginning of the fall 1968 assembly of the Canadian Conference of Catholic Bishops [the name was changed in 1977], the deck was stacked against those who wished to accept the traditional position. Canada's leading progressive bishops, in particular Remi De Roo, head of the theological commission, and Alexander Carter, then president of the CCCB, obtained a consensus of sorts on the Winnipeg Statement. . . . The Canadian bishops, like the Protestant reformers, reversed the order of importance in moral judgement, that is, they put the private, subjective elements of morality before the universal and objective."[11]

What is anathema to Muggeridge is revisionism to Emmett Carter. In Carter's memory there was no "consensus of sorts," but a majority vote with minimal dissent among the bishops. There was no railroading by Alexander, but an open and free exchange of ideas directed by acceptable parliamentary procedure: "The Winnipeg Statement has been totally misread and misrepresented by our dear Ann Roche. Her account of the assembly and the process of composition is comic, fantastic." That may be. But the perception that the Canadian hierarchy was ambivalent in its treatment of the encyclical persists, even in quarters not constricted by reactionary fever.

As late as five years after the Winnipeg Statement, Carter still felt called to defend the document and its fidelity to Rome. In an article sent to the *Catholic Register* on March 29, 1973, Carter invited Catholics to read the Winnipeg Statement analytically, and defied anyone to find the slightest disloyalty to the Holy Father in a statement that was a pastoral one, meant to help the consciences of the faithful either in their acceptance of the papal teaching or with their struggle where acceptance was difficult. But these kinds of defences and explanations were insufficient. Something more substantive was necessary, something more than what the pastoral statement, the clarifying statement and countless columns in newspapers could provide. And so the 1973 "Statement on the Formation of Conscience" came to birth, and Carter was its midwife.

The conference of bishops had promised the conscience document for some time, and because Carter had served as Vice-President of the Faith and Doctrine Department (as it was then called) of the CCC since 1969, and since he had been so crucial a figure in the drafting of the previous statements, it was not unreasonable to see his hand directly in this one. And so it happened that after countless committee sessions and consultations between bishops and theologians, a frustrated James Carney, Archbishop of Vancouver, implored Carter to do something. In the spring of 1973 Carney reminded Carter of the long-promised statement and warned him that with all the committees and sub-committees that were working on various pieces of it, it would never come together. Carter looked ahead at the leisurely summer he had planned, and declined. Carney persisted and told him flatly, "if you don't do it, it won't get done."

Carter concluded that Carney was right. He took all the documentation to his cottage, put the statement together and presented it to the bishops at their fall assembly. The bishops argued, interpolated, deleted and added. But it went back to a delighted Carter, who felt that his statement "was much better after they got through with it." The end result was a well-reasoned, if somewhat dry, examination of the various types of conscience and the processes involved in the formation of a mature conscience. Its references to Scripture are bountiful and it contains ample allusions to the Church Fathers and conciliar documents. It is a careful and intelligent document.

The kind of conscience that today's society needs, the "Statement on the Formation of Conscience" argues in Article 22, is a "dynamic

Christian conscience. This is the conscience which leads us to have a responsible attitude to someone, to Jesus, to the community, to the Church, etc. Every person who fits into this category feels a responsibility for a progressive search and striving to live out a life ideal according to the mind of Christ (Phil. 2:5)."

Having affirmed the role of freedom and the individual conscience, the statement proceeds to remind believing Catholics in Article 28 that, in their tradition, the magisterium is "the definitive cornerstone upon which the whole edifice of conscientious judgement must be built." Catholics must realize that "'to follow one's conscience' and to remain a Catholic, one must take into account first and foremost the teaching of the magisterium." The authority of the magisterium must be clearly distinguished from that of individual theologians and priests. There is nothing brazen or revolutionary in these arguments. They are as conservative as John Henry Newman, the principal force behind Carter's thinking on conscience. But it was this very same Newman who also upheld the priority of conscience over papal authority and who articulated the church's current thinking on consulting the laity on doctrinal matters. There is something of *this* Newman in the conscience statement as well.

The bishops overwhelmingly approved the Statement, and it was released on December 1, 1973.

Within two weeks Carter wrote to his close friend and neighbour, the progressive Archbishop of Detroit, John Cardinal Dearden, claiming that "it is, between us, largely my own brainchild and I am perhaps unduly proud of it."[12] Not surprisingly, under the seal "Personal and Confidential", he forwarded a copy of the Statement to the far less progressive John Wright, the Cardinal Prefect. "This Document on the Formation of Conscience, which has now been accepted and promulgated by the Catholic Bishops, represents something of a mammoth struggle. It took several years to prepare and, at one point, when it was mainly the work of a group of theologians, it appeared to be doomed. It was at that juncture that I was approached by my brother bishops with the proposal that I take it under my wing and rewrite the whole thing. ... [T]he end result, now that it has been studied and improved by the contributions of a number of bishops is, I believe, worthwhile. I am rather proud of it and I wanted you to have a copy as soon as possible."[13]

If Rome was wary of the Canadian hierarchy as a consequence of the 1968 statement, perhaps the 1973 document would go some way to assuage her fears. The latter statement was not a repudiation of the earlier one but a careful amplification. It might appease Rome; it was good theology based on sturdy argumentation. But would it appease the home-front critics?

CHAPTER SEVEN

Reflections on Women and the Priesthood

On October 15, 1976, the Sacred Congregation for the Doctrine of the Faith put its signature to a Vatican statement the implications of which Carter was not to escape as gracefully or as convincingly as he had *Humanae vitae*. Indeed, the fallout from this statement still badgers him. Entitled *Inter insignores*, and generally referred to in English as The Declaration on the Question of the Admission of Women to the Ministerial Priesthood, the document is an official response to initiatives undertaken to no insignificant extent by the Canadian delegation to the 1971 Synod of Bishops in Rome. At that time, speaking on behalf of the Canadian church and addressing that Synod assembly, George B. Cardinal Flahiff had raised the question of the role of women in the church, including their potential ministerial role. Flahiff reviewed the social context of biblical restrictions with respect to a more formal and influential role for women, concluding that, to the best of his knowledge, "there is no dogmatic objection to reconsidering the whole question" as to whether changing ministries in the church should be limited to men's roles.[1] Flahiff completed his presentation with a polite request that the matter be studied, lest the bishops "find themselves behind the course of events", and closed his argument by pointing out that "despite a centuries-old social tradition against a ministry of women in the Church, we are convinced that the signs of the times (and one of those signs is that already women perform many pastoral services and this with great success) strongly urge a study at least both of the present situation and of the possibilities of the future." *Inter insignores* was the papal response to the question, which purported to close the case. But closure does not come as easily as it once did, and not even dating the Declaration on the feast of St. Teresa of Avila, whom Pope Paul

VI had numbered among the doctors (that is, teachers) of the church, could stem the restless tide.

Carter's perception of the role of women in the church has expanded with time and experience, though his own training and his personal sense of obedience to Roman authority has put a lid on the issue as far as he is concerned, at least for purposes of public debate; nonetheless, until Rome defines the matter once and for all, he remains respectful of opposing points of view: *in dubiis libertas* (freedom of opinion in those things which are doubtful).

The Study Commission on Woman in Society and in the Church, established by Pope Paul VI on May 3, 1973, in response to the 1971 Synod, released an interim report to the subsequent Synod of Bishops meeting in the fall of 1974. On that occasion, the Study Commission also made it clear that at the pope's request, their final report would coincide with the United Nation's International Women's Year, 1976. The Commission made several points, two of which are particularly worthy of note. One is that scientific induction (analytical study) and divine revelation speak with one voice on many matters relating to maleness and femaleness. Here, there is a suggestion that the Commission will move beyond traditional deductive reasoning, reasoning which proceeds from abstract philosophical principles as opposed to concrete scientific investigation. Secondly, the Commission stated as its operating principle the concept of complementarity, a concept which has been and remains a contentious one, since even moderate christian feminists see in it a continuation of the church's teaching of male superiority which, Aquinas argued, God had implanted in nature. Nonetheless, the Commissioners reasoned that the thinking of Aquinas and his disciples, like Pius XI, should be modified by contemporary insights. "The New Testament shows Christ breaking through the religious and social values of his time to re-establish woman in the full dignity of her person, as equal to man," the interim report stated. "At the same time Scripture emphasizes the difference between man and woman. This difference does not imply a relationship of superior to inferior: it is a question of mutual complementarity which finds its full meaning in the union of the Church with Christ."[2] This position has often been taken by the church in recent years, especially by Pope John Paul II, and suggests a real willingness to weigh the matter according to contemporary lights, that is, according to modern scholarly signs of the times.[3] Although the winds of change were blowing softly, they were blowing nonetheless, and Carter too decided to take a reading of the times.

In a letter to Cardinal Wright, Carter engages in light banter about a Niagara meeting, and jokes of Wright's apparent invisibility. (Carter and Wright obviously enjoyed their verbal engagement — Wright, Carter observes, was a "brilliant and funny man.") Replying to Wright's written regrets, Carter joked: "To myself I said — not in too audible a voice — 'Aha! he has once more overshot himself. He has forgotten that his episcopal brothers, sundry and not so sundry religious women — most of whom would like to be ordained priests — , a number of stout and dedicated lay persons, who think the Sisters have lost their minds, will all be descending upon Rome for the canonization of Elizabeth Seton.' "[4] Obviously, one ought not to make too much of a private jest — Carter and Wright are fond of engaging in humorous banter and are accustomed to dealing with serious issues by exchanging a light-hearted and satiric verbal cut and thrust. Nor should one ignore altogether the implications of the humour since in the jest something is revealed about the men on both a personal and an intellectual level. No one would question Carter's admiration for the congregations of sisters, but satire is not without its point and beneath the wit there lies a clear attitude towards the question of women's ordination: it is an issue very much on Carter's mind, and he is not positively disposed to the idea.

Two weeks later he wrote for advice, addressing a letter to Lawrence K. Shook, a Basilian priest at the Pontifical Institute for Mediaeval Studies in Toronto. No answer on record. He also wrote to Aloysius M. Ambrozic, a priest and a professor of biblical studies at St. Augustine's Seminary in the Toronto suburb of Scarborough. In his correspondence, Carter pointed out that two current issues needed to be dealt with. One, the question of clerical celibacy, seemed to be cooling off; the other, the question of the ordination of women, seemed to be heating up and he wanted to "orient [his] own thinking and to try to have as wide a spectrum on the topic as possible."

There followed a correspondence between two kindred spirits, at least with respect to the question of the ordination of women. Ambrozic pointed out that should the Commission decide that the ordination of women was desirable, there would remain pastoral difficulties which would take decades to overcome. First of all, proponents of the ordination of women argue their case on the basis of power and not of service; but service, not power, is the essence of priesthood. Carter returned frequently to this distinction, though he shaped it in terms of power and authority. Secondly, Ambrozic argued, parishioners would need time and preparation before they would accept a woman priest. Her introduction would have to be gradual, and the way carefully prepared. There had simply been too many changes too fast in recent years. Ambrozic reasoned that the concept of priesthood is part of a long-standing tradition in which the priest as "a living sign of the presence of Jesus Christ among His people is a reality deeply ingrained in the consciousness of Catholics — even though we have yet to articulate this awareness in a manner which would intellectually satisfy our current ecclesial and theological atmosphere. Real or apparent tampering with this sign too precipitously and without dispassioned and realistic thought will do us a fair amount of harm. And it is far better to be accused of being 'behind time' than to destroy, or give the appearance of destroying, something of permanent value."[5]

Carter's response was in the mail within weeks. He was "almost in total agreement" with Ambrozic's thinking. "There is something in me, I hope it has some tinge of virtue, which makes me most uncomfortable in trying to defend positions with weak arguments. In this particular case, I think it would be much better to face up to the question of the theological problem with a really open mind, but the conviction that, as you have ably stated, no matter what the theological conclusion, this is not the time to ordain women. In fact, this may be the only point in which I disagree with your letter. On the second page you open a paragraph by saying 'Should we decide that the ordination of women to the priesthood is a theological desideratum . . . .' I would not express it that way. I would say if we discover that there is no objection on theological grounds to the ordination. I cannot postulate that this could be a desideratum. From there on we are totally in agreement . . . . I consider that the ordination of women at this point would be a flaming disaster. I say this with all the more vehemence because people are constantly confusing my position of openness on the theological debate with a sophomoric enthusiasm to leap into pools whose depth is unknown and whose rocks may be hidden."[6]

The nature of priesthood and the related matter of clerical celibacy were important and related issues for Carter. In addition, the decline in priestly vocations just at the time when the church was in the process of an historic renewal was a bitter irony for him. As a result, the apparent relationship between the decimation of clerical ranks and the matter of clerical celibacy was cause for concern, as was the question of sexuality in a society suffering from consumptive secularism. Even theologically, Carter knew, there was a kinship between questions of celibacy and female ordination: "It is interesting to contemplate the fact that, everything said and done, celibacy of the clergy and ordination of women might be two matters entirely on the same basis. I mean, there is no reason why the Church should not decide on a discipline which is for the common good whether or not there is a theological obstacle. No one that I know of has ever said that there is a theological obstacle to men being priests and being married. Why should we get so excited about the possibility of there being no theological obstacle to women being ordained, but still not wanting to do it? *Saltem mihi videtur.* [At least it seems that way to me.]"

It seemed that way to Ambrozic too. His response was on the way within the week. "Let me say that I am pleased and flattered that our views of the matter are so much alike. In regard to my 'desideratum', it means in reality no more, or very little more, than your 'there is no objection' — by saying this, I am not pulling in my horns in order to please you."[7] It was an interesting and informative exchange, and a clear converging of minds — which makes all the more puzzling Ambrozic's feeling several years later that he had not been seriously consulted by Carter in the preparation of the Cardinal's own theological definition of priesthood when researching his 1983 *Do This in Memory of Me.*

Carter's position on the ordination of women to the sacramental priesthood was clear: such a move, no matter what obstacles existed or did not exist, would be ill-advised. With the passing of time, however, he has become more and more convinced that one ought to elevate women to positions of authority, and did so himself when he assumed office in Toronto. In addition, during his seventeen years in London, Carter began to take noticeable steps in the direction of the empowerment of women, but he continued to cling to traditional terminology and to stress sexual differentiation without exploring as thoughtfully those points of human convergence, even though he had long maintained that complementarity and equality were not mutually exclusive.

In an analytical reaction to 1968 synodal preparations, for example, Carter observed the human dynamics: "There were the usual characteristics: male arrogance, oversimplification, bravado, the need to pose, to show off, to swagger just a little; the female traits, the cliche in place of the idea, the talking around the subject, the appeal to the emotions, the glorious inconsistencies and the rebuttals of what no one had ever said. Traits, be it said, highly interchangeable between men and women delegates."[8] The final phrase is obviously a disclaimer of sorts, but the thrust is what the scholastic philosopher would tag *ut in pluribus* and, in the eyes of the women's movement or sociologists with an interest in gender definition, it represents mainline thomistic epistemology; that is, Aquinas would argue that this, "for the most part", is the way men and women behave. Although neither man nor woman looks particularly attractive in the caricature, the male characteristics imply relationships to power and reason, the female to sense and the irrational. It is the kind of catalogue sociologists are fond of using in the disclosure of male-female stereotyping, and which the Canadian bishops themselves used in the 1984 Green Kit whose emergence the Cardinal was to find so problematic. It is the kind of catalogue which the Bishop of London was capable of, though one which the Cardinal Archbishop of Toronto would avoid both in principle and as a matter of political sensitivity.

In speaking of women, Carter characteristically portrays them in terms of love and service, characteristics which, he is fond of stressing to the seminarians at St. Peter's, also form the essence of priesthood.[9]

Still, given Carter's view of maleness and femaleness, and given his insistence on the need for adherence to the essentials of Catholic tradition, his active support for the ordination of women to the sacrament of Holy Orders could hardly be expected. In a 1970 address during a nurses' graduation, Carter began with the question of women's liberation, wondering what women want to be liberated from. It could not be "past inequities of law," he reasoned, because they were "mostly gone". Carter then celebrated the women in his life — his mother, sisters, nieces, his "devoted secretaries" — and, true to his traditional vision, he expostulated, "Men have certain talents and abilities. Women have others. *Vive la différence.*" Women, he explained, are "closer to love".[10] *La différence* of the early and mid-1970s suggests that Carter has still not completely internalized the samenesses. Though several see these inclinations as part of Carter's Irish birthright, Carter himself shrugs off the accusations, noting that people are entitled to their opinions but that, for his part, he has always preached complementarity and equality. Many disagree. "He is just typical of the Irish," suggests William Power, retired Bishop of Antigonish. "I'm trying to cure myself of what I think is his attitude: women's place is in the home; don't get too ambitious. What I think is wrong — and it's more of an insight that I wouldn't want to have to prove — is that we are trying to analyze a mystery, or we are trying to analyze the plan of God from a sociological point of view, not from a faith point of view."

Women's liberationists are a problem for Carter, who tends to see in their objectives either the melding of the sexes at the cost of differences which should be celebrated, or the ordination of their gender to the sacramental priesthood. It is not surprising, therefore, that a talk entitled "Women as Agents of Reconciliation" contained many of his anxieties about the objectives of the movement and celebrated the obedience of Mary as exemplified in her *fiat mihi*, her "be it done to me" with which she answered the angel when she was invited to become the mother of the son of God. It is a topic he introduced with a verbal grimace over the "sad spectacle of women activists in the Church." Reconciliation, he argued, cannot come "in the search for predominance and outburst": Carter's epitomizing of the ultimate goal and the intemperate style of the feminist.

Nonetheless, Carter has been listening — and thinking. The persistent objections to Mary as a model for women centre on her role as virgin and mother, an impossible ideal, as well as on her passivity, as represented by the *fiat*. Carter had begun to reshape his discussion of Mary as passive recipient, transforming this ideal of womanhood into an active agent willingly participating in the divine plan. "Tradition and theology agree that her consent was required," required in the sense that she was free to say no. It is a change in emphasis but not in theology, a change which stresses Mary's active role in the mystery of Christ's conception, in her becoming the god-bearer. Indeed, in 1974, Carter told a gathering of Sisters of St. Joseph that Mary's *fiat* was the "greatest act of decision-sharing in the world." But, as Carter explained when discussing the Declaration on the Question of the Admission of Women to the Ministerial Priesthood, "it is fatuous to talk about whether she should or could have been called to the ministerial priesthood. She has simply got another line of redemption." To draw this conclusion of the ideal of womanhood is logically to imply that woman as such simply has another line of redemption. She was not born to be priest.

By December 11, 1977, there were clear signs that Carter knew the thrust of the impending Declaration. Speaking at St. Peter's Cathedral, he mentioned the question of women's ordination and argued that the church was not about to be "shaken by the wind", stating that the "doctrine of Christ is unassailable. Ours is not." The latter observation anticipated (or echoed) the Declaration's assertion that "the Church, in fidelity to the Lord, does not consider herself authorized to admit women to priestly ordination."[11] Then, on January 23, 1977, Carter delivered a homily at St. Peter's Cathedral in London, noting that a statement was imminent and that he would be away for a few weeks; he wanted to address the topic before leaving. Noting that he had been consulted by the Commission, Carter proceeded to outline the difficulty of the Commissioners' task: the decision of the Anglican Church to proceed with the ordination of women, the present agitation by Roman Catholic women, the potential for misunderstanding. It was clear that Carter knew what the document said, and that he was preparing the way for its reception. We are all equal, he argued, though there is a difference in roles, roles decided by God, not by man. Indeed, there is no sign that Christ wanted women to be members of the ministerial priesthood. Two thousand years cannot be cast aside as the result of twenty years of political agitation. "The Church does not consider herself authorized," Carter said, using the exact words of *Inter insignores*, which was yet to be promulgated. He concluded his homily with an exhortation that women "take up the challenge of real superiority. Mother Theresa." Service and love. But no real power to influence change, no authority to alter structures or to celebrate the divine mysteries. Indeed, Mother Theresa ministers to the lowly, and leaves the grand designs to others. Carter himself would argue, as he often does, that woman does in fact have power in the church; it is merely the authority which is missing.

As for Rome's Declaration, Carter can hardly have been disappointed. James Hayes, the Archbishop of Halifax, comments that Carter supported the Declaration very strongly, and frequently, adding, "It was evidently his personal opinion." It was also the position of his mentor, Thomas Aquinas, whose thesis on the derivative and christological nature of priestly power and its exclusively male properties the authors of the Declaration quote directly. Though not wholly convinced of the compelling quality of the argument, Carter walked at least this far with Aquinas and with Rome.

Aquinas had other attitudes toward women which seem to have been at least partially assimilated by Carter, though Aquinas's bottom line was not Carter's. Women, the Angelic Doctor theorized, are excluded from preaching, since "as a rule women are not perfected in wisdom."[12] Although Carter and contemporary church teachings distance themselves at least implicitly from these kinds of thomistic arguments against woman's sacramental ordination, many christian feminists would argue that Aquinas's view of women still forms an intellectual undercurrent within official church teaching, and is especially evident in the church's concept of complementarity. Aquinas reasoned that "since it is not possible for the female sex to signify eminence of degree, for a woman is in the state of subjection, it follows that she cannot receive the sacrament of Order."[13] Similarly, Aquinas explained, only men are able to address entire congregations publicly, since women are subject by nature, but men are not.

Even as Bishop of London, however, Carter could see the benefits of women taking leadership roles — working as instructors in his seminary, for example. Their presence, he said, would provide a warmth, a "dual sexual approach to any subject, since I feel that women bring a perspective that men don't have and vice versa." This perspective, Carter argued, is lacking in the formation of priests, and it is all the more serious, since he sees the church as being too priest-centred and too man-centred. "I have always said that the Church has been overclericalized, over-male also. I wouldn't debate that for a moment. I'm not thinking of over-male simply in the sense of occupying high places and the argument as to whether women can take their place in those positions. I think that is a given. Rather, I mean over-male in the sense that we have not really been sympathetic to or appreciative of the female perspective in our people." Leadership roles, yes, but leadership roles in line with Rome's promulgations and roles whose exercise will necessarily differ not in competence of execution but according to the predilections of the male and female nature.

Although it is true that even as a fledgling priest in the Archdiocese of Montreal Carter had already begun to distance himself from a simple association with Aquinas's teaching on maleness and femaleness, nonetheless as long as his descriptive vocabulary centres on the word complementarity, Carter's message is not likely to receive a sympathetic audience among those schooled in the nuances of cultural history. Hence, given Carter's clear identification with the thomistic tradition; his "clear", "strong" and "frequent" support of the Declaration on the Question of the Admission of Women to the Ministerial Priesthood; and his own sense of ecclesiastical solidarity; and despite his own adaptations to the signs of the times, it is not surprising that the Bishop of London found himself in head-to-head combat on women's issues when he assumed the role of Archbishop of Toronto, Canada's most distinguished centre for theological debate.

CHAPTER EIGHT

The 1970s: Who Speaks for the Church?

No matter what the issue that occupied Carter — ecclesiastical, political or moral — he always had the fifth estate to cope with: the secular press, a seemingly foresworn antagonist. Prelates in the Roman system are accountable only to senior prelates in the same system. It is a remarkably simple and efficient operation in its own way, not always well-oiled and often missing important parts, but still a tested system that has endured for centuries. Carter has made a home in it. But the philosophy on which it is based goes counter to the social dynamic of late-twentieth-century secular Canada.

Educated in the democratic institutions of Canadian society, Carter is fully conscious, and approving, of the integrity of an unhindered press. Nonetheless, he has felt the tension between the authoritative dicta of the church and the press's freedom to poke into controversial corners. Over the years, this has caused him to change his views on the role of the press.

In an address given to the Canadian Managing Editors Conference on February 1, 1955, Carter underlined the commonality of purpose that should unite the church and the press: "I invoke that wonderful saying that might be a slogan of all journalists, '*in necessariis unitas, in contingentibus libertas, in omnibus caritas*' — 'in the fundamental issues, unity; in the area of opinion, freedom; in all things, charity.' If we accept that ours is a religious civilization and that there are certain basic Truths intimately connected with religion upon which our society is built, then in these matters there can be no neutrality. As someone has said in affairs of this nature, 'there may be a horse of another color but there cannot be a horse of no color.' The Church, which is waging a struggle for the preservation of spiritual and moral values, has, in my opinion, the right to count on the support of the

Press. . . . on the active and committed support, not simply an aloof attitude of 'may the best man win'. This does not, or should not make of the Press a 'yes-man'. Once the communion of minds has been established on, at least a certain basic area, it is good for all organizations, even for those of divine institution, to face the light of an informed public, and even, at times if necessary, of a well-intentioned criticism from the Press."[1]

What Carter could presume as true of the largely homogeneous society of pre–Quiet Revolution Quebec (the context in which he gave this speech) was very different from what he could presume to be true of the largely heterogeneous society on the brink of a new century. The role of a secular press in post-christian Canada is fundamentally different from that of a secular press that still acknowledges, at least tacitly, christian hegemony in the nation. Carter adjusted to the changing climate, but the natural tensions that exist between the institutional church and the media were compounded as the church's own considerable political and social clout was waning in proportion to the other forces in a multifaith, pluralistic society. Carter changed and recognized the need for the church to change, to adjust to political reality. At the very least, he always made great copy.

Although Carter would never have been so bold as to deliver to a contemporary secular press the kind of talk he gave in mid-fifties Montreal, he maintained an active interest in the affairs and the direction of the religious media. In an address to the ecumenical Canadian Church Press given in Toronto in the early 1970s, he reminded the assembled editors that their major contribution was "psychological or educational in the full sense. The churches will stand or fall on the faith of their individual members. Nothing in our day is so corrosive of faith as the idea that everyone is losing it. It is like sex and the Kinsey Report."[2]

The role of the church press, in Carter's view, was to be supportive of church morale and not destructive of it, to explode and not disseminate the several distortions of religion that were passing as scientific observation. Ever contemptuous of sociological methodologies, Carter dismissed the accoutrements of poll taking as so much specious science. The church press, he contended, had to be engaged in nothing less than truth-telling, a not-so-novel idea, whose time had just arrived.

But Carter's relationship with the Roman Catholic church press, and particularly the *Catholic Register*, was often a stormy one, marked by his own efforts to influence the direction and management of an organ which, though it published him, also drove him to frustration and acute rage, and never quite as successfully as when it involved Anne Roche Muggeridge.

In a letter to veteran journalist and managing editor Robert Vezina following the *Register*'s publication of an excerpt from Muggeridge's 1972 *Saturday Night* article — a trial run for her longer polemic *The Gates of Hell* — in which she singled out for attack a duplicitous Bishop Carter, he protested that "it would seem fairly clear to the most unskilled observer that an article written by someone who took absolutely no trouble to do her homework, not even a phone call to the CCC headquarters, could hardly be a legitimate source of inspiration or information."[3] He fulminated: "Why then was her name given publicity and her views prominence?"

Vezina responded to Carter's chastisement with alacrity. He acknowledged Carter's anger over Muggeridge's imputation that the Canadian delegation to the 1971 Synod of Bishops had let Canadian Catholics down by encouraging a change in the church's clerical celibacy discipline, but he countered, "I submit that you are overreacting. There is obvious hyperbole in the Roche article, [she had not yet adopted her husband's surname, Muggeridge] perhaps even paranoia, but, again, it is part of an obsessive package. . . . In your letter, you find that the Roche article has glaring errors, that it is fallacious, ignorant, disgusting and garbled nonsense. By imputation and association all this applies to the *Register*."[4] Vezina concluded by inviting the distressed Carter to write for the *Register* on a monthly basis and signs off with the slightly impudent: "I've always been a lousy lackey, and God grant I always will be."

Carter was stung. Piqued by Vezina's reference to ecclesiastical high-handedness, he replied with unqualified bluntness: "And let us get the record straight, my dear Mr. Vezina. Lackeys I do not like. Nor was it my intention in any way to limit your legitimate — and vast — freedom of action in publishing the *Register*. I feel that your 'lackey' reference has misplaced and distorted the whole issue. I shall try to elucidate and I shall emulate your frankness. I hope the day has now arrived when bishops can write honestly to Catholic editors without being accused of trying to bully."[5] He proceeded then to rebut Muggeridge's argument, revealing the imprecise nature of her research. Muggeridge had noted in her article that the bishops had "abused our obedience, the liberalizing Protestantizing Canadian

Bishops", and she singled out Carter for special mention. "Bishop G. Emmett Carter of London, Ont., knew what he was doing when he told us on one of his tapes before the Synod deliberations began that we could expect a change in the traditional rule of celibacy, that the Synod would at last approve the ordination of married men to the priesthood. . . . The last tape from the Synod featured Bishop Carter again, disappointed but not downcast. The proposal for a married clergy had been defeated, but the dinosaurs had received merely a stay of execution. . . . It was wrong of Bishop Carter and the Canadian delegation to try to make us believe that a decision to reverse the Church's celibacy rule was imminent. Those public statements were prejudicial and biased. Very dirty pool. Bishops ought not to behave like that."[6] By way of refutation, Carter simply demolished the credibility of the author by establishing that he hadn't made any tapes and, secondly, he hadn't attended the Synod. She had confused Emmett with Alex. Roche acknowledged the error, and attributed it to a *Saturday Night* researcher. The damage, however, was done.

But it wasn't only his name that he sought to clear; Carter was also anxious to exonerate the Canadian hierarchy of the false charges Roche had brought, in a most public manner, against them. That was the really dirty pool — the implication that the Canadian episcopate was less than fully faithful to Rome.

Now Vezina was stung. The editor wrote that the "Anne Roches, intelligent and fluent and otherwise, seldom do their homework because they willingly choose the agony of polarization and the short view. The basic reason why I published the edited version was to show this, and, perhaps, to show the depth and extent of this type of reasoning. I think we did that, and in the correspondence that flowed from the article we were able to introduce far more light than darkness. And there I leave it, with the decision that Bishop Carter scored more overall points than editor Vezina. The Anne Roches will, in the main, come around to a degree, in the Lord's good time. But, personally I wouldn't want them to come around too abruptly."[7]

Carter was pacified. He accepted Vezina's offer to write occasionally for the *Catholic Register* and noted that the one who "enters the public domain has no right to ask for quarter. All I ask is for equal time. . . . For better or for worse, bishops have to fight with one hand tied behind their backs." It is doubtful that Anne Roche would find this Bishop so easily disabled.

With Anne Roche Muggeridge out of the way — little did he realize in 1972 that she would return with full fury three years later — Carter turned his attention to the series of columns he had been invited to write by Vezina, and determined in the very first of these columns to distinguish between the authority of opinion and the authority of office. When writing on matters of faith and morals, he was writing as a bishop, an overseer, and his authority in the Catholic tradition was unassailable. To strengthen even further the authoritative air of this first "opinion column", Carter invoked no less a figure than John Henry Cardinal Newman: "Read — again, if you like, Newman's *Apologia*. He could find no sufficient reason for leaving his beloved Anglican home except one. And he placed it all on the line of that great Augustinian phrase, '*Securus judicat orbis terrarum*'. The sentence defies literal translation but I believe I do it no violence in rendering it, 'The universal people of God stand secure in their judgement.' Newman wrote: 'He repeated these words again and again, and, when he was gone, they kept ringing in my ears. '*Securus judicat orbis terrarum*'; . . . What a light was hereby thrown upon every controversy in the Church! not that, for the moment, the multitude may not falter in their judgement, — not that, in the Arian hurricane, Sees more than can be numbered did not bend before its fury, and fall off from St. Athanasius, — not that the crowd of Oriental Bishops did not need to be sustained during the contest by the voice and the eye of St. Leo; but that the deliberate judgement, in which the whole Church at length rests and acquiesces, is an infallible prescription and a final sentence against such portions of it as protest and secede. . . .' And that security is guaranteed by the line of the Apostles and through them to Jesus. So judged Augustine. So judged Newman. So has the Catholic world always judged."[8]

And so judges Carter, with one eye on the Anne Roches and the other on the Hans Küngs. He vigorously decries those critics — both reactionary and progressive — who would push the bishops to the side, either questioning their fidelity or dismissing them as a nuisance in a time of renewal. When American publisher and humorist Dan Herr noted in an article quoting historian John Tracy Ellis that "probably the greatest contribution they [the bishops] could make to the Church in transition would be to stay out of the way," he provoked a strong response from Carter. In the mind of the Bishop of London a leader's job was to lead, to get in the way, if necessary to pay a martyr's debt. Carter, of course, had no intention of retreating to the shadows. He would remain centre-stage, under the spotlight, secure in his judgement.

In a letter to Stan Koma in August 1973, the newly appointed managing editor of the *Register*, Carter scolded him for what he considered Koma's sympathetic article/editorial regarding the recent censure of Hans Küng by the Congregation for the Doctrine of the Faith. [This was some time before Pope John Paul II's definitive censure in 1979, when he deprived the controversial and much celebrated Swiss theologian of his *missio canonica*, his canonical mandate to teach in a Catholic theological faculty. Küng has been the *enfant terrible* of Catholic theology from the time of the Council, criticizing the doctrine of papal infallibility among other things.] Carter wrote, "I am rather surprised to see an editorial in the *Register* endorsing this so-called 'creative tension' between theologians and Magisterium. This, as the *Register* should know, is not Catholic thought. Theologians and the Magisterium are not equals who produce progress by some sort of Hegelian or Marxist dialectic. Theologians have a right to explore the truth and to present it, but they do not have a right to contest the Magisterium once the Magisterium has issued a teaching."[9]

These are hardly the views of a "liberal, Protestantizing" bishop, but Roche had cut deep in 1972 and she would again in 1975 with the publication of *The Gates of Hell*. This time round it was a highly sympathetic review of the Roche book by University of Windsor historian John O'Farrell that provoked Carter's wrath. The review appeared in the Saskatoon-based *Chelsea Journal*, a publication with a right-of-centre editorial slant, edited by the highly conservative academic-priest and pro-life activist Alphonse De Valk. Although the review did not mention Carter by name, it cut him to the quick. It looked as if the 1972 Vezina drama would be performed once again, the actors different but the plot the same.

For O'Farrell it all came as a bit of a shock: "In December of 1975 my review was finally published and when I returned to Windsor in January after the Christmas holidays there was a letter from His Lordship. When I got myself settled, I opened up the letter and just about fell off the chesterfield. The bishop was very, very angry and vastly upset with my review. I read and re-read his letter and I was flabbergasted. And, I thought, he's supposed to be an academic. I finally calmed myself down with my crutch, a pot of tea, and showed it to a Basilian colleague and friend, who, although not a die-hard reformer, was certainly more progressive than I. He observed that the letter revealed a 'frightened man, an insecure personality.' What I had before me was not a point of view but an hysterical outburst."

O'Farrell eventually wrote to Carter explaining his own concern about many of the changes in the post-conciliar church, phrasing it all according to a careful, rather laboured etiquette. Carter replied, acknowledging his own anxieties over the present situation of the church and admitting to O'Farrell that the bishops had gone too far too fast. He also sent him the notes that he had made while reading the Roche book at his cottage on Lake Huron. It was a conciliatory gesture, but O'Farrell was contemptuous. "He sent the notes to me to read and comment on, but I didn't want any of this nonsense. I looked through the notes and they were all emotional. 'I don't like this and I don't like that.' But surely that's not the point. You have to absorb the arguments first if you are then going to counter them. You can't say, 'I don't like him', and think that sufficient."

O'Farrell was irritated with the task Carter had imposed on him. He didn't have the time. He wrote Carter begging his indulgence and requesting an extension because of the heavy teaching schedule he faced that winter. Carter didn't reply. In the spring, O'Farrell wrote him thanking him for his thoughts and illuminations, but declined to write a commentary. "I didn't know what on earth I could say about his notes. If an undergraduate had handed them in to me, I would have thought that he had gone off his lid."

The O'Farrell review lacks the vituperative bite of Roche's prose, and pointedly steers clear of naming ecclesiastical culprits. He clearly subscribes, however, to her thesis that although "Vatican II is not found wanting, the liturgical, doctrinal, and pedagogical application of the Council by the Canadian hierarchy and their *periti*, very definitely is."[10] It is in this, the Canadian episcopate's apparent failure to provide true and faithful leadership, that one discovers the hit that smarts. And so Carter lashed out at the hierarchy's detractors irrespective of their academic and spiritual pedigree.

But O'Farrell was not without his own animus toward the renegade ex-Montrealer with a taste for the fashionable and the evanescent. Carter had violated O'Farrell's devotional and aesthetic sense by ordering that the mural of the Jesse Tree in the Cathedral be painted over, and that the use of votive candles in the parishes of the London diocese be suppressed. In addition, his guarantee that O'Farrell

would have complete access to chancery archives for his work on
Carter's controversial London predecessor, Michael Fallon, was not
honoured in the end. An historian aggrieved. Still, Carter was not
named in O'Farrell's review. It is a detached, largely summary assessment of the Roche thesis, and it avoids any mud slinging. The Carter-
initiated correspondence over the review is strikingly out of proportion to the review's contents. It is Carter flailing about, angry, the
wounds of 1972 widening, unhealed.

No sooner had he withstood the assaults of Roche and like-minded
conservatives on the beleaguered integrity of the Canadian bishops
than he found himself embroiled in a controversy with Koma's
successor, Larry Henderson, over a report by Grant Maxwell on the
new China. Maxwell, an employee of the Canadian Catholic Conference, had prepared a report on the changing face of China, and was
favourably disposed to adopting new and positive pastoral approaches
towards that country. Henderson, a convert to Catholicism and a
distinguished Canadian journalist who had served as a correspondent
for the CBC and CTV networks, reacted with some hostility to the
seemingly sanguine approach to marxist China which Maxwell appeared to be encouraging. He fired his first volley in his column of
January 3, 1976.

Carter reacted promptly. As President of the Canadian Catholic
Conference he had to defend Maxwell as well as the integrity of the
Conference. He asked Henderson to hold his fire until he knew better
the target he was shooting at. Henderson responded by distinguishing
between the CCC and one of its employees, but concluded by noting
that he could not remain silent, and if, as a consequence, he was
dismissed, then that was the nature of the game.

Predictably, Carter was furious. The suggestion that he was incapa-
ble of respecting legitimate disagreement, that — as in the case earlier
with Vezina — he wanted lackeys rather than persons with substance,
grated considerably. He wrote back: "My request to 'hold your fire'
was not that you should be silent, but that you should try to be a little
more lucid about what and whom you are attacking. All of which
seems to have had not the slightest effect either upon your thinking or
upon your intentions, since you have reacted not only in disagreement with what I have tried to say, which is totally justifiable and
acceptable, but you even throw in the obviously personal remark
about 'being fired'. This is utterly unacceptable. Is it possible that one

may not suggest disagreement with you without at the same time coming to such fundamental issues?"[11]

The disagreement was papered over, at least for the time being. Yet it was an unfortunate circumstance, for Henderson's concern for the magisterium was comparable to Carter's. "For Henderson the *Catholic Register* must exercise the function of a mediator amongst warring factions within the church, but always serving the authoritative Catholic position, that of the *magisterium* or teaching authority of the church, with aggressive loyalty. ... The didactic strain sometimes detected in the *Catholic Register* during Henderson's leadership reflects the editor's conviction that the beliefs of the Catholic Church have been greatly undermined by the disputes current in contemporary Catholicism, disputes that, in Henderson's mind, unhappily blur the vital distinction that exists between an authoritative utterance and a private opinion."[12] Their sympathies were alike but their styles were markedly different; and when Carter became Archbishop of Toronto, and thus Henderson's boss, their cordiality was strained to the breaking point. In fact, the increasingly conservative direction Henderson was giving the paper occasioned alarm among some of Ontario's bishops, most notably Emmett's brother who, in a letter to Pocock, expressed concern that the *Catholic Register* not "follow the lead of the *National Catholic Register*, the sister paper of *The Wanderer* of the same Frawley Empire, and above all that it will not imitate its negative and reactionary policy."[13]

But the problem was going to be Emmett's, not Pocock's. Larry Henderson, the sometime novelist, a commentator for a Toronto radio station and an aggressively partisan editor, was going to meet his match in Emmett Carter.

Building a theological consensus is no small part of a post-conciliar bishop's responsibility. It isn't enough simply to declaim; the modern bishop must also persuade. Carter realized that rebuking a wayward theologian or the stubborn editor of a Catholic publication was only half the battle. The Bishop had to build constructively, not haphazardly, and he would have to encourage more than correct. Carter the psychologist of education, the master pedagogue, was perfectly suited to the task.

Theologically, the Vatican II "Decree on the Bishops' Pastoral Office in the Church" (*Christus dominus*) put renewed emphasis on the pastoral role of the bishop, in sharp contrast with the juridical emphasis that had dominated since the Council of Trent in the sixteenth century: "In exercising his office of father and pastor, a bishop should stand in the midst of his people as one who serves. Let him be a good shepherd who knows his sheep and whose sheep know him. Let him be a true father who excels in the spirit of love and solicitude for all and to whose divinely conferred authority all gratefully submit themselves. Let him so gather and mold the whole family of his flock that everyone, conscious of his own duties, may live and work in the communion of love."[14]

The Council's definition of a bishop was entirely consonant with Carter's own thinking. He took to heart Pope John XXIII's injunction that this council was not to be characterized by anathemas and condemnations but by a willingness to enter into dialogue in love and good faith with the modern world. But as the years after the Council passed, years of considerable ecclesiastical turmoil, Carter's theological instincts — always conservative — and his unqualified commitment to the institutional church combined to make him more aggressive in rooting out the things that divide, the ideas and people that imperil Catholic unity. Dissent for Carter, particularly public dissent by officers of the church, is a negative feature of Catholic life, and he rarely approves of its expression, although in theory he allows of its genuine possibility. That being said — and it is Carter the administrator who says it — it is important to begin with a positive core of affirmations and legitimate explorations. On this point it is Carter the psychologist who speaks it.

Carter is not technically a theologian, and his forays into the labyrinth of contemporary theological categories and discourse have been few and largely unsuccessful. Carter's intellectual predilections are more in the order of Newman-like lucidity than Germanic opacity, although the rather dense philosophical and theological writings of the Canadian Jesuit Bernard Lonergan have appealed to him since his days with the Thomas More Institute in Montreal.

There are essentially three components in Carter's post-conciliar thinking that constitute his theological viewpoint. First is his understanding of the church's need to re-appropriate an authentic christian humanism, a humanism bereft of the "negative otherworldliness", "false asceticism", and "false stoicism" that prevented it in the immediate past from being a credible sign of the gospel. This re-appropriation began with the Council and is grounded in an incarnational theology, a theology which "is agonizingly preoccupied with the insertion of the Church in the modern world. . . . *It means that God himself has chosen the way of man and the Church can find no other road.* The Church must be totally, completely and unswervingly dedicated to the proposition that she has no other role than the ennobling of man in his fulfillment. Not in some angelic guise, but in his true humanity."[15]

Not only is the church fully enmeshed in human affairs, but there is a radical egalitarianism that runs through Catholicism involving everyone in the mission of the church. This is the conciliar principle of co-responsibility and it is the second essential component of Carter's theology. This principle "does not abolish the hierarchy of authority, which would be a denial of the ordained priesthood, but it insists that all members of the Church, in various ways, must be involved in the problems of her mission and in some ways able to express opinions about administrative matters."[16]

The third component of Carter's thought subsequent to Vatican II is his notion of a vital tradition, a meaningful, non-fossilized, pulsating tradition. "The concept of tradition was radically changed at Vatican II. (Not a fundamental change from the Church's teaching but a clarification of that teaching.) We had been brought up to look at tradition as simply other doctrines which were not written. The concept of the living tradition of the Church is much more than this. It is true that dogmas qua dogmas are not introduced and there is no contradiction between the concept of change and the concept of preservation. This is best illustrated in the human being. For instance, there are changes in life, and yet the basic personality remains untouched. A healthy existentialism is in no way contradictory of a healthy essentialism. Of all historical developments one would have thought that the Church would have understood this better than anyone, simply because the Church is basically a living tradition."[17]

These critical notions — the incarnational theology of the true christian humanist, the all-pervasive role of co-responsibility, and the living tradition that is the church — are post-conciliar, fed by Carter's reading of the *periti* since the Council, and greatly augmented by his attendance at the Congress on the Theology of the Renewal of the Church (Theologo '67) held at the University of Toronto during

Canada's Centennial Year. Without a doubt, Carter is a Council bishop.

But Carter is also a man of eminent pragmatism. He cannot abide grand schemes that remain ever untried by human agency. He likes to enflesh, to incarnate ideas, and the ideas for renewal that he brought back from Rome were ready for incarnation. Never reluctant to make the bold move, Carter launched his own diocesan synod — "the first synod in modern history which represents all levels of a diocese"[18] — in March 1966. He appointed a Secretary-General and a Co-ordinating Commission to oversee the entire operation. The work of the London Synod was divided into four phases covering three years, and was responsible for the establishment of such consultative and deliberative bodies as the Diocesan Pastoral Council, the Senate of Priests and Parish Councils at the parish level. Every section in the community was represented — it was as comprehensive and democratic as its Catholic nature would allow — and it served as a perfect illustration of the papal social principle of subsidiarity (the freedom to make decisions at a specific level without fear of having that authority subsumed by a higher power).

Carter was very proud of the Synod's myriad accomplishments: "Perhaps I am overly proud, overly sanguine, or have simply enjoyed you all too much. But I feel that we have even gone further than the idea of loyal opposition. This concept of opposition is based upon the parliamentary idea of a party being in government and another having the obligation of pointing out the errors of that government. From the very beginning we have tried to achieve a notion of the Church which is not primarily one of authoritarian government but rather of a common effort to find the truth, that truth which would make us free. We have been dedicated to the proposition that the Holy Spirit moves in each of the members of the Church in the hierarchically lowliest as well as in the highest, and that His wisdom is manifest in every person of faith, courage and truth; that the government of the Church is a protection of this notion of the Spirit, guiding it and regulating it as all human beings must be. We have not denied the charism and authority given to the Apostles and their successors, but we have understood that this authority is sterile and hopeless except in juxtaposition to the movement of the Spirit in the whole believing community."

The Synod embodied the objectives of the Council; it represented, in Bishop John Sherlock's words, "Carter's ecclesiology, the ecclesiology of Vatican II." But it was also the consummate administrator's practical realization of reasonable goals, leaving little time for either flights of fantasy or grounds of complaint about lack of consultation. Carter's trustworthy aide, Father Joe Snyder, confides that when Carter first broached the idea of a synod, "the bishops of Canada thought he was nuts. He had everybody running from every end of the diocese. Practically everyone was on some commission or other — priests, religious, lay people from every parish. There were several meetings, and grand sessions as well. It was an horrendous undertaking. In the long run it served to diffuse a lot of mounting energies and frustrations: the liberal wing complaining that things were not changing fast enough and the conservative wing complaining that there were changes at all. I think that Carter achieved through the Synod a means of eliminating a lot of confusion and disillusionment. It was a grassroots experiment and we tinkered. And then the time came after two years when Carter said, 'It's time to stop tinkering with the car and to put it back on the road.' I think the church of London is better because of the Synod he called."

It was therapy, it was catharsis, it was political and it was brilliant. It was clearly not nuts.

The London Synod was a master stroke, a carefully orchestrated project designed to engage as many baptized Catholics as possible in a decision-making exercise that would have direct significance for their lives. And it worked. It also prepared Carter admirably for synodal work, or at least synodal work of a kind.

When he was elected by his brother bishops to be one of the delegates to the 1974 Synod of Bishops in Rome, he knew that this was a different kind of beast from the London variety, and his experience as a Council Father and member of the consilium and ICEL ably acquainted him with Roman means and manners. Still, for all that, someone with the democratic and open leanings of Carter could not help but feel some annoyance when coping with the often convoluted and occasionally secretive operations of the curial machine. To work with Rome demands more than a mite of patience and forbearance. One waits. Carter has always known that. "In Rome everything moves slowly. It is the nature of the animal. Rome moves for the whole world. You have five continents that you are making decisions for. So Rome takes a long time to move; you must expect to keep pressure going for some time."

Carter knew that the episcopal synods were not legislative but advisory only and he was prepared, in print at least, to admit to their

efficacy. Unlike his episcopal colleague, the Winnipeg-based Ukrai-
nian Archbishop Maxim Hermaniuk, who has been present at every
one of the synods since their legal re-establishment by Pope Paul VI
in 1965, Carter has never made war with the limited function of the
episcopal synods. He sees genuine value in their bringing together, at
regular intervals of three years, various episcopal representatives from
the universal church, and he welcomes the opportunity the synod
provides for the pontiff to hear his brother bishops address issues of
common pastoral concern.

But the real work of the synod occurs outside of Rome. "We had a
philosophy, a procedure, that we worked out very early in the history
of the synods, that the important work is not what is done in Rome for
a month in the Fall. It's what goes on before the synod convenes as we
define the problem, let our people know what the problem is, and
then report back to our people after the synod in order to say 'Well
here's what happened in Rome and here's what should happen now
and here.' It is the preparation and the follow-up that is important."
Ever the pragmatist, Carter would defer to Rome and Roman procedure when necessary, for he was not one to contest authority, but
the "real" work could be managed at a safe distance, and under local
initiative. Carter's synod experiences — he was elected to the '74, '77,
and '80 Synods — confirmed his conviction, if it ever wavered, that it
is the branch office, not home office, that gets done what needs to be
done.

The theme of the 1974 Synod was Evangelization, and Carter
prepared himself and his diocese in several ways. He accepted Henderson's invitation like Vezina's before him to write a column (once
every three weeks) and to devote a substantial number of these
columns to the Synod; he attended an Inter-American Bishops' Assembly meeting in Miami and took part in a CBS panel discussion with
the formidable John Cardinal Krol of Philadelphia and Bishop Luis
Aponte Martinez of San Juan de Puerto Rico, where he made clear his
understanding that the synod is not, strictly speaking, an exercise in
collegiality; and because he was Vice-President of the Canadian
Catholic Conference, he took an active role in encouraging discussion and feedback at the national level.

But perhaps most importantly, Carter understood long before
many others that *the* major problem of the Synod lay in its communications apparatus — the rather arcane Sala Stampa Della Sante
Sede (Press Office of the Holy See) — as well as in the false expecta-

tions generated by the media: "During the last Synod [1971], there were three times more journalists and media people in Rome than there were bishops. Put yourself in the place of one of these fortunate or unfortunate persons who must cover the Synod in Rome. The deliberations of the bishops may or may not be interesting. The structure of the Synod is such that interest can be a very low factor. The official meetings . . . were mostly composed of a series of mono- logues. The situation is not unlike the parliaments of the world where members are making speeches for the people back home. . . . In such a situation, journalists are hard-pressed for copy to send back to their editors. . . . This leads us to the situation where the journalists have to make copy at all costs. Their copy may frequently consist of scuttle- butt obtained through various hangers-on in the Roman Curia over a bottle of wine on the Via della Conciliazione or in even less reputable situations. . . . If we had a few well prepared and well informed journalists and media people covering the event, who could under- stand its nature and not build up impossible expectations, the Church and the world would be much better off."[19] That was in 1974.

In 1985 one Canadian journalist was moved to remark on the communications problems at the Extraordinary Synod held in that year: "Many of the press are eager for stories that touch the lives of their readers; their editors hound them for ideas that are recognizable and credible. The irritation experienced by some of the press, includ- ing myself, is palpable. Controversy is courted when obscurity is normative. In the absence of the full texts, and with a dearth of 'real issues', the powers of invention become fully activated and the inter- ests of truth are, as a consequence, ill-served. The press should be helped, not hindered, in their work and they should, in turn, come prepared — apprised of the issues and comfortable with the lan- guage."[20] *Plus ça change, plus c'est la même chose.*

Although Carter would continue to worry about the sad nature of the media coverage of the Synod, by 1977 there were more pressing things at hand. The topic was Catechetics, and he was the President of the Canadian Conference of Catholic Bishops (1977 was the year that the Canadian Catholic Conference changed its name to the Canadian Conference of Catholic Bishops). Besides his own personal interest in the topic and his international reputation as a catechist, as the presi- dent of the Canadian episcopal conference, he had much more at stake with this Synod than with the previous one. There was no doubt in anyone's mind who the leader of this delegation would be.

Each episcopal conference prepares a series of interventions or short addresses for several of its delegates. These interventions are approved, in Canada, by the Plenary Assembly of the Conference and are not necessarily representative of the views of the particular delegate charged to read them at the Synod. In a letter sent to Father Guy Poisson, the Secretary-General (French) of the CCCB, concerning an intervention composed by Father Gilles Langevin for the Canadian delegation at the 1977 Synod, Carter reminds the Secretary-General that a "synodal intervention has to be unified, has to say one thing and has to say it very directly and rather provocatively."[21] This letter reveals a great deal not only about Carter's active role in the preparation of the interventions, but also about his keen sense that for the intervention to be relevant to Canadians, it must spurn the rarefied language and myopic preoccupation of the specialist. It must have the broadest appeal and it must be immediately intelligible. The teacher and the journalist in him balked at the futility of a narrowly conceived intervention. The intervention written by amanuensis Langevin was too insular, too religious and, in Carter's mind, it did not adequately represent the consensus of those bishops gathered at St. Jérôme, Quebec, before the Plenary Assembly. And he said so.

"Among other things, the Christian community to which the paper appears to refer would seem to be only the structured Church. I really do not recall that as having been the majority position of the delegates of St. Jérôme. Quite to the contrary. I felt that, while recognizing the value of the parish and the diocese, we considered the problem to be at a much broader and deeper stage. I think my ideas are sufficiently well known . . . that no one will attribute to me a tendency to 'play down' the official Church, which includes the diocese and the parish. But to place all of our emphasis upon it — or almost all of it — is, in my opinion, a mistake. . . . I understood our effort at being directed towards the whole atmosphere of present day society, with its electronic media and all the rest of it."

In the end, he had his way. He found *this* synod experience rich and productive, the more so as it endorsed a catechetical model he had been advocating for years. He wrote with elation to his old friend and colleague at the Thomas More Institute, Charlotte Tansey, confiding to her that he detected "a flowering of the very philosophy which we have so long espoused in our movement. . . . I sat there bemused while I listened to bishop after bishop from various sections of the world saying roughly the same thing we have been saying over these years. We have clearly come away from the idea that the presentation of the gospel can be in terms of answers. I would be afraid to put this in most popular journals. But I know that this idea is in safe hands with you. The conclusion was that we have to proceed by questions. And we have to make sure that we reach other people's questions instead of our own answers. The Church has too long been caught in a framework of answers handed down from on high, without care as to whether they were relevant to the questions being asked. The best answer is useless unless it corresponds to a question in the mind of the person to whom the answer is directed. I do not know if I ever told you Gregory Zilboorg's analysis of Heaven. I think it is delightful. Zilboorg [a Catholic psychiatrist] said as he was dying of cancer, 'I really look forward to Heaven. All my life I have been going around saying, "What are the answers?" When I get to Heaven, I will be saying, "What are the questions?" ' The questions which people are asking today are the same questions which they always ask. What is the meaning of life? of death? of love? of rejection? of sin? of God? of prayer? of communication? But we have frequently allowed our gospel answers to become stultified and codified and classified. So they remained in one corner while the questions prowled around the world unanswered. As you may guess, I am not against answers; I am against answers that do not meet questions."[22]

Although sanguine about this Synod, at the controversial 1980 Synod on the Family, Carter would be far from convinced that the church had moved away from the position of providing "answers that do not meet questions." But for the moment, sweet victory, a sense that his life's work as an educator had been vindicated. There was also the sweet taste of victory when, in 1977 he became the first Canadian ever elected to the Administrative Council of the Permanent Secretariat of the Synod of Bishops.

Carter's election to the Permanent Secretariat came at a particularly appropriate time. He was concluding his four years (1973 to 1977) on the executive of the Canadian Conference of Catholic Bishops, two as Vice-President and two as President, and he could now devote some time to new responsibilities. "To understand the full import of the post-conciliar implementations in Canada, it is essential to appreciate the critical role exercised by the Canadian Conference of Catholic Bishops, the national episcopal assembly. Even before the Second

Vatican Council encouraged the establishment of national episcopal conferences, the Canadian bishops had created precisely such a structure in 1943. . . . The Conference consists of the General Assembly, which is the body of highest authority; the Permanent Council, whose principal responsibility is to oversee the work and direction of the Conference; the Executive Committee, which is responsible for the promotion and co-ordination of all Conference initiatives; and the Presidency, which alternates between the two linguistic sectors of the Conference, so that when the president is an Anglophone the vice-president is a Francophone and vice versa."[23] Carter knew the machine intimately.

Carter's term on the CCCB had been demanding. In his presiding role Carter had had to attend all the executive meetings, all Administrative Board sessions, the two annual meetings of the entire assembly of bishops, and the international and national meetings. He had also undertaken several new initiatives, including direct contact with the hierarchies of Poland, France and Germany. At the same time, he maintained close links with the United States Catholic Conference executive — especially with the influential Archbishop of Cincinatti, Joseph Bernardin (soon to become Cardinal Archbishop of Chicago) and the *éminence grise* of the American hierarchy, his old friend Cardinal Dearden of Detroit.

His years on the CCCB executive had revealed both his strong hand as a bishop-administrator and his political savvy. Msgr. Dennis Murphy, one-time Secretary-General (English) of the CCCB and Director of Ontario's Institute for Catholic Education, remembers a no-nonsense president who "knew his way around politically. He knew how to handle the papal pro-nuncio, Angelo Palmas, he knew how to make his opinion about episcopal candidates heard and heard seriously and in places where it mattered, and he knew how to work with and, if necessary, around bureaucracies."

His old friend Archbishop Joseph-Aurèle Plourde of Ottawa remembers Carter's consistently moderate voice. "I think that Carter would like to be considered not a progressive but a moderate. That was certainly his style at the bishops' conference. Whenever we met as a group he was always the moderate, although deep down, I would say, he is inclined to be conservative." Plourde should know. As a member of that select body, "The Gang of Five" — Alex, Emmett, Pocock, and Flahiff — Plourde would vacation with Carter and indulge in general banter, light comedy and bouts of Gallic and Hibernian rhetoric.

Bernardin recalls a vibrant mind, both confident and unwavering. "A very intelligent and perceptive man, Carter knew how to handle a meeting, how to penetrate through the flowery language, the lofty vision, the tiresome periphrasis. He could be very direct in a North American way." He could also be direct in a Roman way, asking politely of authority but obliquely critical of the status quo at the same time: "We feel that it would be a wonderful development in the Church at this time," he wrote to the papal Secretary of State in 1977, "if the Synod of Bishops were to become more and more a privileged expression of episcopal communion and that it be seen to be more and more a key advisory body for the Holy Father."[24] Translated, this means: If we are to be advisory, then let us be truly advisory; communion does not mean subjugation.

To ask firmly for one's right is one thing; to dissent freely and publicly, with no accountability to legitimate authority, is another. Carter was clear on the difference: responsible bishops engage in the former, and renegade theologians in the latter. As the 1970s progressed, Carter became more and more open in his disapproval of dissident theologians. When the Sacred Congregation for the Doctrine of the Faith issued its Declaration on Certain Questions Concerning Christian Ethics in January 1976, several Catholic ethicists and many moral theologians in positions of church leadership took strong exception to the document's juridical tone and traditionalist methodology. It was the *Humanae vitae* debates all over again. Carter was alarmed. In a sermon he gave at St. Peter's Cathedral in London, he denounced the disloyalty rampant in various Catholic circles and singled out for particular reprimand Toronto's Gregory Baum and New York's Jesuit advocate for Gay rights, John MacNeil. "What I say, I say without apology; it is the teaching of the Church."[25] *Roma locuta est*: Rome has spoken.

Carter values a public gesture of defiance when necessary, but he is adamant that the context and the authority being defied must be meticulously examined and weighed.

When, as President of the CCCB, he received invitations in 1977 to visit Poland from Cardinals Stefan Wyszynski and Karol Wojtyla, of Warsaw and Cracow respectively, he gladly accepted. The visit was profoundly emotional. He discovered truths about the Polish experience during the Second World War of which he had been sadly ignorant, and he witnessed again and again the Polish hierarchy's resolute opposition to communist rule. Church leaders defied their government with seeming impunity. What government could possibly act against a church so obviously popular and powerful? In the pre-Solidarity days of the 1970s, the church in Poland, hampered in its work by bureaucratic obstacles but supported with a visceral instinctiveness by the patriotic and the devout, was the only credible alternative to the hated regime.

Carter celebrated mass at the famous shrine of Jasna Gora, the shrine of Our Lady of Czestochowa, and was overwhelmed by the size of the multitude and its palpable piety. "As I spoke to the people jam-packed in the shrine of the miraculous picture of the Black Madonna, and particularly while I was being interpreted I could observe a long line of pilgrims, threading their way in a single file to spend a moment or two on their knees before the Madonna. Their faces were lined and tired — work faces. Old, many of them, before their time. People. People who had known persecution and war and hunger and the death of their loved ones. I was so touched I had trouble completing my homily."[26]

But he did *not* have trouble recording his impressions of the Polish visit upon his return for his brother bishops, the Catholic populace and the Canadian community at large, which he did in numerous articles. Poland impressed Carter and Carter impressed his host, the Cardinal Archbishop of Cracow, who, within a year, would be elected pontiff, and take the name John Paul (II).

The respect of the Polish people for the hierarchy and the hierarchy's willingness to offer firm leadership struck Carter as signs of a vital Catholic culture. At home, the situation was the opposite: the public frequently showed disrespect for rightful ecclesiastical authority, a disrespect, a disloyalty, that are especially heinous when they come from those who owe a particular obedience to the magisterium. In a homily given at a Catholics United for the Faith Congress, Carter reminded his singularly devout congregation of both the limits and the prerogatives of the teaching authority of the church: "The magisterium is not, as some conceive, the source of revelation nor of theology nor even of initiative. The role of the official teachers of the Church, the Pope, the bishops and the priests who are associated with them in Holy Orders . . . these official teachers do have the duty to attempt, in cooperation with the operation of the faith in the believing people, to examine the times, the moods, the dangers, to speak authoritatively on the message of Jesus and to apply Christian values to the development of the Kingdom in any time and place. . . . [E]verything said and done, the Pope and the bishops speak in the name of Christ. Once again, it is unpopular for any man to assume such authority in a period which despises authority. But there is no other way. . . . [T]o say that all in the Church have an equal voice, that the speculation of theologians is on an equal footing with the magisterium, or simply to refuse to speak on grounds of a search for popularity or false humility, is actually the denial of one of the vital presences of Christ."[27]

A bishop must be a bishop; he must lead like Wojtyla of Poland. Still, Carter the intellectual would not abide a facile opposition between theologian and bishop as if it were a law of nature. It was rather a law of the media, the managed opposition of a power external to the church, that prompted his strong words on Catholic dissidence. He reminded his fellow bishops at the Ontario Bishops' Meeting in April 1978 that there is as great a role for the theologian as for the bishop, but their gifts are different, their office is different: "No one denies the legitimacy of both charisms in the Church. However, there have been misunderstandings and, at times, tensions, some of them valid and healthy — others ill-directed and mischievous. On the part of the hierarchy, the latter have been caused by arrogance and authoritarianism; a lack of openness involving a certain fear of the whole truth; mistrust of theologians. On the part of the theologians, it may have been caused by a certain theological misdirection; a form of self-aggrandizement; mistaking authority for power; a unionized attitude which has prevented theologians from policing themselves. As a result, at times, two camps have formed and dialogue has been inhibited."[28]

In Carter's view the camps seemed poised to do battle, because of grandstanding theologian-media stars, a confusion over the precise and essentially different mandates of theologians and bishops, and the dangerous polarization to be found in contemporary Catholicism, a polarization fed by an uncomprehending or hostile secular press and an often unwitting religious press. But the occasional skirmishes of the London years were but mild preparation for the future.

When a dying Pope Paul VI named Carter the Archbishop of Toronto, a new era was about to begin.

PART III

ORONTO

(1978–1990)

CHAPTER NINE

The Toronto Challenge

Carter's appointment to the largest English-speaking archdiocese in the country seemed inevitable, in retrospect, though at the time it came as a surprise. Pocock was a tired and sick man. Although he had yet to reach the retirement age of seventy-five, he wanted to resign. Carter had more than an inkling that the Toronto See would soon be vacant. Pocock had a sister living in London, and when he came to visit her, he would often stay with Carter. One winter day in 1978 he arrived at Carter's house, sat down and lit his customary cigar and without ado pulled out a letter of resignation which he had shown to no one else. He told Carter that he had cancer and that he couldn't carry on as before. Carter had noticed that his energy was diminishing and that at meetings of the Ontario bishops Pocock frequently appeared to be absent-minded and that, as a consequence, the meetings were often run by the secretary, Jesuit Father Angus MacDougall, rather than by Pocock himself.

Carter's thoughts immediately turned to the succession. Convinced that he was too old to assume such a demanding leadership role, for he was sixty-six at the time, Carter was concerned about the quality of candidate who would succeed Pocock. He worried and the Gang of Five worried. He spoke to Baggio, still at the helm of the Congregation of Bishops, and he waited anxiously while Pocock dithered. Then the letter was sent and Rome accepted. The nuncio called from Ottawa and spoke of Pocock's resignation. It was a fact. The king is dead; long live the king. But *who was* the king?

Baggio informed Carter that his age was a difficulty. Carter conceded that it was and that he didn't expect to be considered. And then the nuncio called again; the Holy Father wanted Carter to accept the appointment as the new Archbishop of Toronto.

It was as if Toronto was waiting for him: the pastoral problems appeared insuperable. The burden of overseeing so many agencies and structures under the aegis of the CEO, the Archbishop, was daunting. But Carter was ready.

There were some in London who were glad that the appointment had come through. For Professor John O'Farrell, there would perhaps be some light in London now: "Carter was born on March 1st and so he's a Pisces. They are very ambivalent — the twin fish, always chasing each other's tails. Carter, to my mind, is typically Piscean. He can entertain several ideas and believe in them all at the same time. Just exactly which one will prevail will depend on the mood of the moment. He had turned what the Anglicans used to call Huron's Darkest London darker."

Not all judgements were so severe; many lamented the departure of a bishop who had given national, indeed international, prominence to a basically rural diocese. But he seemed destined all along for something greater than London. It was no surprise that he'd been appointed to Toronto; the surprise was that he'd been appointed so late in life. But his vigour surprised no one. In an interview with Tom Harpur, then religion editor of the *Toronto Star*, just days before his installation as Toronto's archbishop, Carter spoke with candour and self-assurance of his strong media image and the problems that some priests and laypeople would have because of it. But he reminded his critics that although he would run a tight ship, he respected the consensus model advocated by the Second Vatican Council, a model implemented successfully in London these last several years. He was no autocrat, he said.

At least, not in his own mind. Many others, however, in London and Toronto, were otherwise persuaded. Ambrose McInnis, an aesthetician, biographer and Dominican friar who spent but a brief time in university chaplaincy during Carter's early London tenure, watched the Carter regime unfold from New Orleans. He didn't like the style of the man then and he doesn't like it now. But he concedes that Carter has finesse in securing the patronage of those in power, of knowing whom to pursue and when: "I think that Carter is a man who sees that it is absolutely crucial to cultivate people with power, whether political power, financial power, or ecclesiastical power. These people are the key to getting what you want to have, to doing what you want accomplished."

Carter has always known how to wield power and how to court it. Toronto merely gave him a wider field for going about his Father's business. At the time of his appointment, the city was on the brink of a new confidence: aggressive, affluent, cocksure and inclined to bully. It had enormous immigrant potential — and that largely Catholic — and it needed a new kind of episcopal leadership. Philip Francis Pocock, tired and ill, could not provide the kind of innovation needed to cope with the burgeoning Catholic population of Toronto. Emmett Carter was the man of the hour.

Pocock had been, in turn, a seminary professor, Bishop of Saskatoon, Archbishop of Winnipeg, and for several years the Coadjutor Archbishop of Toronto during the declining years (and they were many) of Cardinal McGuigan. As his friend Vern Moore, an advertising executive and prominent Toronto layman, observed to journalist Warren Gerard, he was a "truly gentle man". Few would gainsay such a judgement. Pocock could inspire affection and respect, but he lacked the fire and the combative spirit that the new Toronto demanded. Carter could provide such fire and such spirit.

And so on June 5, 1978, Carter was installed as the eighth Archbishop of Toronto at St. Michael's Cathedral. It was a grand affair, with a plenitude of prelates, clerics, civic dignitaries, exalted members of the judiciary and a handsome complement of ecumenical and interfaith representatives. Carter praised his predecessor generously and then spoke plainly, some would say ominously, of his own appointment: "You are not getting a young archbishop, which in some ways is unfortunate, but the Holy See has judged that I may — for a few years — make some contribution to leadership. For better, or for worse, you will be hearing from me all too frequently in the months ahead."[1]

Those months would bring rapid changes, changes that proved off-putting for some and jarring for many but invigorating for the majority. One newer-generation Canadian bishop, who had some acquaintance with the Toronto scene, witnessed the inauguration of the Carter years with considerable foreboding: "As the pastor of pastors, which is what I understand the bishop to be, he is zilch, a failure, despised by most, save those who admire the way he can handle a press conference, the *Globe and Mail*, and tell people to go to hell yet maintain credibility. As a public relations guy he is without equal, but as to communicating the essence of the Gospel, he is a disaster."

Although this opinion is held by only a few of the hierarchy and clergy, it is broadly representative of that segment of the clerical ranks which views Carter, the perfect corporation man, with considerable spiritual disquiet.

In contrast, clergy like Carter's one-time auxiliary bishop, John Sherlock, felt the new archbishop would prove to be Toronto's salvation. In Sherlock's view, Carter was not only a man with a vision, but one who could implement it, who could create the structures needed to realize that vision. This he did with dispatch. He arranged to receive three new auxiliary bishops, and with them and the already present Auxiliary Bishop, Aloysius Ambrozic, he would divide the archdiocese into three regions. He saw this division as a "pastoral allocation of responsibility and an attempt to make sure that there is episcopal leadership as close to the scene of action as possible. It is patently impossible for one man to be present except on very rare occasions in all of the parishes and institutions of this Archdiocese. In this new fashion everyone will have access to a bishop who will be, in effect, his pastor, while at the same time we maintain an overall unity in this Archdiocese."[2]

With his auxiliaries strategically placed in the east, the centre and the west, he could achieve his goal of making the bishop accessible, of centralizing at the same time as he was decentralizing — "controlled subsidiarity" once again. Emmett Carter had arrived.

And that arrival was noted by the press. The *Toronto Star* was particularly well-disposed to provide ample coverage of the new Archbishop's comings and goings. The *Globe and Mail* was another matter. Carter arranged to meet with then-publisher Brigadier Malone. They had a pleasant luncheon, at which Carter drew to the attention of an initially incredulous Malone his conviction that the *Globe and Mail* had a reputation in several quarters as an anti-Catholic paper. Malone became quite distressed at hearing this, though Carter was adamant that the reputation, rightly or wrongly, was rooted in more than a few cursory or summary bits of coverage. Within a short time Carter would have all the evidence he needed.

In the *Weekend Magazine* of March 3, 1979 — an insert then carried by the *Globe* — an article on the ex-Basilian Paul Speck, an entrepreneurial educator with a touch of panache, prompted an angry Carter to write to Editor-in-Chief Richard J. Doyle, attacking the paper for publishing such a "scurrilous article". Outlining what he considered some of the more egregious errors of the piece — they were nothing more than the usual sentiments of liberal ex-clerics — Carter proceeded to remind Doyle of the anti-Catholic charge levelled at the *Globe*, the very charge that had so disturbed publisher Malone. Here, claimed Carter, was solid evidence.

Carter used the Speck piece to underline the slavish attention the secular press gave to dissenters. The time had come to move beyond dissent to reaffirmation. "My opinion, which is the only one that I can honestly reflect to you, is that we indeed needed what I might qualify as the 'theology' or 'ecclesiology' of dissent in the '60s. For that matter, this was the decade of dissent in almost every field. We in the Church certainly needed it. Pope John saw the need and called the Council. The Council was a very critical instrument, if you analyze it, but it did not stop at criticism. It proposed things in very positive ways. After the Council we had a host of theological dissenters. Gregory Baum, Charles Curran, Bernard Haring, Hans Küng and a whole host of others put the spotlight on the weaknesses of the Church. In some ways they rendered a very real service. But dissent is always a negative thing and the time soon comes when we have to say what we affirm as well as what we disaffirm. I am convinced that the last part of the '70s and '80s into which we rapidly enter are a period of reaffirmation. I would hope that the reaffirmation would take place in the political, the economic and the social order. Is it too much to hope that we can find it also in the theological order?"[3]

Annoyed by the media's habitual preoccupation with the maverick, the rebel, Carter the institution man asked only for equal time, determined to counter the slanted coverage of church affairs by taking a more aggressive *public* posture on dissent, the psychology of dissent and certain notorious dissenters. In a hard-hitting address to the Ontario Catholic Supervisory Officers at the Royal York Hotel in Toronto just a month after the Speck article appeared, Carter bemoaned the sad fact that many things emerged from the Council that remained untempered by its wisdom. "It became popular and profitable to dissent. The great theologians of the Council, the Rahners, the Congars, the De Lubacs, the Lonergans, were replaced in the public eye by the dissenters, some of whom we would never otherwise have heard of. *Humanae vitae* produced Charles Curran; sociology produced Gregory Baum; popularization produced Charles Davis, and so on. Not that they did not have their value, but they were dissenters first and theologians second."[4]

This sentiment, and the increasing boldness with which it was expressed, could not have comforted the professional theologians — Roman Catholic or otherwise — of the Toronto School of Theology. But there was more in store.

Knowing Carter's ecclesiology, his reputation as a strong leader in London and his conservative connections in Rome, the nervously curious theologians of his new diocese were not surprised at the role he played in the controversy following the "Küng Affair". Swiss theologian Hans Küng had a long history of badgering Rome, prompting an official inquiry into the orthodoxy of his several books and occasioning a veritable tempest in the Catholic world over various issues, including the rights and prerogatives of a theologian, the nature of a scholar's free search for the truth, the function of the papacy and the limits of the magisterium. From the mid-sixties until 1979 Rome exercised considerable restraint. Then it struck. Küng was deprived of his right to teach as a Catholic theologian, although he was neither suspended from the priesthood nor deprived of his position as a teacher in an ecumenical setting. Rome's censure was viewed in numerous quarters as a throwback to the Modernist persecutions of the turn of the century and as the latest instance of Rome's incurable villainy.

Much of the ensuing dispute revolved around the procedures adopted to carry out Küng's censure. Many theologians who shared strong reservations about Küng's Catholic theology were nonetheless keenly disturbed by the antiquated adjudication process that resulted in his being disbarred as an official theologian in the Roman Catholic Church. Surely there had to be something better than the system used on Galileo.

Carter had very little sympathy for Küng, who was, in his mind, a master dissenter, but he was aware of the public relations disaster Rome had created for the magisterium. He struck while the iron was hot. In an article on the Features Page in the *Globe and Mail*, Carter addressed two of the key issues in the Küng Affair in a way that guaranteed his *bona fide* credentials as a Roman prelate and a Canadian democrat. "The Church has the right and the duty to tell a theologian he has erred. The Church can never tell a theologian or all theologians to stop searching. . . . It seems to me infinitely regrettable that the general public perception, due in part to hasty and irresponsible statements by a few theologians, but most of all by the typical orientation of the media to the spectacular, is that an adversarial situation has been created between the official Church and the body of theologians. I am convinced that . . . the vast majority of Catholic theologians have repudiated Küng in the very areas where he has been challenged. There are numerous statements and even publications of many respected theologians to that intent. But, might we not have put that integrity and orthodoxy of the main body of theologians to better use? My disquiet in this dimension is admittedly inspired by my upbringing in a Western democracy permeated by a passionate dedication to due process and the principle of appearing to be just, as well as actually being so. . . . I suggest that in such cases as Küng's, somewhere in the procedure, a truly representative group of theologians would be called upon for a relatively open examination and a report of findings. . . . I know that ours is not the only model of democracy, but I believe we have something to offer in this matter."[5]

Carter has long deplored Rome's obsession with secrecy, especially with respect to financial matters, and its sometimes callous disregard for human rights, but he will not denounce the institution to which he has solemnly pledged his fidelity. That doesn't mean he won't criticize, that he won't work behind the scenes to effect change, that he won't sputter with rage when encountering Roman intransigence. He will do all these things and more. But he will remain, particularly in the public court, in full conformity of mind if not heart with the Roman position. When authority speaks, it must be obeyed. And authority in the Catholic tradition must be one and entire, not fragmented, personal or parallel. Authority divided against itself is without divine foundation, it is a magisterium sundered and incredible. Final authority is not resident in the halls of academe.

On this matter of the magisterium Carter was categorical: "In some manner which is very difficult to pinpoint an impression has grown in the Catholic world and even around it that the Council created what has been termed, with remarkable inaccuracy, a 'Parallel Magisterium'. This concept has been inflated and crystallized into an opinion that in some way a substantial body of theologians, on almost any given subject, has an equal voice with the successors of Peter and the Apostles. The vast majority of the Fathers of Vatican II were anxious to acknowledge and encourage the work of theologians. Indeed much of the wisdom of the Council owed its origin to the experts, the 'periti' in so many fields who advised and suggested concerning the subjects before us. We recognized that theologians have not always been well or fairly treated, we decried past abuses, the silencing without recourse, the condemnation without defense and a host of other historical aberrations which threw up the image of a central dogmatic despotism that is foreign to the Church of Christ. But one excess need not breed another. To go from that legitimate defense of the rights of theologians, human and ecclesial, to establishing a teaching body other than that of the bishops in union with Rome is a far cry from due process."[6]

Carter knew his authority, the authority of office if not of personality, and he was prepared to attack any violators of its legitimate jurisdiction.

At the same time, Carter valued the multiplicity of gifts that the various members of the church can bring to its life. He was not a supreme clericalist, in that he felt comfortable supporting authorized developments for the non-ordained constituency of the Roman Church. The intellectuals and the ordinary folk, he acknowledged, can be of enormous service to the church. As he noted in his 1986 pastoral letter, "There have been great theologians officially recognized who are lay people and there still are. The names of Gilson and Maritain come readily to mind, as to a Canadian do the names of Charles deKonick or Anton Pegis. But we would be very unwise to limit our considerations just to the formal teaching of theology. Think of the value which has been brought to Catholic thought by people like Chesterton, Mounier, or for that matter by poets like Thompson and Noyes, or novelists like Waugh and Greene. Again it would be a mistake to feel that we have to aim as high as the expertise and professionalism which these people have brought to their work. What of the wisdom of the ordinary people who have the 'sensus fidei' [the insight of faith]. Why are lay people either so loath to speak up on matters which concern the Church or why are they discouraged from doing so? There is a great deal of wisdom out there to be tapped."[7]

In this document Carter reminds Catholics of their common obligation as full members of the church. He dispenses with elitism. He celebrates worthy Catholic names — although they date his literary and philosophical interests specifically to the Catholic renascence of the 1930s and 1940s in France and England — but he refuses to downplay the role of the average believer, the humble but resolute folk — people like Minnie Carter. Catholicism, he writes, is remarkably more democratic than its critics will allow.

For all his willingness to rebuke Catholic dissenters in the secular as well as the religious press, Carter possessed a moderate view of the power of the papacy and was fully aware of the dangers of curial centralization. His consilium and ICEL fights left their mark. Carter is no ultramontane; he is no supporter of extravagant claims for the pope and papal prerogatives.

In an address he gave to the exclusive Michaelmas Conference in 1979, Carter celebrated the rightful integrity of the local church. This Conference, an annual event held at St. Michael's College in Toronto, provided a perfect venue for Carter's "democratic" ruminations. Composed only of men drawn from the professional classes and including such luminaries as John Turner, former Cabinet minister Mark McGuigan and several of the foremost chief executive officers of the land, the Michaelmas is a storehouse of old money, political connections and strong intelligence. Carter was at home in their company.

He told the assembled gentlemen — all leaders in their respective fields, all accustomed to the exercise of power — that "we Catholics are ... notorious for having sometimes set up a concept of the hierarchical structure which does not bear the tradition of Catholicism. We have, if anything, interpolated the systems of the armies which we know. We give the impression that we accept a sort of superior-subordinate chain of command. In our thoughts and sometimes in our words and actions we seem to postulate that the Pope is a Commander-in-Chief, the Cardinals are the Generals, the Archbishops are the Colonels, the Bishops are the Majors, the Priests are the Captains, and the laity run through the subaltern states to the lowly Private. Nothing could be further from the truth. The fact of the matter is that each Bishop, who is what we call the 'Ordinary', i.e. the Bishop in charge of a Diocese, is in every sense the spiritual leader of that community. *Lumen gentium* [Vatican II's Dogmatic Constitution on the Church] boldly calls the bishop the 'Vicar of Christ' in his own Church. Until the Second Vatican Council we had reserved that title to the Holy Father. Now we clearly establish the fact that while he is the Vicar of Christ for the Universal Church, each Bishop also has the right to that title with his local authority. It follows from this that one Bishop does not have a right of supervision over another Bishop. Even the Bishop of Rome does not unnecessarily and unduly interfere in the affairs of the other Bishops of the Church."[8]

What Carter expounded before the businessmen, lawyers, engineers and physicians was clearly articulated post-conciliar theology. He does not subscribe to a romanticized view of the papal office; he is not a maximalist, one of those who would attribute extraordinary authority to every papal utterance and move; and he does not condone the pious adulation that accompanies a cult of the pope. In fact, in an article published in *Saturday Night* on the very eve of the papal visit to Canada in the fall of 1984, Carter warned against the nostalgic revival of the concept of the papacy that is destructive of the true Catholic perspective: "The strength of [Pope John Paul II's] personality and the enthusiasm he arouses may not only obscure the gospel that he is trying to teach, it may also reinforce a false and exaggerated view of the papacy. The hype promotes the notion of the pope as a kind of super-bishop, between us and God, with the other bishops little more than branch managers. This is bad theology. . . . The concept of the local church suffers when Catholics refer only to the pope without recognizing the authority of the local church, without placing the pope in his proper role as bishop of Rome, chief bishop among the bishops, sign and cause of unity."[9]

It is surprising, then, that he would pen a letter to the Catholics of Toronto at about the same time that his *Saturday Night* article was scheduled to appear, encouraging the flock to attend the various papal events because "to be in the presence of the Spiritual Father of the Catholic Church is a privilege and an Act of Faith as well as a memorable historic event."[10] Such a claim may well be a measure of Carter's desperation concerning the mounting rumours of "poor" attendance at the papal events in *his* Toronto, but it is also the kind of claim he forcefully repudiates as distorting the papal office. An "Act of Faith"? The theologians cringed, the media appeared puzzled and the flock made up their own minds.

But by the time the pope came to Toronto in September 1984, the colonel of the garrison had been promoted to general. Toronto's Archbishop was a Cardinal, one of the pope's inner circle, a prince.

Only a pope can name cardinals. The Sacred College to which they are named performs the function of electing a new pontiff upon the death of an old one. But the members of this elite body in the church also exercise a considerable extrajurisdictional influence on papal policy. Hence, the appointment of a cardinal is always a matter of major interest.

For his first consistory following his election as pope in October 1978, John Paul II chose to elevate fourteen prelates to the cardinalate. They included: Agostino Casaroli, Vatican Secretary of State; Giuseppe Caprio, President of the Administration of the Patrimony of the Holy See; Ernesto Civardi, a Vatican official; Egano Righi-Lambertini, papal nuncio to France; Wladyslaw Rubin, Secretary-General of the Synod of Bishops; as well as the Archbishops of Turin, Venice, Hanoi, Marseilles, Mexico City, Armagh, Krakow and Toronto.

And Toronto! The city had been without a cardinal for some years, and Philip Pocock was considered somewhat suspect in various Roman quarters because of his perceived ambivalence on *Humanae vitae*. It was a spurious charge in many ways because Pocock was loyal to the Holy See and no different in his approach than the vast majority of Canadian bishops who had been part of the 1968 Winnipeg Statement and the subsequent controversy. His qualified support of the "pill" as a way of regulating the menstrual cycle was distorted into a general approval of its use — and Pocock was labelled "Phil the Pill". Pocock would not be a cardinal.

Although Toronto, as the major English-speaking Canadian diocese, could reasonably expect its Ordinary to be elevated to the red, Carter was surprised when his appointment came. He received the news from the papal pro-nuncio on Friday morning, May 25, with the traditional caveat that there should be a twenty-four-hour news embargo. "I wondered if I was really hearing it . . . so I made him repeat it. . . . I had the strong impression I was dreaming, and I told him so."[11]

There were a number of sceptics, however, who remained convinced that the announcement was no surprise but a realized goal. Carter, they argued, with all his Roman connections, his personal friendship with the pope, his administrative prowess and his increasingly hardline view on dissent and its practitioners, deliberately sought the honour. Yet Carter denied this vigorously: "In response to repeated questions from the media people about whether he 'lobbied for the appointment', the archbishop made it clear that in his opinion 'that is ridiculous.' 'First of all,' he said, 'the surest way not to get it would be to lobby for it, and, in the second place, anyone in the church who is looking for this sort of thing shows immediately that he shouldn't have it.' "[12]

Vintage Carter, but not entirely persuasive. He was conscious of the easier access to the pontiff a cardinal's hat could provide, and hence the added impact he could have on papal decision-making at the highest levels; he was also aware of the significant prestige such an exalted rank would bring Toronto's Archbishop and the additional clout he could wield in socially conscious, corporate Toronto. Carter and his Roman friends, particularly the still-powerful Sebastiano Baggio, could not have been unaware of the propitiousness of the hour. Carter, the accomplished politician, had always had a sense of the moment, whether one called it the moment to lobby or the providential moment.

However it happened, he was named, and a new phase in the church career of Emmett Carter began. But there was a kind of shadow cast over the elevation, a shadow close to home. The more liberal Bishop, Carter's brother Alex, had noted in an interview with *Ave Maria*, a U.S. publication, in their February 22, 1969, issue that "it would not be a tragedy if Rome's authorities decided that the College of Cardinals had outlived its usefulness. . . . It is almost unbelievable that we will go on forever having people electing a pope who have not themselves been elected by their peers."[13]

How would Alex, who had such outspoken views and was universally respected for his fraternal candour, respond to the news of Emmett's appointment? He is reported to have reacted to Emmett's phone call with the laconic, "Well, you can help the church in this way." Clearly, Alex would have delighted in his brother's good news precisely because it was *his* good news, and the church in Toronto could benefit from just such a promotion. Emmett would see to it. But the liberal bishop from Ontario's north would never seek such a preferment for himself. It wasn't his style. Besides, Rome has a long memory.

Emmett's big day in Rome was distinguished by the solemn, the absurd, the grand and the touching. But it started inauspiciously. A number of Carter's family; his housekeeper; friends from Montreal, London and Toronto; several clergymen; a dozen reporters; and various political dignitaries, including Steve Paproski (federal Minister of Fitness and Multiculturalism), Tom Wells (Intergovernmental Affairs Minister in the provincial Cabinet and the formal delegate for the Ontario government), Gordon Walker (Correctional Services Minister) and René Brunelle (Secretary for Resources Development), numbering about 225 in total, rented a DC-8 scheduled to fly from Toronto to Rome's Ciampino Airport. It arrived several hours later than scheduled, after the Pope's Wednesday audience, and with no offical greeting party from the Canadian Ambassador to the Holy See, Yvon Beaulne.

Evergreen International, the airline responsible for getting the Carter party to Rome, had made several errors: they incorrectly advised Ambassador Beaulne's office of the time of arrival; in the estimation of at least one reporter they provided the "most excruciatingly uncomfortable flight" he had ever experienced; and their seating allotment prompted Carter to quip: "It just goes to show that if God had meant people to fly economy He would have made them midgets." The expense for the return fare (assumed by each traveller) was $600. The price proved the only reliable "guarantee" Evergreen offered.

But Carter quickly put the annoyance behind him, and he and his entourage were swept away by the pageantry and pace of the ensuing days. And so the ceremonies began on June 30, in the Consistorial Hall of the Apostolic Palace. "Fifty-two existing cardinals were present. Other secret consistorial business was transacted, including the nomination of bishops and archbishops and the nomination of the Camerlengo of the Sacred College. An hour or so later in the morning, in the Paul VI audience hall, the dean of the college handed the new cardinals their *biglietti*, or certificates. The new cardinals then took their oath of faithfulness and obedience to the Pope and his successor. Then the Pope went through the ceremony of imposing the biretta on each of the new cardinals kneeling before him and assigning to each the title of a Roman see, in the presence of the other cardinals, many bishops, members of the diplomatic corps and four thousand of the faithful. The next day, July 1, the Pope concelebrated Mass with the new cardinals and gave them their rings in the Basilica of St. Peter's. And on July 2, with friends and members of their families, they were received by the Pope in audience."[14] Most of Carter's family and friends were thrilled. Alex, however, was missing. He foresook the pleasures of Evergreen International because he was physically indisposed to travel. A telling absence. A telling comment?

All that was left now was to take possession of his titular church in Rome, Santa Maria in Traspontina, a seventeenth-century church administered by Carmelite friars and strategically situated on the Via della Conciliazione, virtually adjacent to the Vatican. The church's proximity to the pope was not lost on Carter: "I am grateful to Pope John Paul II . . . for having chosen this church, which is so close to his own seat of government and to his own church of St. Peter. I have celebrated Mass here many times before, when I was working in Rome, and therefore it is not as a stranger that I come. It is rather as a brother and a father that I would remain."[15]

Carter spoke in Italian and English and was enthusiastically received, but he understood what it all meant. "Title to the church is a formality in a way. It makes Carter a leader of the church in Rome, an ancient tradition which preserves the early practice whereby the clergy of Rome elected the Bishop of Rome — the Pope. Privately, Carter says that having title to the church will probably mean 'shelling out some money now and again' for a new organ or whatever."[16] Ever the practical man; ever the light touch.

On July 5, two days after he returned to Canada, he addressed a liturgical reception at St. Michael's Cathedral of more than one thousand church and government officials, including William Davis and several members of the Ontario government, as well as such prominent figures as Conrad Black, John Turner and Pauline McGibbon. He followed this feat with a mass for ten thousand of the Toronto faithful in Varsity Stadium the same evening. The next day, it was on to a reception in his honour at Toronto's city hall, where he informed a delighted Mayor John Sewell that he would gladly accept the mayor's invitation to occasionally address city council meetings.

All in all, the schedule would have defeated a lesser figure than Gerald Emmett. He, however, thrived on it. He was ready for Toronto, and so far, Toronto was in love with its new celebrity.

But Carter could never forget Montreal, the Montreal that had nurtured him, educated him and continued to fill him with love and anxiety. He returned there, the triumphant son, to dinners and receptions in his honour. After all, Toronto's Cardinal Archbishop was a Montreal boy; the old geographical rivalries embrace even the ecclesiastical order.

He came to remind them of his deep respect for Quebec culture and of the priority of the French language in *la belle province*. He came to remind them of his opposition to the restrictive language legislation, Bill 101, and of his support for the "legitimate aspiration of the Francophone minority in Ontario". And then he spoke of Newman: "One of the most thrilling experiences I have had is to be named a Cardinal almost exactly one hundred years after the appointment of John Henry Newman. As you probably know, Newman was in obscurity and even in a certain sense rejected, not only by the An-

glican establishment which he had left, but by the Catholic community which had doubts about his authenticity. It was the strong action
of Pope Leo XIII which named him a Cardinal and which gave him
status in the Catholic world, which he would not otherwise have
achieved. Without any comparison whatsoever, I found it most exhilarating to be named one hundred years later in his succession. So
much so that I even tried to see if the church of which he was titular in
Rome was not open. . . . What I am saying is that I would like to be in
Newman's tradition as well as, in a certain sense, his succession.
Newman's motto, which is engraved upon the crozier which was so
graciously presented to me by the Newman Clubs of Canada, is 'Cor
ad Cor loquitur.' This is the charge which I would want to make to
you today. Whatever your contribution, and sometimes that contribution must be made with difficulty, make sure that you do it with love.
Love . . . is not a soft sort of emotional thing. It may be of steel.
Remember the text — 'The Kingdom of heaven suffers violence, and
the violent bear it away.' But it is the violence of love to which I
appeal."[17]

Inspired by Newman and driven by a love made of steel, Carter
launched into areas where angels and lesser bishops feared to tread. It
is not that he was timid before and only now found his voice and
authority. Quite the contrary. It is simply that as the Archbishop of
Toronto, and now a Cardinal, he was in a position of greater influence
than ever before. Emboldened by Mayor Sewell's invitation, and
convinced that as a cardinal he could bring a power of moral suasion
to bear on the political order that lesser rank would not provide,
Carter began his new regime with uninhibited panache.

In an address he gave on October 22, 1979, at a dinner in his honour
sponsored by the Ontario government, Carter accepted the generous
accolades of his friend Premier Davis and his ministers and MPPs with
good grace and a measure of self-deprecating humour. But he also
used the occasion to speak about the role of a truly participatory
democracy and of the essential need for leaders gripped by a cause,
not by self-aggrandizement. He spoke of the common values that
unite all civic and religious leaders — the cement that holds the
pluralistic community together — and he reminded the large gathering, which included the occasional civil servant, that all leadership is
ultimately service. He drove the point home with a personal reference. "It is not for nothing that the Cardinal's robes are red, and
whether that be the physical sacrifice which is so seldom called upon,

or the outpouring of one's energies, there can be no doubt that the higher the honour, the greater the onus. There is no other possible formula in the Church and I believe, that everything said and done, there is no other possible formula in leadership of any kind."[18]

Carter's taste for high theatre and the royal gesture can deteriorate into ecclesiastical melodrama, and the allusion to martyrdom seemed a bit misplaced. But perhaps it was appropriate after all, because within a week of the dinner he found himself at the centre of a political maelstrom. Politicians not of the Progressive Conservative Party were infuriated by the Cardinal's generous homage to premiers Leslie Frost, John Robarts and William Davis, all of whom had denied the extension of funding to the upper secondary grades in the Ontario separate school system. Ron Van Horne, Liberal MPP for London North, berated the Cardinal in the bluntest terms: "I must express to you my absolute dismay and concern about your words of praise and commendation for a Conservative Government which steadfastly refuses to extend support to Grades 11 to 13 of the separate school system in Ontario. . . . The agony felt by me and many of my Catholic colleagues over your words of praise for the Government was and is sharpened by my own feeling of hypocrisy in even attending an affair with such political overtones."[19]

Other Opposition members beside Van Horne responded in similar ways, parliamentarians both Catholic and non-Catholic, including Eli Martel, New Democratic member for Sudbury East; Ross McClellan, NDP, Bellwoods; Liberal member Alfred Stong of York Centre; and Robert Nixon, Liberal House Leader, who remarked that the dinner proved "the most disconcerting evening of my political life. . . . To use some of the terms His Eminence used seemed to me to show a devastating lack of information or pure hypocrisy." Or perhaps it showed uncharacteristic ecclesiastical savvy.

The offending passage appeared to be Carter's observation that Roman Catholic churchmen are not "in the least likelihood of forming some sort of power-block to force our opinions and our ways of looking at things upon other people. . . . I must insist that although we have no desire to form power-blocks, we will close ranks if our rights and traditions are challenged."[20] But such a statement in itself was reasonable, acknowledging the pluralistic status of contemporary society and the foreswearing of direct ecclesiastical interference in the operations of government. It is what followed that piqued the Opposition. Having outlined his position, Carter paid tribute to the men who, the other political parties logically argue, prevented full funding from occurring. The Cardinal was too Tory for their liking. And the issue would surface again.

When the Cardinal attended an annual fund-raising dinner for the Progressive Conservatives chaired by Davis, followed a day later by Davis's attendance at the head table of Carter's annual Catholic Charities dinner, the combination proved too much for many non-Tory Catholic politicians. Sean Conway, Deputy Leader of the Ontario Liberal Party, complained to Carter in a letter co-signed by eleven other like-minded Catholics that the "Conservative Party is obviously making a vigorous play for the Catholic vote here in Toronto and they seem to be doing so with the comfort of His Eminence Cardinal Carter. . . . He purposefully, or otherwise, is lending the very considerable prestige of his red hat to the partisan activities of the Big Blue Machine in this province."

Accusing Carter of a "regular duet" between himself and the Premier, Conway warned the Cardinal of the dangerous pathways of such blatant partisanship, particularly on the part of a Catholic churchman of his prominence. The New Democratic member for Downsview, Odoardo Di Santo, struck deeper: "When the bishops issued their letter on the status of the economy he said that it was too political and that it is not the role of the church to be involved in the political process. . . . I think that it's a little bit contradictory when he attends Tory fund-raising."

Red robes of martyrdom indeed!

Carter was pledged, by his own words and the logic of his thomistic reasoning, to reject the Lutheran theory of the two kingdoms and to insert himself directly into the life of the body of Christ as well as of the body politic. He could rise above the criticism of Conway, Van Horne and the others because in his own mind Carter had *never* been partisan. Political, yes; partisan, no. At the level of general principles he could articulate the overarching design without attending to the minute details. As a Lord Spiritual, he would enlighten, exhort, admonish and prod, but he would not interfere. He would not interfere as a churchman, but as a citizen he would exercise the rights and responsibilities that citizenship entails.

On another occasion he warned that "participatory-democracy does not mean that each one of the citizens of any country takes over the role of government. But it does mean that at least a large number will have the maturity, the courage and the vision to be able to make judgements not based upon the passing whims of the day or the expression of opinions of this or that commentator or this or that journalist but against a background of values that endure and which are based on something more than the here and now and allow us to give ourselves in the service of others."[21] Participatory democracy is the ecclesial principle of subsidiarity applied to the political order. Authority isn't imperilled; it's enabled.

Given Carter's willingness to speak publicly and boldly on issues that touched him as a citizen in a pluralistic society, given his capacity to mingle comfortably with the social and political elite, given his democratic belief regarding the accountability of elected authorities and given the leadership initiatives that flowed from his elevation to the cardinalate, it is not surprising that when Metro Toronto's Chairman, Paul Godfrey, approached him to write a report on the problem of racism and the Metropolitan Toronto Police, he accepted.

After the fatal shooting of Jamaican immigrant Albert Johnson, the relationship between the police commissioners and the city's black leaders had deteriorated to a dangerous point. Something needed to be done and quickly. Carter was the choice. He took two months to write his report. He did not mince words.

In the report he concluded that racial minorities did have some cause for complaint and that the complaint procedures presently in place were ineffective. He noted that "retaliation or the fear of retaliation [was] widespread" among minorities and as a consequence they were not likely to complain of abuse. An independent review board operated by civilians, he suggested, would be the only reasonable course to follow. In addition, Carter encouraged the use of more foot patrols, the establishment of a police officer's bill of rights, the elimination of inflexible height and weight restrictions and better training and selection procedures.

The Carter report was applauded by a number of civic and religious leaders and endorsed in the lead editorial of the *Toronto Star* (October 30, 1979). Carter had acquitted himself with distinction.

Ten years later, after delivering his 1988 New Year's Statement, which called on the community to work towards a just resolution of the Toronto housing crisis, Carter again found himself working in close association with municipal and provincial politicians, in this case Chaviva Hosek, Minister of Housing for Ontario.

Condemned by Catholics of the left for his seeming insensitivity to social justice issues, Carter points to justice initiatives like this to disprove their charge. He rightly reminds them that he has been stinting neither with his time nor with his financial support.

But Carter's whirlwind pace of involvement came to an abrupt halt barely two years after his nomination as Cardinal.

On the morning of May 29, 1981, he found himself engaged in the usual routine of meetings and conferences. He had summoned the Rector of St. Augustine's Seminary, Brian Clough, to discuss with him a complaint that had arisen over the publication of an article on the priesthood written by a member of Clough's faculty. Clough remembers an exhausted and unusually disturbed Carter: "He appeared very tired while I was talking to him and I attributed his weariness to a heavy morning of meetings. While we were talking he continued to rub his left wrist and his forehead and appeared a little distracted. But he was not agitated by the discussion, so I concluded that he was overly tired."

When they had finished their business Clough took his leave of the Cardinal. He stood briefly outside Carter's office speaking with Mary Frances Keating, Carter's executive secretary, when the Director of Communications, Brad Massman, arrived for a quick chat with the Cardinal before his lunch. "I walked in and for some reason, I don't know why, I was pacing nervously up and down his office. I kept talking and he didn't answer. I turned around, looked at him, and said, 'Your Eminence?' He said: 'Brad, I think I'm having a stroke.' I went over to him and put my arms around him. I said, 'Just take it easy.' And then I rushed out to Mary Frances and asked her to call an ambulance immediately. I went back to him and waited. He said that he preferred if I would drive him. I thought, 'Oh, God! I can't do that; I'm not that good a driver. I'll go down a one-way street or get lost or something.' But he insisted that I drive him. So we passed the ambulance on the way to the hospital. When we arrived in the parking lot of St. Michael's Hospital, Sister Mary Zimmerman, executive director of the hospital, and Dr. John Killoran Wilson, his physician and chief of cardiology at St. Michael's, were waiting for him. I quipped that my mother would say that I hope you're wearing clean underwear. He simply said, 'Brad, I have got to slow down. I gave three major talks this week alone.' But the worst was yet to come. He had a devastating stroke in the afternoon, and we were worried that he would not make it. I slept the night in his room in Intensive Care."

But make it he did. What he was to discover, now that he had looked death in the face and won a reprieve, were aspects of his personality that had hitherto eluded him. He discovered the crushing humiliation of physical incapacity; he discovered the frustrating rage that accompanies one's total reliance on others; he discovered his mortality. As he noted in a reflective reminiscence a year later: "The impact on the psyche is hard to describe. And I was one of the lucky ones. My speech was blurred for a day or two, but I could always speak adequately. I never lost consciousness or had any memory failure or confusion of mind. But I, who was a doer — a self-propelled, take-control guy — was reduced to a ludicrous, humiliating dependence on all about me. When I was named and consecrated bishop in Montreal in 1962, the students at McGill where I was a chaplain presented me with a crozier, or pastoral staff. It comes in four sections and is fitted together. Someone was trying to assemble it at the reception in my honour. I left my chair, took it in my own hands and fitted it. Dr. W.J. McNally of the Royal Victoria said with a smile, 'I don't think you are quite ready to be a bishop, yet.' Well, if being a bishop meant not doing things for myself, I wasn't. I'm not yet."[22]

But bishop or no, Carter learned the terrible lesson only the shattering of stubborn self-reliance can provide. Carter discovered the dark night of the soul. The masterful administrator, accomplished educator, eloquent public speaker and deft manipulator of political and ecclesiastical forces, was brought low, humbled, reminded in the starkest terms of his dependence on God alone. He discovered his spirituality.

Not a particularly pious man, Carter faithfully says his daily prayers, his office, and finds in the celebration of the mass the spiritual nourishment necessary for his tasks. It is a traditional spirituality, a spirituality of the seminary, of an earlier age. It is simple, inclined to be private and very priestly. But it didn't suffice. Carter had to plumb deeper into his own inner resources. It was a trip he hadn't previously taken; the terrain was new and a little alarming. His convalescence helped to mould a more mature spirituality and, ever the communicator, he decided to share his new insights — wrung from him in blood, suffering and impatience — with the people he served as a pastor: the priests and the laity of Toronto.

Within a month of his "cerebral vascular accident" (he shuns the word "stroke"), Carter wrote a pastoral letter outlining the details of his malady, the slow progress of his healing, his determination to serve as steward as long as he was able and his resolve that he not become a burden for the church. The letter also recorded his meditation on the state of his suffering: "A cerebral accident like this carries us within the camp of death. I have felt a little as if I were assisting at my own funeral."[23]

He then shared with his people two spiritual truths that had come to him with particular force during his convalescence. The first truth was theological in nature and concerned the sacrificial character of suffering, the participation of the afflicted believer in the redemptive suffering of Jesus. For Carter, the *alter Christus* (the other Christ), schooled in a theology of the priesthood that places a specific emphasis on the sacrificial aspect of the presbyterate, *his* suffering had a communal and cultic dimension. "The sacerdotium of Christ is primarily a sacrificial sacerdotium. It was when He offered Himself upon the *ara crucis* that He expiated for our sins. And it has been the constant tradition of the Church that our greatest privilege is to be associated with Him in that expiatory action which reconciled the Father to His sinful people. Therefore when we suffer and above all when we suffer as He suffered, helpless and held back, we may be at the highest point of our lives, not the lowest."

The other truth was more psychological in nature and centred on his realization that when the chips are down, one's spirituality is all that is left. "Don't lose sight of your spirituality. The day may come when it is all you've got. When I crumbled and found that I could not move my left leg or my left arm, when I had to be led like a little child, when I didn't know if the next few hours were going to be life or death, all I had was my spiritual peace and confidence in the Lord."

This letter was written during his early convalescence and had an effect on his clergy and Catholic faithful strikingly out of proportion to that of his previous writings. He spoke in a new way to them; he spoke as a man whose pride had been irrevocably broken; he spoke humbly and from the heart. This new voice lacked the usual self-confidence; it seemed more tentative. It was a confessional, not an official, voice, and it spoke movingly of a man's discovery — late perhaps for a churchman — of how utterly vulnerable we are. Upon receiving the letter, one young Toronto priest, known as a critic of the

Cardinal's conservative style and thought, was prompted to reassess favourably his opinion of his leader. But even at this point of humiliation and humility, there were the critics. A religious order priest who insists Carter once connived to have him sent into exile by his order, noted how late in the game it was for the Cardinal to happen upon the most self-evident of spiritual truths.

It was far from the last word from the spiritual *paterfamilias* of Toronto, but coming as it did from a man struggling to reclaim his dignity, from a man unaccustomed to speak of his frailty in public, it underscored a dimension of the man very few ever witnessed: his spirituality. People caught a glimpse of a different Carter — more human, less remote, splendid in his weakness.

But the old Carter was only temporarily in remission. There were battles to be fought, and no one was in any doubt as to who was the General, least of all the Premier of the Province of Ontario.

CHAPTER TEN

Educator and Lobbyist: Carter the Politician

On a wall to the left of Bill Davis's desk at the law firm of Tory, Tory, Deslauriers, and Binnington there hangs an Andy Donato cartoon from the *Toronto Sun* depicting Gerald Emmett Carter bedecked in full cardinal's dress and to his side, in happy compliance, Bill Davis, the Premier of Ontario; under the picture there is the caption: "Bless you my son!" The place of honour accorded Donato's caricature of the two old friends underlines the misperceptions inherent in Edouard Cardinal Gagnon's candid explanation that Carter's successes in Toronto are the simple and direct result of an apprenticeship served in Montreal while working with Quebec's politicians. This widely held supposition is also reflected in Claire Hoy's biography of Bill Davis. Its heavy-handed thesis is that Carter pressured an unwilling premier into extending full grants to the province's Roman Catholic separate schools during the heady days of June 1984.[1] The thesis does not do justice to the character of the Cardinal or of his friends who often point out that intelligent people are influenced by intelligent arguments, but they are intimidated by no one. As for close friends, they are in the happy position of being able to exchange intelligent arguments without rancour, and hence to enjoy some ultimate influence, if the arguments are sound ones.

The long-time friendship between Carter and Davis has drawn the Cardinal to Davis's PC fund-raising events and the Premier to Carter's annual Cardinal's Dinner, itself a fund raiser for local charities. Indeed, Bill Davis has continued to share Cardinal Carter's head table even though he has long since left public office.

Public signs of friendship. When Carter rose to speak at the Ontario Provincial Dinner in 1979, he spoke as a long-time friend being feasted by a long-time friend: "I am honoured to have been honoured for many years by the friendship of the Premier. We have worked together and even laughed together on a number of occasions. . . . Nor do I forget that I have many friends in the ranks of his Party and also in the Parties represented by the Opposition."[2]

Carter began his 1983 Cardinal's Dinner address in a similar vein. He welcomed the Premier to the event, noting: "It is good of you, Mr. Premier, to come . . . particularly since you knew the risks to which you are exposing yourself. You see, Sir, for reasons well known to you and Senator Kelly I cannot afford a speechwriter. So you should prepare for the worst." In the text of the speech, the phrase "for reasons well known to you and Senator Kelly" appears in longhand, replacing the original text which reads: "in view of the tremendous drain on our finances because we are obliged to support the 11th, 12th and 13th grades of a public school system".[3] The emendations indicate both tact and diplomacy, but they also betray a standing private joke shared publicly by two good friends. Friendship may preclude public embarrassment, or public harassment, but it does not preclude the private debating of dearly held principles.

One year later, on November 8, 1984, Carter began his after-dinner address by recognizing "the presence of the Premier of the Province, Mr. William Davis, whom I am honoured to call friend and who has saddened us to some degree by his decision to withdraw as the premier of this great province. . . . On the twelfth day of June of this year [however], Premier Davis made an historical announcement establishing at long last the Catholic Public School System of Ontario on the same footing as the Common School System."

When Bill Davis rose in the House to speak on that historic June 12, 1984, his 1971 speech was far behind him. The altered provincial demographics which Bishop Cody had spoken of in 1963 were now upon him, since the influx of Roman Catholic immigrants had begun to tilt the numerical electoral balance in their favour. More to the point, however, Toronto's former Archbishop, Philip Pocock, now lived across the street from Davis in cordial retirement at St. Mary Church in Brampton, and Toronto's new Cardinal Archbishop often enjoyed the Premier's hospitality. Moreover, as Davis explained to Lewis Garnsworthy, the retired Anglican Archbishop of Toronto and vehement opponent of full funding, it was from that same sitting room that the Premier could see "all these little Catholic kids" about whom he had asked the Archbishop rhetorically, "What is it you want me to do?"[4] In the minds of many, Davis was the dupe of partisan politics in an increasingly Roman Catholic province. No doubt practical political considerations played their part, but more likely the principal motivations influencing the Premier's decision to back full funding for the separate school system, even in the face of heavy opposition mounted within his own government, were fairness, right reason and personal friendships.

In his statement to the House, Davis explained: "If we are to serve the spirit and the realities of 1867, we should acknowledge that basic education was what was recognized then and, today, basic education requires a secondary, as well as an elementary, education. As the nondenominational system has evolved to meet society's needs, so too has the Roman Catholic system." Bishop John Cody had presented this argument in 1963 when Davis was Minister of Education and Carter had repeated it many times since, but Davis had explicitly rejected it before the 1971 provincial election, arguing that a fully funded Roman Catholic school system would be educationally divisive.

Conrad Black sees the change of heart largely in personal terms, noting that it was "clear that Bill Davis was enormously impressed with Cardinal Carter as an individual and still is. And there is no reason why he shouldn't be. I think it is a legitimate case of someone being impressive. And my judgement is that the personal relationship between these two was a terribly important element in the funding issue. I think that Bill Davis was absolutely sincere in coming around to his change of view. And I think it was a great testament to his fairmindedness, particularly given someone who had been Minister of Education under John Robarts and who would have been aware that such a change would not be well received among those with whom he had worked so closely for so long. It was also, of course, a credit to the Cardinal's persuasive abilities. And I think he had a rather good argument to make. These were two reasonable people having a prolonged reasonable discussion, demonstrating the truthfulness of the old saying that when intelligent and fair-minded people can fully possess the same facts they come to the same decision."

Conrad Black's judgement of the situation and William Davis's recounting of events square exactly with Carter's own recollections. Carter does suggest that "friendship had a lot to do with it. We became very friendly and we were able to put our cause to him in a way that he was prepared to listen. I wouldn't really want to go any further than that. I don't think there's any doubt that I had some influence on him, but I'm not sure it was preponderant. I don't want to overstress my friendship with him, not to the point of becoming stupid — Bill Davis never became stupid. He was well aware that half the population of Toronto was Catholic, that the Catholic community was becoming more and more effective on the political scene in Ontario. And he was also a good friend of Archbishop Pocock." John Fraser, now the editor of *Saturday Night*, takes a more pragmatic view of the matter. Speaking of Carter, he sums up the question: "It was a great coup. He campaigned, he played a political game and he won. He had the demographics going for him too. It was quite straightforward."

Nonetheless, the Carter-Davis friendship was such that shortly before the announcement was made in the House — Carter suggests it was probably two weeks before — Davis phoned to inform him of the government's intention, even giving him the day and the hour, should Carter want to be in the public gallery for the announcement. Carter declined the invitation, though he did accept the offer that certain key figures be informed under the strictest of confidence. The two weeks which followed were difficult ones for Carter as he awaited the formal fulfillment of a promise, and as he fretted that the confidentiality might somehow be broken.

Despite Davis's acknowledgement of the rightness of the case, the full-funding agreement was not achieved without some bargaining. Davis asked for and received certain assurances. "He wanted to make sure that we would not ask for a teachers' college, he wanted to make sure that we would not sell our properties, but that we would turn our properties over to the school boards, and that we would cooperate in the transfer of properties — a few things of that nature. And, of course, we were only too happy to agree. The diocesan properties were prepared to transfer, but that's been put off for some years and with good reason. But we did agree to all of that. So we had a kind of regulation on the arrangement, in a broad sense, beforehand. Then he called me to tell me what day he was going to do it."

True to his word, Carter urged the Roman Catholic community to respond to the government's initiative with generosity, broadmindedness and cooperation. While maintaining his traditional stance that Catholics had asked only for what was right, and no more, that the concerted pressure had been for Roman Catholic tax dollars to pay for a Roman Catholic public school system, Carter also maintained that the new arrangement ought not to spawn exclusivist or triumphalist reactions on the part of Roman Catholics. Speaking at an Education

Dinner in Thunder Bay in October 1984, he argued that the Catholic school boards must be willing to absorb "a certain number" of non-Catholic teachers and non-Catholic children into the separate public school system. In that same speech he made public his own opinion that the success of the full-funding lobby could be attributed to no particular group. He gave credit to a series of Ontario bishops (Reding of Hamilton, Pocock of Toronto, Alex Carter of Sault Ste. Marie, Sherlock of London, Doyle of Peterborough), to the school trustees, to the Ontario English Catholic Teachers' Association, to the parents and to the taxpayers. His own name he left off the list.

Carter repeated similar messages for cooperation at an assembly of Catholic High School Officials and Teachers at St. Michael's College School in Toronto in February 1985. At the same time he began to face the new issue: "There is no point in having a Catholic School System unless it is Catholic." As a result, his speeches began to echo themes initiated in London and repeated in Toronto. In a secularized society, the Roman Catholic school is the only public educational venue capable of asking the "big questions": "Who am I? Where do I come from? Where am I going? What is the nature of the universe? What is the dynamism behind life itself? What is behind all of the suffering and struggling of our human existence, our loves and our hatreds, etc., etc." Roman Catholics, he reiterated, have always held to the conviction that each generation has the responsibility of transmitting the articles of the Catholic faith from one generation to the next, and that, he argued, is a responsibility to be shared by their schools.[5]

With the principal financial problems resolved, philosophical and logistical issues remained still to be addressed. The key philosophical issue for Carter was clearly centred on the teaching of the faith. The teaching of catechetics, although not the issue it was for him in Montreal and London, remained a problem in Toronto since it was the teaching of the faith that would obviously make Catholic schools Catholic. And Carter is not one to be silent in the face of a perceived problem. Hence his August 14, 1987 letter to the officers of the school boards in his archdiocese lamenting the overemphasis on sociology and psychology in the teaching of religion and the apparent reluctance to celebrate the Catholic faith, to teach the gospel of love or to present Christ as the exemplary hero Carter has always maintained he should be for Catholic youth.

Carter had earlier exercised a similar impulse to speak out on the teaching of the faith. It was at a higher level, however, and was necessitated when the orthodoxy of Catholic teaching and the lived example of Catholic teachers and seminarians were in serious question at his seminary. The letter to the officers of the school boards had been a minor irritant for some, but the St. Augustine's affair became a matter of public controversy.

The crisis was precipitated by an internal letter issued in March 1984 under the signatures of M. Cenerini, Fr. B. Clough, J. Murphy and D. Reilander. Entitled "A Dialogue of Trust", the document was an internal and strictly confidential recollection of a series of meetings which had taken place between Brian Clough and groups of St. Augustine's seminarians. The issues, as they are recorded in the confidential correspondence, centred on conflicts between two segments of the student body, termed the "macho" and the "effeminate", and seem to have been causing a serious deterioration of morale.[6] Aside from the suggestions of homoerotic behaviour, there seem also to have been tensions between those members of the seminary community who were theologically liberal and those who were theologically traditional. When the letter fell into Carter's hands, he felt that he had no choice but to act, which he did — though some who were close to the scene argue that he did so precipitously, thereby creating a public furor out of a situation that might have been quietly and efficiently resolved in private. Turning to his friend Marcel Gervais, who was then the Auxiliary Bishop of London, Carter immediately initiated an inquiry.

When Gervais's report reached the Cardinal's hands, he cleaned house, expelling two students, dismissing a professor of church history, Father John Tulk, and accepting the resignations of the rector, Father Brian Clough, and a professor of moral theology, Father Thomas Dailey.

It had to be a bitter pill for the Cardinal to swallow, since he had taken some pride in beginning the rebuilding of St. Augustine's almost as soon as he arrived in Toronto. Shocked at the deep-seated morale problems resulting from a local seminary whose teaching staff consisted almost entirely of outsiders with no particular commitment to his archdiocese, Carter had arranged to send his men to Rome for training, and things seemed to be on the mend; in fact, Carter suggests that the situation at St. Augustine's had been so bad that had he

Sharing a papal greeting with Paul VI. FOTO FELICI, ROMA.
(Below) Polish promenade with future Pope John Paul II in
Krakow, 1977.

(Top) The new Cardinal Archbishop of Toronto approaches his
titular church, Santa Maria in Traspontina, in Rome, 1979.
ARTURO MARI/L'OSSERVATORE ROMANO CITTA DEL VATICANO.
The inner circle in Carter's new domain: Bishops Clune,
Ambrozic, Pocock, Carter, Lacey, Wall.

Carter knows the advantages — and the dangers — of close association with temporal power. With Trudeau, 1983 (DICK DARRELL); and as the political manipulator in a famous Donato cartoon during the school funding debate.

The "Gang of Five": Pocock, Plourde, Emmett and Alex, Flahiff — bishops all. (Below) Carter with provincial cabinet ministers Leo Bernier (left), and Allan Pope after unveiling the cairn at Carter Falls at Oak Lake, Ontario, 1983.

A sharp-edged caricature in *Toronto* magazine had the Cardinal hob-nobbing with controversial developers Huang and Danczkay ("But we *do* like people. It's just that we like them in bunches."); urban planner Jane Jacobs (". . . your buildings suck"); fur merchant Paul Magder; animal-rights activist Vicki Miller; Craig Russell ("So I like to wear nice things. This makes me a bad person?"); Sue Johanson; Gar Mahood (Non-Smokers Rights Association); Robert Fulford and Conrad Black tussling over *Saturday Night*; Johnny Arena; and food columnist Joanne Kates.

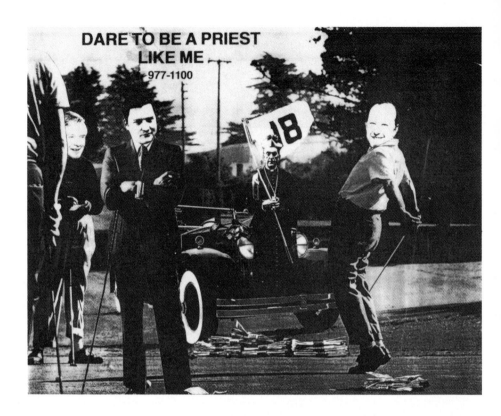

A critic of the Cardinal parodied Carter's recruiting campaign with this collage of Premier Davis (left), Conrad Black, Carter, and William Mulholland, CEO at the Bank of Montreal. (Right) Making melody with a mandolin.

Recognition of long and varied service to many Canadians: honorary degree, University of Waterloo, 1989 (with President Wright, past-President Choate and Chancellor Wadsworth). UNIVERSITY OF WATERLOO. (Below) Honorary degree, University of Notre Dame, 1981 (with U.S. President Ronald Reagan).

Cardinal Carter receives the Order of Canada from Governor
General Edward Schreyer, 1983. JOHN EVANS, OTTAWA

understood its magnitude he would not have accepted the position in Toronto.

Although Gervais's report remains confidential, allegations of widespread homosexuality seem to have been ill-founded, and Carter's particular concern as the local Ordinary seems rather to have centred on questions of religious orthodoxy and lived example on the part of his faculty. While in London, Carter had often insisted that theologians were free to ask the basic questions, that there was a wide range of freedom in theology, but that the freedom of the Catholic theologian was ultimately answerable to the magisterium.[7] It is a position whose application to St. Augustine's received very wide support among Canada's bishops and local senior administrators, although the University of Toronto's senior administration moved to dissociate St. Augustine's from the Toronto School of Theology, arguing that the dismissals had not been carried out according to U of T protocol and with due respect for academic freedom. To the University of Toronto's published insistence that "[t]he principle of academic freedom is central to a university,"[8] Carter responded that the principle of academic freedom was equally important to him, but that when it came to individuals employed by the church, with the express permission of the church, to teach in the name of the church, then the same rules do not apply. A Catholic professor, as Catholic professor, has to be mandated by the local authority. In the cases of such individuals, fidelity to the magisterium, the official teaching authority of the church, is a prerequisite and it is his obligation as bishop of his diocese to ensure the orthodoxy of the teaching in his seminary. In support of Carter's position, Father James McConica, president of the University of St. Michael's College, observed of the negotiations which followed the embargo of St. Augustine's: "To put it bluntly, it was never in the minds of those of us representing the Roman Catholic constituency that professional competence would not include, in the case of the theologians, doctrinal integrity."

In fact, few within the Catholic community would fault Carter on the theory, though there are not a few who would fault him on procedure. (One of those who would not fault Carter either on theory or practice is his educational specialist and one-time Professor of Sacred Scripture at St. Augustine's, Archbishop Ambrozic: "I know that the theological crowd thinks otherwise, but everything was done absolutely in keeping with the by-laws of St. Augustine's Seminary.")

Carter responds to his detractors by arguing that he "would never take any unilateral action without great consultation"; in the university setting, there is, nonetheless, a large gulf between consultation and due process. Fidelity to the magisterium and an impulse not to wash the church's soiled linens in public figured prominently in Carter's decision making. They were overriding considerations. *In necessariis unitas*: we must be of one mind with respect to those things which are necessary to the faith.

In a 1988 address to his seminarians he provided what he no doubt hoped would be the last words on the St. Augustine's affair. Commenting briefly on the history of the seminary, Carter observed that, "We came to the post-conciliar years, the loss of priests, some of them on the staff of the seminary, the diminution of vocations, and finally, our present days in which in insisting on the rights of a major seminary to guide its own destiny in those things pertaining to the Church and the formation of men to the priesthood, above all in the tradition of the orthodoxy and the purity of doctrine, we have been criticised at least by a small number of persons. Today therefore I say to you that we must never lose sight of the transcendence of our mission and consequently of our teaching."[9]

The future of the Roman Catholic tradition is intimately linked with the future of its educational system, and no other single individual has influenced that system, either in Ontario or in Quebec, as substantially as has G. Emmett Cardinal Carter.

CHAPTER ELEVEN

Women and the Church:
The Controversy Continues

Toronto provided the ideal testing ground for Carter to act out his evolving convictions about the nature and role of women in the church, including his theories about the complementary nature of men and women. The drastic reduction of the numbers of priests able and available to serve a burgeoning Roman Catholic population also provided a high-profile and thorny issue which needed to be addressed. And, in Toronto, Carter's successes as well as his failures came under close public scrutiny.

Convinced of the church's need to empower competent women and of the virtue of adding a female dimension to the education of priests, Carter decided to undertake some bold initiatives at St. Augustine's Seminary, including granting permission for the hiring of women instructors. Mary Malone, for example, a classicist and a popular professor of church history, was appointed and taught at St. Augustine's for some ten years before being lured to the University of St. Jerome's College at the University of Waterloo. Malone's was a departure Carter was sorry to witness, and he took the unusual step of writing to her to say just that. Offering his congratulations on her new appointment, he added: "You will be much missed at the Seminary I am sure. The reviews in the paper were, as usual, somewhat provocative as they normally are on such subjects but I, too, am very pleased to see that women are able to be recognized as having skills of this order and ready and able to share their gifts with the whole community. . . . I am sure that the students will benefit a great deal from your presence as will the other members of the faculty."[1]

When Carter gave Mary Malone a mandate to teach at St. Augustine's he was making a bold move since Rome has had its visions and revisions with respect to allowing women to teach in its seminaries. The permission was, nonetheless, wholly consistent with Carter's own wish to empower women within the church to the extent permitted by official Catholic teaching. In this instance, two opposing forces were clearly at work in Carter's own mind: the definition and support of the ministerial priesthood, and the just role of women in the church — both of them causes on which he had had much to say and for which he offered outspoken support, especially in the 1970s and 1980s.

Questions of priesthood had been pressing and sometimes agonizing for Carter since his elevation to the episcopacy. During a homily that he gave relatively early in his tenure in London, Carter had explained that for the priest, "leaving is a failure to be understood and aided in sympathy."[2] Carter's own actions have been true to this counsel. Many priests — like Joe Snyder in St. Thomas and the late Sean O'Sullivan, who served in Toronto — have recounted touching examples of fellow priests in difficulty who approached Carter for help, and received it wholly and without reservation. Many have marvelled that behind the clip and cerebral demeanour is a sympathetic and sensitive man whom only those in need have come to know — and many have remarked that it is a pity that only a few have come to know this side of the Cardinal.

Unfortunately, for most of his priests Carter seems to be perceived as a shadowy abstraction. Even in London, where he knew his men by name and consulted them personally on decisions affecting their professional well-being, Carter was an intimidating presence. He never seemed to have time for small talk and appeared to be ill at ease in casual social settings. In Toronto, the size of his archdiocese removed him even farther from direct contact with his priests and forced him to appoint sociable and truly pastoral bishops like Robert Clune and Pearse Lacey to represent him personally. No longer could Carter consult with his priests individually about matters affecting their personal lives; no longer could he call them by name. The size of the task was impossible and the demands on a cardinal archbishop unrelenting. As a result, many note that morale among the Toronto clergy is at a low ebb. They are overextended, serving a volatile, cosmopolitan and mobile people in an increasingly secularized society. They too have trouble knowing their people. And their archbishop seemed to have no time for them.

Describing the low morale of Toronto's clergy, Sean O'Sullivan recounted what he claimed was a standing joke amongst Carter's priests. A synod of priests is in session when an announcement is made that the Cardinal is sorry, but he cannot be personally present. Instead, a video of his greetings flickers on a television screen, while the rumble of a jet whisking him off to perform foreign and important tasks vibrates throughout the meeting hall. Mission impossible.

While in London, Carter spoke often of the need for the priest to find his self-identity. He sorrowed at the declining numbers of priests just at the time that Vatican II was being implemented and the church was being modernized; and he worried about the cause and the effect. He worried about clericalism and about the lack of confidence his priests were beginning to show in themselves and in their calling. He worried about the apologetic attitudes some had adopted towards their calling, the "little-boy-lost attitude" of some, the "good guy, good companion" complex of others — there were, he suggested, enough matinee idols to go around. He worried about the "hail-fellow-well-met attitude which says, 'See, I'm no better than you.' " Priesthood is a privilege, a call to service, an invitation to model the life of Christ, an elevation of the human condition, a challenge to sacralize society. The objective of his seminary in London was to produce self-starters, proud of their calling, self-assured men who do not need sets of rules to regulate their lives. London ideals, London problems, translated to Toronto.

To solve the numbers problem, Carter appointed the newly ordained, ex-MP, and unabashed admirer of the Cardinal, Sean O'Sullivan, as Director of Vocations. O'Sullivan's "Dare to Be a Priest Like Me" billboards soon dotted the Toronto landscape. The image of the crucified Christ superimposed on a Toronto cityscape enraged local feminists, who had been agitating for a more flexible, more inclusive definition of priesthood: the identification of priesthood with Christ was a vivid reminder of the Declaration on the Question of the Admission of Women to the Ministerial Priesthood and Rome's association of the priest with the maleness of Christ; in addition, it seemed to ignore the growing role which Vatican II envisaged for the common priesthood, which all the Catholic laity possess by virtue of their baptism.

The style and flair of the billboard also conjured up images of questionable advertisements a religious order in the United States had placed in *Playboy* not long before. Satiric composite photographs of the "Dare to Be a Priest Like Me" slogan began to circulate; there was widespread protest and the billboard posters quietly disappeared. It

was a high-profile campaign, one which Sean O'Sullivan admitted
was a public relations blunder, one he swore never to repeat. Nonetheless, the seriousness of the church's recruitment problem had
been laid bare for all to see.

Of course, the shortage of priests added additional fuel to the
heated arguments being articulated by those who were agitating for
the ordination of women to the ministerial priesthood. For his initial
reasoned response to their demands Carter returned to his thesis
concerning authority and power. Ron Graham recalls Cardinal Carter's reaction to a member of Canadian Catholics for the Ordination of
Women, who, after a 1981 meeting, wrote to Carter to register the
feeling of unfulfillment in the Catholic Church which many women
were experiencing: "I wrote back and said that feeling fulfilled in the
church is not a question of power structure. If priesthood is just to get
power, then forget it, it's not worth it. That's where many of these
ladies are hung up, in the power structure."[3]

Carter has commented on the question of power and authority in
many contexts, and when he has, he has inevitably made reference to
the question of women's ordination and the women's movement, at
least by way of footnote. So in a homily given to a congregation of
lawyers at the Red Mass for 1983, three months before issuing his
famous pastoral letter on priesthood, Carter's theme was not priesthood or the role of women in society, but questions of law. He began
his discussion on freedom and authority by reiterating his personal
pet distinctions: "Authority is based upon the right to make ultimate
decisions which is placed in the hands of an individual or a group.
Power, on the other hand, is the inner dynamism that moves human
forces to a determined end. . . . The bishop has the final authority but
the power is very diffused. . . . Another example of that distinction
which I shall approach with great wariness [the text reads "weariness"] is that of the male and the female in human affairs. I have long
been convinced that whereas in most of our present civilization
authority resides in the men more frequently than in the women,
power, on the other hand, is the other way around. I certainly saw this
carried out in my own family, where my mother never contested my
father on matters of authority, but there was no doubt about where the
power resided."[4] These identical points he had made in his presentation at the September 11, 1978, Red Mass, and they clearly reinforced
both his own thinking and the familial influence on that thinking.
Women ought to accept the fact that, in the church, ultimate author-

ity is not to be theirs; they ought also to understand that there is power in the roles which nature has assigned to them.

Power and priesthood became recurrent themes as Carter tried to rally his beleaguered troops. Making a scholastic distinction between temporal and spiritual power, Carter suggested that the women's movement has confused the two, though he argued that certain types of spiritual power can be exercised by men only. "The priesthood is widely misunderstood in the trend of modern calculations," he said in a homily delivered in 1987. "It is seen as an instrument of power in a very secular sense of that term. Much of the controversy about the ordination of women to the priesthood is based on a raw drive to power.... But we cannot deny that there is power in the priesthood."[5] Women, it seems, are by nature excluded from both the authority and the power which reside in the ministerial priesthood.

What is the nature of this priestly power? During the ordination mass for Sean O'Sullivan, Carter noted that priesthood "confers very real power. The Council which is so often quoted wrongly says very clearly: 'The ministerial priest, by the sacred power he enjoys, molds and rules the priestly people. Acting in the person of Christ he brings about the eucharistic sacrifice and offers it to God in the name of all the people.' "[6]

He returned to these concepts and elaborated on them at some length at the ordination mass of Richard McKnight, an Anglican priest who was converted to Roman Catholicism. Carter explained that "there are three powers granted to the priest, the power to teach, the power to assist in the governance of the Church and the power to sanctify."[7] His homily consists of an exposition of each of these powers. One cannot help but wonder if it is fair to characterize woman's desire to share in one or more of these powers "a raw drive to power." Philosophically this was a peculiar tack for Carter to take, given his agreement with Ambrozic that priesthood is not about power.

However, priestly authority (and power) are not matters of degree for Carter but matters of natural birthright. Men and women, he argues, simply have different callings. He has therefore concluded that Christ is the liberator of women and the christian tradition is the tradition of liberation for women. "However," he said in an address to the Theresians of Toronto, "as is true of all people, 'to grow to maturity we must realize that there are some things we cannot achieve,' so people should avoid unrealistic expectations. 'I deplore the idea that women can do everything,' he said. Addressing a mainly female audience, the archbishop warned good-naturedly: 'If you want to appear in the Grey Cup, you have my blessing. I'll conduct the funeral."[8] Or, as he said to Ron Graham in an interview with *Saturday Night*, "there's no point in wasting time and credibility on issues like ordination. That's like trying to score a touchdown every time you get the ball."[9]

As a matter of clerical morale and Roman politics, however, Carter really did have to take a formal public stand on the issue. Speaking of the St. Augustine's Affair, Mary Jo Leddy, a founding editor of *Catholic New Times* and a socially active Sister of Sion, recalled the common wisdom that there are three issues on which a bishop is judged: abortion, the orthodoxy of one's seminary, and one's stand on the matter of women's ordination. In Sean O'Sullivan's eyes, "the whole question was under siege, particularly here, and there is always that feeling that if there is ferment in your archdiocese you have as a bishop aided and abetted this sort of thing. Obviously you end that speculation in a hurry by bringing out your own mini-encyclical."

There seems to be something to Leddy's and O'Sullivan's observations. In the winter of 1981-82, for example, an article entitled "The Roman Catholic Church and Sexism" appeared in *Status*, an article forcefully cataloguing the evils of sexism in the church. For Carter it was aggression not in his backyard, but actually in his own front yard. The authors, Ellen Leonard and Mary R. D'Angelo, insisted that their presentation represented the views of women professors and students in the Department of Religious Studies and the Faculty of Theology at the University of St. Michael's College — the Catholic College of which he was the Chancellor. The article concluded with a note on the establishment of the CCWO (Canadian Catholics for Women's Ordination), a group whose appearance cannot have been well received by the Cardinal. Indeed, the inaugural meeting of CCWO envisioned the establishing of local groups across the country, so that Carter's bush fire had the potential for a national conflagration spreading east and west from his own archdiocese. Aiding and abetting on a grand scale.

And so, on the feast of the Immaculate Conception, the day Carter had traditionally reserved for homilies to his seminarians, the two crucial issues of priesthood and women's role in the church became one. That is the promulgation date appearing on Carter's pastoral statement on priesthood, *Do This in Memory of Me.*

Although Carter has consistently argued that *Do This in Memory of Me* is, in fact, a statement on priesthood and not on the ordination of women, the thrust of the document, the origin of the document and the reception of the document suggest otherwise. It is a statement on priesthood to the extent that the 1976 Vatican Declaration on the Admission of Women to the Ministerial Priesthood is a statement on priesthood. Both provide a philosophical discussion of priesthood, and both expressly exclude women from participation. The Declaration proceeds largely by way of biblical argument with a philosophical-theological underpinning; *Do This in Memory of Me* proceeds by way of philosophical-theological argument with a biblical underpinning.

Carter's personal secretary, Mary Frances Keating, carefully filed the *Do This in Memory of Me* materials under the title "Discussion Re: Ordination of Women, 1981", and the document is very similar in content and style to an article by Marquette University's Jesuit theologian Donald J. Keefe entitled "Sacramental sexuality and the ordination of women",[10] that had appeared a few years earlier. The terminology, the issues and to a large degree the order of the argument are strikingly similar to Carter's. In addition, Jerome Cardinal Hamer, Prefect of the Sacred Congregation of Religious, wrote to Carter on September 29, 1984, noting that he had seen mention in the French press of "an important letter regarding the question of admission of women to priestly ordination" issued by Carter, and that he wanted to receive a copy. Then, on November 12, 1984, Hamer sent Carter his congratulations, commenting on his appreciation of *Do This in Memory of Me* as a study of the question of women's ordination.

The argument of the text itself centres on maleness and femaleness. Carter's thesis is based at the outset on the order of the goodness of creation and the "uniquely and qualitatively distinct human existence of a man or a woman with personal responsibility and historical freedom." There follows a discussion of the covenantal relationship of creation to creature, and the marital imagery on which it is structured in the Jewish tradition. The applicability of the Jewish to the christian tradition resides in the pauline hierarchical definition of the "headship of the husband over his wife [as] an analogy of the headship of God over Christ." Mary enters into the christian tradition with her willing and active *fiat mihi*, so that her generative role is ultimately the origin of the marital relationship of Christ the High

Priest to his church: Christ is the Head of his bridal church. The church, therefore, is the "covenantal Flesh of the New Adam [Christ] and the New Eve [Mary]." Therefore, only a man can stand in imitation of Christ, since the relation of priest to church is the relationship of Head to Body and Bridegroom to Bride. It is a divinely ordained relationship and, according to the theory, can therefore not be altered. The nature of the arguments reflects Keefe's theological ruminations, and the reasoning is a reinforcement of the 1976 Declaration, though on another level. The argumentation is also wholly consonant with Carter's thinking on the distinction between power and authority, the priest's authority being "different", not "greater". The scholarship inherent in the presentation is borrowed, perhaps eclectically, but the sentiments are vintage Carter.

Carter's pastoral letter also calls for freedom and fulfillment of women in the church, while at the same time arguing for equality in dignity, difference in function. These are all arguments which have some currency for Carter, so that even though he seems to have borrowed elements of Keefe's argumentation and even his terminology, the conviction is clearly Carter's own. And there is no question but that Carter is speaking about pristehood, but his stress on the marital covenant, the marital relationship of priest and church, is a discussion of male and female roles — the concentration on marital relationships is the beginning, middle, and end of the pastoral.

In a speech he made to the Catholic Women's League after the pastoral letter appeared, he summed up his position this way: "It is not a question of worth or ability or dignity or equality. It is a question of the will of God who alone can call to the priesthood. No one has a right. Secondly, the Church has the tradition from Jesus on to call only men to that role. This position is formal and normative, and we are required as Catholics to respect and obey it."[11]

Since the pastoral letter was an explicit response to Cardinal Ratzinger's "Letter to the Bishops of the Catholic Church on Certain Questions Concerning the Minister of the Eucharist", since Carter noted in his own text that the representation "of the ordained priest acting *in persona Christi* . . . is being questioned" and since "[t]he unity of the Church is at stake," for Carter there was only one thing to do: in those things deemed essential to the church there must be unity — *in necessariis unitas*. As teacher he had to take a stand in favour of tradition, in light of the Roman position, and in support of his priests who were, after all, a beleaguered and declining cohort.

Carter's old friend Joseph-Aurèle Plourde, the archbishop of Ottawa, summed up Carter's thinking with respect to the role of women in the church: "He was not at all opposed to recognizing the women, because the Canadian bishops had won on that question. But he was very, very opposed to the extreme feminism, women wanting to be priests. He's dead set against that." As for the pastoral letter, Plourde said, "He should be satisfied because the Pope congratulated him on it."

Is it any wonder that Joseph Cardinal Ratzinger, Prefect of the Congregation for the Doctrine of the Faith, spoke in glowing terms of *Do This in Memory of Me*? "I think it's a very excellent document and I think it would merit to be better read and better known, not only in the English-speaking world. It is precise and brief, but really deep and profound with all the tradition of the Church, with also a richness of the great tradition. Tradition really actualized. I think it's one of the best documents about priesthood I know." If the question of women's ordination is the second touchstone of episcopal orthodoxy, Carter's stock was obviously high in Rome.

In fact, Carter had gone to some pains to get a wider readership for *Do This in Memory of Me*. His correspondence with Donald J. Keefe centred on this very issue. Keefe took the initiative to contact Chauncey Stillman, the founder of the Stillman Chair in Catholic Theology at Harvard University, to see if Stillman would support distribution in the United States.[12] Keefe's intention was to arrange for publication of *Do This in Memory of Me* through the Catholic Truth Society since *The Wanderer* had declined publication.[13] Keefe was joined in his efforts by fellow Jesuit Brian Van Hove whose communication with another Jesuit, Gustave Martelet of the French province, suggested the possibility of a French translation.

In the long run it was the ponderous style (more Keefe's than Carter's) which doomed *Do This in Memory of Me* to lie unread on clerical and college bookshelves. There is a cruel irony in this. From the beginning of his educational career Carter had insisted that the church should teach in the language of the people, not in scholastic argot. But one could hardly expect the average priest or teacher (a good part of the intended audience) to make too much of an argument that concluded its discussions of the equal dignity of man and woman with a statement like: "To move from this position to the necessity of ordaining women is to impose, for the most part unreflectively, a monadic logic upon a trinitarian and covenantal equality. Equal monads are qualitatively indistinct; their differentiation is quantitative only." This kind of language was far too weighty to give the document a wide readership.

Little wonder that the editor of the Catholic Truth Society of London, England, should send Carter this honest, if somewhat ingenuous rejection letter: "Many thanks for your kind letter of 2 November and for the copy of your Pastoral Letter, Do this in memory of me. To be truthful this has rather stumped us; our authors' brief is usually 'imagine an audience of bright fifteen year olds' and our instinct is not to publish anything we cannot readily understand unless it is a papal encyclical."[14]

Stateside, Chauncey Stillman wrote to Donald Keefe suggesting the letter be "rewritten in language of the middlebrow like myself ", suggesting Carter consider "dumbing it down." He assured Keefe: "It is easy to see why, a year after publication, it has gone almost unnoticed. It's too abstruse by far. No wonder *The Wanderer* didn't print it. I would wager that the clergy to whom it is addressed have treated it with respectful neglect, read by a small fraction of them only."[15] Even Carter's good friends in the chancery office do not reject the Stillman analysis. Aloysius Ambrozic laments its lack of biblical orientation, but then he claims that he was not consulted (and he is a biblical scholar); Brad Massman writes in puzzled bemusement, wondering who might do a final edit on a text such as this.

Many did read and understand, however. The Toronto School of Theology mounted a public protest as well as a public study session of the document. *Catholic New Times* printed a feature analysis and ran a personal interview with Carter, in which he assured Janet Somerville and Grant Jahnke that "[t]he ordination of women is — well, not a false issue, but a bad one strategically. We should be pushing hard in areas where we can get consensus, along the lines of the paragraph in my pastoral where I speak of how women haven't been given fair treatment in the church. If we can get together on that, we can discuss ordination ten years from now, or twenty, God knows how long from now. Talking about it now falsifies the issue . . . . But we're overdue for a whole rehabilitation of women in what you might call the power structure of the church, the administrative structure. I'm always telling them that when I go to Rome."[16]

Others too have read and understood. Anne Roche Muggeridge wrote to Carter twice, explaining that she was in sympathy with the pastoral, but worried that it rested on the acceptance of a single premise on which the argument stands or falls. She said she was also puzzled by the article in *Catholic New Times*. Is Carter's argument a philosophical and theological truism which is valid for all times, or is the question of the ordination of women an open issue which can be altered in ten or twenty years as he suggested in his interview? Carter's response is typical of him — the thomist and the churchman. His explanation is also a useful corrective with respect to the whole issue of ordination of women to the ministerial priesthood. "The arguments which I used in my Pastoral," he said, "are in my opinion, irreversible. They are the constant teaching of the Church. However, the question which was raised was one of a juridical nature, not a basically theological argument. The fact is that the official Church, speaking universally, has taken a position only through a decree of the Sacred Congregation for the Doctrine of the Faith although approved by the Holy Father. This, in itself, and in juridical terms is not irreversible."[17]

Father Anthony Durand sent a four-page analysis. As a retired professor of philosophy at St. Peter's Seminary, he took a particular interest in *Do This in Memory of Me*, on the basis of both style and content. And he had to confess that there were places where even he had difficulty following the argument. With respect to the question of the ordination of women to the ministerial priesthood, however, he understood quite well the implication of Carter's thesis; nor did he see the question as something of passing interest within the flow of the pastoral letter. On the contrary, the logic of *Do This in Memory of Me* had convinced Durand that the question of the ordination of women was inevitably more than some contemporary fad destined to fade inconsequentially; the issue struck at the very heart of the sacramental nature of priesthood. Like Ratzinger, Durand saw in Carter's pastoral a compelling statement on the issue of priesthood, one which deserved serious analytical attention.[18]

Although Carter's own attitude toward the ordination of women to the ministerial priesthood was firm and clear enough, he did remain flexible on the question. The church's position could change with time, and, theoretically at least, so could his. *In dubiis libertas.* "As far as anyone's opinion goes about the ordination of women, it disturbs me not at all," he has said. "I am not sure that the last word has been said on this subject and a counter position to what the Church has taught so far is not, in my view, heretical, at least not yet."[19] In fact, Carter has suggested that there are certain topics he could not write about because of his responsibilities as Cardinal, and that one of those topics was the role of women in the Church — "[b]ecause my position is, I think, a little more advanced than the Pope's, and therefore I should not parade it in public."

Carter's thinking with respect to the role of women in society and in the church has certainly evolved with the times. Although for at least pastoral, perhaps even theological reasons, he is not ready to see women ordained to the ministerial priesthood, he does argue for and work at providing authoritative roles for women within existing structures. Margaret McLaughlin, for example, speaks enthusiastically about her former boss, and reflects with some animation about his inviting her to join him and Brad Massman in Toronto as Assistant Director of the Office of Communications almost a year after their first meeting during a radio interview on CFRB. During that initial encounter in 1977 McLaughlin was moved spontaneously to ask for a private session with Carter, where she expressed her wish to work for the church. McLaughlin recalls the interview ending with Carter's counsel: "Don't ask me why or how I know this, but one day, young lady, you and I are going to be working very closely together." McLaughlin's appointment, which was announced in an April 28, 1979, *Catholic Register* item entitled "Women hold key Toronto jobs," was to be a sign of efforts to empower women in Carter's corner of the church.

Carter's professional experiences with women communications officers had been good ones. He and Bonnie Brennan, the Information Officer for the Canadian Conference of Catholic Bishops in Ottawa, had obviously had a frank and fruitful working relationship during his years as president of the Canadian Conference. It too was a relationship built on respect and confidence, and like the Margaret McLaughlin association, it began with Emmett Carter doing the unexpected. That story has become somewhat legendary. It took place during Vatican II, apparently during the 1964 session, when Bonnie Brennan and Bernard Daly were working the Council as reporters. Both were anxious to get into the Council hall, which was under tight security, and the chances of getting anyone, much less a woman, into the hall were very slim indeed. Nonetheless, Brennan lobbied on Daly's behalf, and unbeknownst to them, a group of Canadian bishops managed to secure a pass for the two of them. When confronted with the request of the twenty bishops, and knowing they could not issue press passes to the two laypeople, the Vatican Press

Office finally decided to provide passes for "reverends" Daly and Brennan. And so they got into the hall for almost two full days before they were found out. After her summary dismissal, Brennan went to lunch to brood over the situation. Everyone, she says, was very nice about it, but Alex Carter, Emmett Carter and a third member of the delegation sought her out, lamenting her expulsion. "But it was Emmett who said, 'Well, darn it, kid, you are not going to miss this morning.' And he stood there and translated for me, because the Council was all in Latin. He stood there and made sure I got what was being said and knew what was going on." It was an inspired meeting for two business-like people, a meeting which became the stuff of legend and the providential source of a solid working relationship many years later.

Carter has a knack for attracting dedicated people around him, and the women on his team are wholly devoted to him. This is certainly true of Araceli Echebarria, a Basque and a member of the Institute of Secular Missionaries, who was his housekeeper in London and who moved to Toronto with him. Araceli is an excellent cook and an extended member of the family. Brad Massman suggests that Carter "treats her with respect, but he's tough on her as he is on all of us. She has to bear the brunt, just like when you or I go home, or when somebody has had a bad day. If the food's cold or if you really don't want to talk and you really can't take it out on anybody else, I'm sure that Araceli's the one to whom he can say 'Don't bother me.' Just kiddingly. He enjoys kidding people he likes." For her part, Araceli obviously enjoys working for the Cardinal, though she demurs when asked leading questions, feeling she is too close to the scene.

Among the other ladies to share in the Cardinal's professional life was Mary Frances Keating, whose appointment was announced in the *Catholic Register* simultaneously with Margaret McLaughlin's. Keating had been the president of the board for the Council of Catholic Charities, cultural life convenor for the Catholic Women's League in Canada and past president of the Catholic Women's League in the Archdiocese of Toronto. Carter appointed her his executive secretary, a position which she held until her death.

Carter respects intelligent and efficient women, and he found another in the person of Suzanne Scorsone, a convert to Roman Catholicism who holds a doctoral degree in anthropology. She became the director of the archdiocese's Office for Family Life. She is a bright lady whose thoroughly traditional inclinations suit Carter's own progressively conservative predilections perfectly in the areas in which she works, and it is clear from the confidential correspondence between them that she has served the Cardinal well.

Despite popular opinion to the contrary, Carter also values women academics working in theological and ecclesiastical areas, as long as they are not one-issue people whose professional motivation is fuelled by an overriding desire to argue the case for women's ordination. In the case of Mary Malone, for example, not only did he take the time to make it clear to her that he was sorry to see her leave the teaching staff of St. Augustine's Seminary, but he had previously written to her to congratulate her on the publication of her book on the Virgin Mary, *Who is My Mother?*, in which Carter had found much to be admired.[20] That was no little accolade, given his own particular devotion to the Mary of the Annunciation. Malone is a christian feminist who understands the ins and outs of the ordination issue, but who has never aligned herself specifically with it. As an academic who is Roman Catholic, Malone has taken a scholarly and personal interest in the history and nature of her church; as a christian feminist, she is eager to see that history and nature interpreted through women's eyes. Intellectual qualities Carter can admire.

Nonetheless, Carter drew persistent and unflattering national headlines with his response to a special report prepared by an ad hoc Women's Committee on the Role of Women in the Church presented to the Canadian Conference of Catholic Bishops in the fall of 1984. The report made a series of twelve recommendations on the status of women in the church, one of which proposed a work kit to be administered at the parish level — the Green Kit — in order to raise consciousness and to improve woman's lot within the church.[21] The controversy over the report raged for some time: an English professor from the University of St. Michael's College, David Dooley, argued in the *Catholic Register* that the effort at conscientization "amounts to a deliberate effort to create discontent among women who have probably not been discontent in the past";[22] and an Edmonton-based group, Women for Life, Faith, and Family, countered Archbishop Joseph MacNeil's quick endorsement of the report and the Green Kit by issuing their own counter-kit, which was immediately tagged the Blue Kit. But it was Carter who was in the middle of the storm.

The Women's Committee, consisting of up to twelve women (their membership was not constant over the life of the Committee) and two bishops, had been working for the better part of two years, and their report was slated for presentation at the October 1984 Plenary Assembly of the Canadian Conference of Catholic Bishops scheduled for the last week of October. The Ontario bishops met in advance to plan their strategy, and the southern Ontario bishops, for the most part, apparently decided to rally around Carter as their focal point. In doing this, they antagonized the Quebec delegation in particular — not to mention women and journalists of both sexes across the country. Unfortunately, Carter was taken ill and forced to return to Toronto on the opening day of the session, Monday, October 22, where he was hospitalized with influenza. The Committee report was presented on Tuesday the 23rd, with thirteen bishops in opposition to the use of the Green Kit as it stood, ten in favour of using it in every diocese and forty-seven in favour of distributing it. With Carter in Toronto, his auxiliary, Leonard Wall, read the Carter response on Wednesday, October 24. One bishop close to the scene blamed the uproar which followed on Wall's presentation — his booming voice and lack of diplomacy: "Len boomed it out like it was the Archangel Gabriel coming down from heaven. He pontificated as if it were almost coming from the Holy Father. I don't think it was one of Emmett's best interventions, but he would have done it differently. He would have relieved the tension with a wisecrack or such — he has that knack." As it was, every major newspaper in the country was on Carter's neck. It was not his finest moment.

Alex Carter recalls that some of the women were pleased, others furious with the bishops' response that Wednesday. "The ones who were very avant-garde were very annoyed. Furious. I thought that there were one or two excellent ones among the six, but they could have done without one or two of the ones who almost came with a chip on their shoulder and wanted to let the bishops know it's about time that they did this, that and the other thing."

Emmett Carter's intervention had, in fact, quoted his *Do This in Memory of Me* insofar as it relates to sexual equality and the need to find expression within the church for the dignity of women. However, Carter had problems with both the content of the presentation and the procedures followed by that committee. "To begin with the latter," Carter wrote, "it seems well established that not only was this committee selected with only one viewpoint in mind, dissenting voices were not encouraged, in fact they were pretty well gagged. Time does not permit me to produce the factual evidence, but many of us have received reports to that conclusion. It is open to serious doubt as to whether this committee really represents the majority of the Catholic women of Canada. Secondly, the tone of the documents is negative to the point of being almost abusive in places. Instead of presenting questions and perspectives that are suggested to the Conference of Bishops for our consideration, we are rather patronizingly told what we must think and what we must do."[23] He concluded by calling for a more balanced report.

Thursday's newspapers across the country roared their disapproval. Women took to their telephones to register their dismay. Ottawa mayor Marion Dewar, who was one of the thousand or so women to provide the Committee with her story, contacted Ottawa's Archbishop Plourde, requesting that he dissociate himself from the Carter attack. According to Paul DeGroot of the *Edmonton Journal*, "[a]t the opening of proceedings Thursday, Vachon read a letter whose intent, he said, was 'reconciliation'. The bishops had also heard from women in their dioceses overnight. Bishop Remi De Roo of Victoria said the head of his women's organization had protested the bishops' actions Wednesday."[24] Thursday's journalistic hue and cry was replaced by Friday's peacemaking. Emmett Carter, his most vocal ally, Bishop Marcel Gervais (who had argued that the documents promoted contraception and women's ordination), and the president of the Conference, John Sherlock (who repeatedly ruled the Committee chairperson, Professor Elisabeth Lacelle, out of order when she tried to explain the contents of the report), were undercut by the proceedings that followed. In the long run, the Committee recommendations were passed with only minor alterations, and Canada's bishops became the darlings of the press. Carter was left to bear the national wrath.

The *Globe and Mail* carried a headline announcing "Bishops brush aside cardinal's objections,"[25] the *Edmonton Journal* headlined its article "Carter's mistake against women"[26] and the *London Free Press* introduced the topic under the heading "Bishops make amends to women's panel shocked by attack from Cardinal Carter."[27] Carter was forced to defend himself, and did so in a letter to the editor of the *Globe and Mail* printed on November 12, 1984. In his response, Carter argued that he had been vilified by the *Globe*, that in fact he was not the villain of the piece: many bishops had called to thank him for his intervention and the dialogue which resulted from it. He also insisted that had he been present he would have supported all of the propositions without amendment except one, Proposition 9 (dealing with the

Kit), which he would have voted to amend. "My objection was and is to the tone of the document. This tone, negative and shrill, was not to be found in the propositions, which were reasonable enough, but in the considerations, 'whereases' that made the women in the Church appear to be a beleaguered, oppressed, and persecuted minority. This I reject, and I believe it is equally rejected by most women in the Church who do not feel alienated. The considerations made it sound as if we have achieved nothing in giving a larger liturgical, ministerial and administrative role to women. The record says otherwise."

The Green Kit lies for the most part unused, most dioceses lacking the expertise (and some the will) to implement it. But most, including Cardinal Carter, have become more sensitive to the issues. The bishops have taken a strong stand in favour of the use of inclusive language (their August 16, 1989, pastoral message, "To Speak as a Christian Community", is a forceful and sensitive response to the issue of exclusive language — the use of words and phrases like "mankind" and "good will toward men", which seem to relate to men only — a response with which Carter is in agreement); Canada's bishops, already among the most progressive in the world on women's issues (arguably the most progressive), have continued to foster the CCCB objectives of sexual equality. Indeed, the January 1990 report of the Quebec bishops, *Violence en héritage*, though clearly a Quebec and not a national statement, is seen by many to be a remarkably sensitive response and a milestone on the road to understanding and renewal.

For his part, Carter has struggled with Roman decrees and journalistic reporting. Faithful to his tradition, he has supported Rome's Declaration on the Question of the Admission of Women to the Ministerial Priesthood. Faithful to Rome, he suffered the effects of journalistic newsmongering in uncomfortable silence as the nation was informed about Sandra Bernier's summary dismissal from the altar for the one hundredth anniversary of Sacré-Coeur parish in Toronto. Carter was blamed for a lower-level decision, not of his making, which enforced Rome's directive against the use of altar girls. No one took note, however, that when Carter celebrated mass in Montreal a week later, it was served by girls. And no one bothered to point out publicly that girls regularly serve mass at Carter's church in Rome, Santa Maria in Traspontina. Carter has empowered women where he could, turned a blind eye to lower-level initiatives where he should and supported the church where Rome expected he would.

In a 1988 address Carter repeated his vision of the role of women in the church, and added to it his growing sensitivity to the use of language. Addressing a Catholic Women's League gathering, he explained: "We do not subscribe to the excessive and bitter accusations of patriarchal domination, alienation and discrimination which have such a place in feminist literature of the times. We rather rejoice in the evidence of a great number of Catholic women who feel at home in the Church, do not feel put upon and who are very conscious of the great contribution that they are making. If time permits we will come back to the subject of sex and God and inclusive language. But even postulating that there is a common-sense middle ground in all of these problems there can be no denying the tendencies to discrimination which history has witnessed."[28]

Carter understands history and he abhors discrimination. He understands clericalism and appreciates the giftedness of women. He is also every inch a churchman, and has devoted his life to a church whose central authority is wary of moving too quickly in the empowering of women. As a result, he urges Catholic women to exercise their gifts with patience, with love, and with understanding. Catholic tradition allows him to do no more.

CHAPTER TWELVE

The Modern Family in Crisis

For Carter there is no question that the history of women in western society is a history of injustice, and he often argues for the righting of the wrong. Always, he rejects extremist views and extremist actions. Nowhere does he make this case better than in his statements on family — especially in the series of articles he wrote for the *Catholic Register* in connection with the 1980 episcopal Synod on the Family. There is also no question for him that the family is the cornerstone of our civilization, and that the family as we have known it is in trouble. Part of the problem is the increasingly secularist and humanistic nature of our society, one expression of which is the extremist position in the Women's Liberation movement which "actually sneers at motherhood and at caring for the home."[1]

As the Canadian Conference of Catholic Bishops prepared for the 1980 Synod, Carter urged sensitivity for change both in the church and in society, hoping earnestly that the Synod on the Family would provide the context for this renewal: "It seems to me that what is required is a change of attitude towards the role of women in the Church and an enhancing of their contribution. There are riches here which have been sadly neglected. It is also beyond question that we have excluded women from many echelons where they legitimately belong whatever the question of their involvement in the hierarchy. This, then, would be the first position for the Synod to take: A strong call for recognition of the true rights of women in the Church and their importance. Then the door would be open for us to affirm the importance of women in the family, in the re-establishment and redirection of sexual morality, in parenting and in all of the other aspects which preside over the destinies of the family."

In the early sixties Carter had talked to Ron Locas, student at St. Joseph's Teacher's College, about the heroism required in marriage. He repeated that point of view in a 1976 homily at St. Peter's Cathedral, and the same message has come through in his synodal interventions. (Thomas Francoeur suggests that this sensitivity springs from Carter's own experience of his sister Margaret's troubled marriage.) Carter spoke of the need to take the unpopular stand, to speak the hard truths, but to do so in a manner which does not smack of unilateral proclamation, but of understanding and empathy. "We feel very strongly, without any discernible negative voice, that we must, at all costs, avoid trying to 'lay down the law' to the real and already agonized Christian families, who are not abstractions, but tangible, vibrating human beings, caught up in the problems of human relations in all of their stark dimensions."

Our materialistic society, Carter pointed out in the homily he delivered when he was installed as archbishop of Toronto, preaches selfishness and impermanence; there is no longer the willingness to opt for permanent commitment. Yet the family is the bulwark of society, and "everything tells us that a stable home is absolutely of the essence in self-development." The Synod on the Family, therefore, must be pastoral, it must inculcate the teaching of responsible parenthood, a healthy sexuality, the dignity of motherhood and the role of the housewife. It must do this by speaking in the language people use, by convincing rather than dictating, by teaching compassion through compassion. Carter argued for a more sympathetic approach to the reception of the sacraments by those facing marital breakdown, and he reiterated the need to appreciate "the importance of women in our civilization, particularly the equality which must be granted to them."

The document which was released by the Vatican in the name of the Synod does nothing of the kind. It is authoritarian in tone, harsh in its analysis, insensitive to its audience. Carter was disappointed, and he said so publicly. His openness earned him yet another set of scars.

Carter's call for sensitivity to human suffering and for the legitimacy of the quest for women's equality is a matter of both pastoral care and human justice, but it should not in any way be seen as a breaking of ranks. On essential issues, Carter and Rome are as one. On the question of abortion, therefore, he is unambiguous: human life is sacred at all its stages. Such is the message of the Judeo-Christian tradition since Cain's killing of Abel.[2] Indeed, the attitude of society

— any society — toward life is the touchstone of the quality of that society's civilization.[3] So, as Carter planted his episcopal flag on Toronto soil, he spoke his thank-yous and outlined his agenda in his mass of installation at St. Michael's Cathedral on June 6, 1978. At that time, he assured his congregation that he would like to see Toronto's leadership in English-Catholic Canada continue along recently established lines: "standing for the forces of life, the enduring values of morality, and the nobility of the human spirit."

In his *Catholics against the Church: Anti-Abortion Protest in Toronto, 1969 – 1985*, Michael W. Cuneo documents Carter's role in Toronto's anti-abortion scene, and outlines the pro-life movement's vacillation between dismay, confusion and celebration over the direction and commitment of Carter to their cause. For his part, Carter has often felt misunderstood, unheard or misjudged. Accordingly, as his theme for the 1986 Cardinal's Dinner, he turned his attention to a familiar topic, the question of leadership. Canadians, he said, are ambivalent about leadership. "With one breath we extol it and demand it. With the next we vilify and ridicule it. Let's take the first stance. Speaking for myself and the almost 25 years I have had as a bishop, my mail must run at least 3 to 1 in demands or suggestions that I take action on one or another front. To give only one example: I must have made or joined in making some 10 or 15 statements against abortion on demand. Yet, yesterday or tomorrow my mail will ask me at least once why I don't make a statement."[4] It is an obvious frustration for Carter, who complains that since much of what he does cannot be done in full public view, people assume he's doing nothing. But "you can't write back and say, 'I am doing something, dammit.' "

While Bishop of London, Carter had indeed spoken out on the question of abortion on numerous occasions so that his installation pledge in Toronto was hardly the embracing of a new direction or the mouthing of platitudes. He had argued, for example, that the selfishness of modern society is a threat to life itself, since it is a selfishness which promotes pollution, abortion, euthanasia and which strikes out at the stability of marriage.[5] Ours, he asserted, is a society which would silence Beethoven in the womb, a society which is inherently self-destructive, since "Life, my friends, is the true basis of democracy and freedom. Respect it not at your own personal peril."[6] Indeed, in communist countries, Yugoslavia for example, even a philosophy of secular humanism finds abortion contrary to its moral values.[7] For our part, bespeaking a cultural arrogance, we have decided that life is not sufficient, and we have begun to debate the quality of life by adverting to the convenience of the pregnant mother as a justification for the termination of embryonic existence.[8] Because of these attitudes, the womb, the place in which the child ought to feel most safe, has come rather to resemble the tomb.[9] And in 1976, when Henry Morgentaler's abortions were reaching proportions which aroused national concern, Carter announced that he refused to "see the other side — whatever it is. Over 50,000 innocent children slain in their mother's womb in the last year! THE OTHER SIDE!" If the question of abortion is, in fact, the third test of episcopal orthodoxy, there is no question but that Carter has long met the mark on this issue too.

On the matter of abortion, therefore, Carter also brought well-established attitudes to Toronto, but, as on so many other issues, he was to find Toronto a far greater task than London had been. Carter was to learn with a vengeance that both the political climate and, therefore, the issues themselves were much more volatile in Toronto than in smaller Ontario centres.

While in London, Carter had written to Larry Henderson, editor of the *Catholic Register*, to congratulate him on his stand on abortion as articulated in an issue of that journal. "It has moved me to contemplate a series of actions. The first is to put all of the candidates in the forthcoming federal election on a publicity griddle in my own diocese. I plan to challenge them on their position on abortion and to notify them in so doing that I intend to publish the results."[10] At the same time, however, Carter was always mindful of the way clerics had interfered with the political process in Duplessis's Quebec, and he was a democrat by nature: he would not publicly advocate the support or rejection of any particular candidate; he had refused to do so over the separate school issue in 1971, he refused to do it in 1978 and he would refuse to do it in the federal elections of 1984 and 1988. So, when in 1984 Henderson exhorted his *Register* readers to spoil their ballots, Carter publicly dissociated himself from Henderson's position. Privately, Carter described the position to us as "awfully stupid". Instead, Carter urged his parishioners in a pastoral letter to "challenge the candidates in regard to their philosophy of human life." He urged the Catholics of his archdiocese to make a careful choice of their candidate, and warned them that "In truth we really get what we deserve [by way of elected representation]."[11]

In the same pastoral letter, Carter clarified his own position on the question of abortion. He traced the slaughter of the innocent to the days of King Herod, and wondered about the logic of permitting the killing of a child within the womb when the perpetrator of such an act would be subject to the full force of the law if that same innocent were disposed of outside the womb. This we do in the name of freedom of choice?

Questions concerning Carter's support for the anti-abortion lobby and his vision of law and order also emerged in other contexts during his tenure in Toronto. Carter's outright advocacy for the picketing of the Morgentaler clinic in 1985, for example, was prompted by his own right-to-life principles as well as his repugnance at Morgentaler's flouting of the law. At the same time, Carter's subsequent urgings for peaceful demonstration were motivated by a respect for the law coupled with his own legitimate concerns for the safety of those living within the vicinity of the clinic, though the reality of the danger and the wisdom of Carter's involvement do not lie unchallenged. While not faulting the logic of Carter's response, Michael Cuneo, who spent a good bit of time on the scene, outrightly rejects Carter's calculation concerning the degree of actual danger involved in the Morgentaler picketing.[12] In the eyes of some, Carter had been manipulated by the pro-abortion troops.

Carter has often used the occasion of the annual Metropolitan Toronto Police Breakfast as a venue for a discussion of law, life and abortion. In 1987, for instance, he took the occasion to speak about matters relating to life and death, noting that police officers "have a stake in life." Carter quoted the presentation of an unnamed Jewish doctor who, when speaking to the Canadian bishops, observed that "We have lost the battle on contraception; we are in the process of losing it on abortion; we are on our way to euthanasia."[13] And in 1990, while not advocating civil disobedience, Carter defended the action of Constable David Packer, who had refused to do guard duty outside the Morgentaler clinic, an action for which he was dismissed, rehired and demoted, in turn. True to his principles, Carter encouraged those gathered for the twenty-sixth annual Metro Toronto Police Mass and Communion Breakfast to follow their consciences, as, indeed, Packer had done, even though the following of conscience ultimately led to the Constable's own resignation.[14]

No doubt the most contentious encounter involving Carter, abortion and the law centres on the Trudeau government's 1981 efforts to repatriate the Canadian Constitution, complete with a new Charter of Rights. It was a debate in which the pro-life forces mounted a concerted effort to protect in law the rights of the unborn. But Carter was unable to accept the combative tactics used by Campaign Life, and he and the right-to-life movement were on a collision course. Ultimately, that movement concluded that its Roman Catholic thrust was being undermined by Carter when the prelate publicly accepted the assurances of long-time friend and Prime Minister, Pierre Elliott Trudeau, that nothing in the proposed Charter could be used to sustain a woman's right to freedom of choice with respect to abortion.[15] The relationship between Carter and the right-to-life movement grew bitter.

As a result, when the Supreme Court of Canada struck down the country's abortion law on January 28, 1988, by using as its principal reference point the Charter of Rights and Freedoms, Carter bristled as one betrayed. The resulting strongly worded open letter addressed to Prime Minister Brian Mulroney reminded the new prime minister of the assurances Carter had previously received: "We point out that the Constitution of Canada gives to the Federal Government the power to override the Charter of Rights in appropriate circumstances. During the repatriation process and the enactment of the Charter of Rights, we were assured by the government then in power that should the Courts at any point upset the existing abortion law, the override would be put into effect."[16]

Carter argued a passionate case, insisting that "We are in a state of lawlessness." He also made it clear that no compromise was possible, since a human fetus in the womb one week, three weeks or twenty-four weeks was a human fetus. Nonetheless, true to his democratic principles (and no doubt quite aware of the practical impossibility of doing otherwise), Carter noted that it is not within the purview of the church to dictate to its flock how to cast its vote. However, he continued, Roman Catholics would be encouraged to ask their candidates where they stood on the question of the protection of human life.

In light of the internal acrimony that marked the Roman Catholic aspects of the abortion debate, Carter must have taken some comfort in the CBC's summary of the man and his record when, on the occasion of his March 17, 1990, announcement that he had handed

over the responsibilities of office to Archbishop Ambrozic, the public
network stressed in particular the Cardinal's aggressive position
against the abortion-on-demand lobby.

Carter's successor, Aloysius Ambrozic, gives the Cardinal full
marks for courage and conviction. "He never curried favour with
certain extreme Campaign Life stratagems," Ambrozic pointed out.
"Certainly the abortion issue is a very important one, but it's not the
only one. Also, the other fact is that the majority of Canadians are not
exactly on our side. I think we have to face that fact. Certainly the
legal side has to be addressed, but we are not going to solve the
problem by having them write a law only. There is so much else that
has to be done and addressed. In each individual case, in each
individual instance, I can sometimes listen to the one side and agree
with it, and then I listen to the other side and agree with it — and I
thank God I don't have to make the decisions. Ultimately, these are
practical decisions. As far as principle is concerned, there is no
question about it. But what do you do in a given situation without
compromising the principle when you live in a society which is
pluralistic?"

How does Ambrozic react to Henderson's call for an effective
boycott where no pro-life candidate can be found? "This is the kind of
thing that the single issue people would do — let's put it that way. But,
to me, this is simply an acceptance of the fact that when you have
three people who are all pro-abortionists, what do you do? Vote for
none or vote for the best? Personally, I vote for the best."

The abortion issue is a complex one, and it is bound to affect any
archbishop of Toronto in many ways. Archbishop Philip Pocock and
the United Way had come to a confrontation over the question of
funding abortions and abortion counselling, and in the end they
parted company, Pocock forming ShareLife and opting out of the
United Way. When Carter arrived on the scene, Conrad Black, a
patron of ShareLife, entered into discussions with United Way to
explore the possibility of a truce. According to Black, United Way was
willing to guarantee Carter that they would "reaffirm publicly that
they would not fund abortions and they would not fund organizations
that sought to or did if the law ultimately permitted operating abortion clinics. But they could not and would not say that they would not
give funds to organizations that gave advice that ultimately led to the
person being advised seeking an abortion."

The idea was to work out a wording acceptable to both parties and hence to provide a basis of cooperation. Black explained: "I am not one to sweep legitimate and profoundly held differences under the rug, but to the extent that you can get people of good will to cooperate, then for heaven's sake let's do that." Black understood that Carter would recommend the deal to ShareLife with his strong recommendation that it be accepted, but the advisory council of ShareLife unanimously rejected the arrangement. Black felt that Carter had not seriously let the council know that he expected approval, and therefore he felt personally compromised by the decision. As a matter of principle, he would have to withdraw as a patron of ShareLife. Black reflected on the process: Carter had to decide "whether it was more inconvenient to incur the reservations or disquietudes of more conservative elements in the Catholic community, or more inconvenient to him to incur the disappointment of friendly elements in the non-Catholic community. And he chose to do the second and avoid the first. Nothing wrong with that. But it left me in a rather odd position, so I discreetly retired as a patron of ShareLife."

Clearly, Carter is his own man: not Trudeau's, not Black's.

In his 1985 recommendation to William Ryan, English secretary to the Canadian Conference of Catholic Bishops, Carter provided a philosophical summary of his approach to the abortion issue and, indirectly, to most other issues. He argued that the bishops should yield nothing on the principle of abortion, though they "have been tarred with the stick of 'one issue' and an unwillingness to see the other side." Nonetheless, and understanding that such a move would be misinterpreted by some in the right-to-life group, he advocated understanding and compassion for women who were contemplating an abortion, urging that society provide "every possible assistance to those so burdened." To which he added: "We should present this in such a context that it becomes very clear that we would support these plans [to be supportive, helpful and sympathetic] even if the person who enters [a counselling refuge] then decides in the final analysis to have an abortion."

At the same time, Carter urged dialogue, the discarding of the "combative and confrontational poses of some of our extreme wings" and "respect for those who do not agree with us." "While we must keep up the struggle to save the lives of the unborn, we cannot continue to do it at the cost of sacrificing our respect for those who do not agree with us or even contributing to the loss of self-respect of those who fail to measure up to the standards we think are proper through a condemnatory, abrasive and unforgiving attitude."[17]

True to his word, Carter established Rosalie Hall as a way of reaching out to the hurting women of Toronto, those who were pregnant with no one to turn to, and Rosalie Hall became one recipient of the funds raised at the 1986 Cardinal's Dinner. Carter also embraced the 1990 recommendations of the Options of Life Committee to provide a social framework to assist pregnant women of Toronto who were reaching out for help.

Despite his tough-mindedness, Carter has always acted sympathetically to those in need — the socially underprivileged, the poor, the ill or the homeless.

CHAPTER THIRTEEN
End of an Era

What constitutes "need"? In attempting to answer this question Carter has been the focus of no little controversy over the years, particularly during his Toronto years. Social justice issues have involved him in colourful debates with sections of the public, the Catholic community and the episcopacy, and these issues have continually captured the national headlines.

His first major social justice clash in Toronto came over his decision in the summer of 1982 to reduce the amount of money allocated by the Archdiocese of Toronto to the Canadian Catholic Organization for Development and Peace (the CCODP). This agency was established by Canada's bishops in 1967 to provide funds and support for overseas development projects, but in Carter's estimation it had become, particularly through Québécois influence, a basically socioeconomic enterprise with a left-wing slant. He was determined to curtail its increasingly socioeconomic orientation by providing a counterbalance through support of more traditional catechetical projects. Rather than attempt a radical restructuring of the CCODP — the Quebec hold on the organization was too great — he opted to channel some of the monies raised for CCODP into his newly formed Toronto Pastoral Missionary Council. Then, following the ShareLife Campaign of 1982, Carter announced that of the nearly $5,000,000 dollars raised, $500,000 will go to the CCODP, $600,000 less than was given the previous year. In addition, he allocated $750,000 to his new Missionary Council.

Carter's action unleashed a torrent of criticism from various liberal Catholic organizations, including *Catholic New Times*, Toronto CCODP workers and campaigners and the Scarboro Foreign Mission Society. By shifting his priorities to the more transparently evangelical and less political enterprises to be sponsored by the Missionary Council, Carter was sending notice that he had little in common with liberation theology's sympathy with marxism, a sympathy all too apparent in the CCODP.

As far back as 1940 Carter had expressed the anti-Bolshevik sentiments characteristic of Pope Pius XII and the anti-Red fears endemic in North American society on the eve of the McCarthy Trials: "Communism is not a political party. That is just a front. It is a religion, a philosophy, a way of life. It is fundamentally opposed to everything decent people have ever held dear. You don't stand just to lose your car or your business. You lose your right to worship as you please, to speak as you please, to work as you please. They can't destroy your ability to think as you please, but let them come to power and they will see to it that your children will think the 'right' way, the 'party' way."[1]

The tone and style of his anti-communist statements were more in the manner of a Fulton Sheen, the urbane U.S. television bishop, than Charles Coughlin, the rabid Detroit "radio priest", but they did incline to categorical judgements, and were completely representative of official Roman thinking. In later years they became considerably more nuanced, but they remained substantially the same. In an address to the Canadian Club in London in 1977, he reminded his listeners that marxism's appeal was grounded in a dangerous confounding of true community with collectivity. "If ever there was stark opposition, Jesus and Marx are it: both are insisting on community, but one is a community of hatred, contestation, opposition and total materialism. And in Marx, remember, no solution is possible. By definition all solutions must be immediately attacked. It is the thesis, antithesis, synthesis of Hegel. And the synthesis, once reached, becomes a thesis to begin again the eternal process of conflict. And what do you think is happening in some of our labour unions if not that?"[2]

Class warfare is at the heart of any marxist critique, argued Carter, although "there is no doubt that the Hegelian-Marxist theory that tensions are necessary for growth in any society is basically true. But what is distressing is the development of the idea to a necessary and an essential pitting of one part of society against the other. This has its necessary concomitant hatred, animosity and warfare. Jesus said, 'Love thy neighbour.' Marx postulates class warfare as the necessary stage to the solution. In 1849 he wrote, 'We are ruthless; we expect no consideration from you. And when our turn comes, we shall not disguise terrorism.' "[3] Carter was convinced that marxism, whatever clone, hyphenated or derivative strain one might have in mind, was ultimately pledged to conflict and was, therefore, irreconcilable with the type of integral humanism espoused by Catholicism. We dabble with marxism at great cost.

The CCODP had so dabbled and the time had come to seek some kind of redress, some kind of balance. Carter was adamant that projects that assuage the hunger of the flesh *only* are insufficiently christian. After a visit in 1973 to the region in Peru where the Diocese of London had sent a missionary team, Carter concluded, quoting scripture, that christians are responsible for keeping before the eyes of all the saving truth that "we have not here a lasting dwelling" and that "man does not live on bread alone but on every word which proceeds from the mouth of God." This is traditional missiology with a vengeance. The missionary, for Carter, should be principally engaged in evangelization and not social work.

It was not surprising, then, given his views on marxism and the missionary apostolate, that he would try to offset the imbalance he saw in CCODP priorities. When the *Globe and Mail*'s provocative headline, "Cardinal under fire for giving less to poor"[4] highlighted the dramatic response to his curtailing of CCODP funds, Carter could easily counter with this passage from his recent Canadian Club address: "The idea that the poor cannot be happy is a fallacious one. The worst hunger is the hunger of the spirit. Those who would give the poor nothing except bread are very poor providers."[5]

For all Carter's reservations concerning policy and procedure at CCODP's head office, he was persuaded that its goals were fundamentally good and that the organization must continue to be supported by the Canadian hierarchy. But he would correct the CCODP's excesses, to the degree that he was allowed, by complementing its social justice labours with more conventional pastoring. But there was a cost to pay, and not only in fiscal terms. The CCODP debacle would draw the fire and focused attention of the woman who would become his strongest critic, the philosopher-activist nun, Mary Joe Leddy, a member of the women's religious congregation, Our Lady of Sion (Notre Dame de Sion).

In her column of October 2, 1982, in the *Toronto Star*, she probed beneath the surface of fund allocation to the undergirding principles that governed ShareLife and wondered aloud why the new Missionary Council's pastoral efforts need to be supported through a cutback to Third World development projects. It was lightly ironic, she implied, that the old maxim "charity begins at home" should be applied with a vengeance just when the people of the Third World needed it more than ever. Her investigation did not stop with her *Toronto Star* column.

A central figure in all the decisions affecting ShareLife was its Executive Director, Paul Anthony Robinson. At one time Robinson had served as President of the Toronto section of the CCODP, but in 1976, when Pocock withdrew from the United Way and established his own Catholic parallel organization, the ShareLife Trust, Robinson was named Executive Director. His record for effective lobbying and volunteer work was exemplary by any standard. ShareLife flourished under his leadership.

Then, in December 1982, the Montreal head office of the CCODP contacted the Chancellor of the Toronto Archdiocese, Bishop Leonard Wall, indicating that ShareLife was $450,000 behind in the promised 1982 disbursement of funds. Wall requested an explanation from Robinson and Robinson assured the Chancellor that the mistake was Montreal's. After further inquiries, it became clear that Montreal was not mistaken. Wall informed Carter and the Cardinal instituted a pay check. Robinson was caught virtually with his hand in the till. He resigned as executive director on December 14 after first acknowledging in a letter to Wall that he was guilty of misappropriation of ShareLife funds over a good number of years. A conservative estimate of the total misappropriation, not counting loss of interest, amounted to $593,913. Subsequently sentenced to jail for six years, Robinson admitted spending the money on 168 luxury vacations and other extravagant ventures. Carter quickly moved in to limit the publicity damage, and in a press release following Robinson's sentence, guaranteed that ShareLife would not be out of pocket because the stolen funds would be replaced by money from a reserve fund. He conceded that because of the complete confidence placed in Robinson by senior church authorities and ShareLife personnel, various deficiencies went unattended to and various internal controls had been neglected.

But Leddy, among others, was not satisfied by this explanation. Little in the way of discipline or checks and balances appeared to be in place. At the time of the theft, Carter was out of action with his stroke, and Wall was undergoing cancer treatments: they could in no way be held accountable. And yet, as editor of *Catholic New Times* and with a taste for investigative research, Leddy persisted in asking uncomfortable questions. She dug deeper and deeper and explored the financial connections of the various high-profile people who had worked with Robinson as patrons and chairmen of the ShareLife campaigns.

Coming so soon after Carter's June decision to diminish Share-Life's financial contribution to the CCODP, the Robinson scandal profoundly weakened, in liberal Catholic circles at least, the impeccable credentials of Carter the fund raiser. But in other circles, the circles that have always mattered most to him, his reputation and that of ShareLife remained untainted.

In 1981 Carter instituted the Cardinal's Dinner, an annual black-tie event which served both to highlight specific charities and to bring into full public view a corporate leadership with a conscience. He was persuaded to establish the dinner by Joseph J. Barnicke, a Prairie boy of Polish background, who has earned himself a reputation as one of Canada's wealthiest and most inventive realtors. Barnicke was a prominent Catholic from the Pocock era who sat on the board of ShareLife and the Emmanuel Convalescent Foundation, or South-down (a rehabilitation centre for dysfunctional clergy). After hearing of the fund-raising success of the annual Bishop's Dinner held in the Archdiocese of Detroit, Barnicke decided that the time was ripe to mount a similiar event in increasingly Catholic Toronto. Carter, Barnicke reasoned, was the right man to bring it off. Carter agreed.

It was a tame social justice statement, too tame for the liberals. Carter's chairpersons over the years included only the socially prominent and wealthy. Besides Barnicke, they included Douglas G. Bassett, Bill Davis, John Craig Eaton, Paul Higgins (President of Mother Parker's Foods), William D. Mulholland (Chief Executive Officer of the Bank of Montreal), Hal Jackman and the vivacious Hilary Weston (Vice-Chairman of Holt Renfrew and founder of the Ireland Fund of Canada). They were all his friends. He valued them and they valued him. There wasn't a rag picker among them.

Long before he arrived in Toronto, Carter had chosen to move among the elite of society. He felt comfortable in their presence and they genuinely liked his style, wit and intelligence. He would serve the church from above, not from below. He would hear the cry of the destitute but he would answer that cry by helping to shape the moral sensibilities of the movers and shakers. It was the politics of a different era and he practised it with a master hand. He kept the tradition alive during his administration, but it was the man and not the office that determined the style and made it pay. But the price could be very high.

The social justice teaching of the Roman Catholic Church dates back to the publication of Pope Leo XIII's *Rerum novarum* in 1891. That encyclical was a serious response to the problems of acute industrialization and *laissez-faire* capitalism in the Europe of the declining years of the nineteenth century. Since Leo, several popes have addressed socioeconomic problems from the vantage point of an evolving Catholic social doctrine, and following the Second Vatican Council and the two critical and prophetic sessions of the Latin American Episcopal Conferences (CELAM) in Medellín, Colombia (1968), and in Puebla, Mexico (1979), the church's social voice has become increasingly assertive. The Canadian bishops have been in the vanguard in developing a credible and practical social critique grounded on the gospel and papal teachings. They have, most importantly, been profoundly respectful of the Canadian reality.

As President of the CCCB from 1975 to 1977 and as Vice-President for the two years before that, Carter had a central role to play during the development of the Canadian episcopate's social justice teaching. In 1976 the bishops collaborated on an ecumenically produced document entitled "Justice Demands Action". This brief was subsequently presented by several church leaders, including Carter, to Pierre Trudeau and some select members of his cabinet: Judd Buchanan, Alistair Gillespie, Marc Lalonde, Allan MacEachen, Bryce Mackasey, John Munro and Mitchell Sharp. It proved to be a highly revealing encounter, in no small part because of what the occasion revealed of Carter's understanding of the issues under discussion.

Dr. Tony Clarke, a social ethicist and staff member of the Social Affairs Office of the CCCB, recalls the easy kibitzing that Trudeau and Carter engaged in at the meeting when Trudeau joked with his fellow cabinet ministers: "Well, which one is your bishop? Mine's Carter." But he also recalls Carter's illuminating admission in front of the whole cabinet: "'Well, I believe that the poor will always be with us. This is what's in Scripture and our concern is simply to take care of the poor.' What became clear is that Carter subscribed to the 'charity model' as opposed to the 'transformation model' advocated by contemporary Catholic ethicists and liberation theologians." Collision was inevitable. With one school of thinking supporting radical changes in our social structures to effect justice, and the other school arguing that we must give of our "superflua" and provide leadership in charity, the Social Affairs Office of the CCCB became the terrain on which this ideological clash would take place.

In 1980 the CCCB, under the authority of its Administrative Board (now called the Permanent Council), published "Unemployment: The Human Costs", in which it stated that "unemployment is not simply a political or economic or social problem. It is a profoundly moral and spiritual problem in our times."[6] Fair enough. At the level of general principle, no bishop would argue with this sentiment. It was when the document became specific, suggesting alternative industrial strategies and various guidelines for action, that Carter became anxious. No longer president but an *ex officio* member of the Permanent Council, Carter had his oar in the water early in the proceedings. He protested vigorously against the document in a nine-page critique that he submitted to then-president, Archbishop Gilles Ouellet of Rimouski. He was the only bishop to protest. But this "in-house tug-of-war," as Tony Clarke calls it, was merely a prologue to the battle looming on the horizon.

The years 1981 and 1982 were bleak years in Canada, years of mounting unemployment, skyrocketing inflation, wage restraint and desperately high interest rates. The Social Affairs Commission of the CCCB knew that it had to do something. Social Affairs Officer Tony Clarke recounts that "it was becoming very evident that there was no consistent voice in the community speaking out against the economic injustices affecting so many people. Ever since the November 1981 Parliament Hill demonstration that garnered 100,000 people, the largest ever in the history of Canada, to protest against high interest rates, there was a dramatic downside and no one was speaking, no one was addressing the pain of unemployment. Trudeau had gone on television in October of 1982 to give his three sermonettes, advising us that we were moving into a tough new world of international competition and employing a 'survival of the fittest' kind of language. The Trudeau prognosis revolutionised us. The government's analysis was not ours. We had John Paul's *Laborem exercens* with its ethical framework and priority-of-labour principle to support our social and economic analyses. In addition, just after the Trudeau TV commentaries, we had our plenary Assembly of the CCCB, and the corridor discussions amongst the bishops underscored the national despair and sense of crisis. We prepared something for the Social Affairs Commission to present to the Plenary Assembly by way of an open letter to Prime Minister Trudeau, but the President of the Conference, Archbishop Henri Légaré of Grouard-McLennan, Alberta, said no."

The executive of the Social Affairs Commission — the bishops, in other words — decided that they would take the Commission's final draft — it had gone through seven or eight of them — and move on its authority and that of the President to publish a statement bypassing the Administrative Board. They had attempted, vainly, to have it on the agenda of the Plenary Assembly and it appeared that Légaré was waffling, reluctant to insert a potentially divisive social justice statement before the Assembly of Bishops, yet conscious of the need for leadership in these economically depressed times. The chairman of the Social Affairs Commission was the irrepressible leftist Bishop of Victoria, B.C., Remi De Roo.

De Roo had no qualms about harassing the cautious Légaré: "I waited until early December and then I went after him again. I said to him, 'Hey! This document is important, very important to the nation, and you have been sitting on it. What are you going to do?' Even at that time he was seriously reluctant to bring our statement out; he was busy preparing his own Christmas Message and he had the option of electing to publish an economic statement being prepared by someone at head office. I went after him. I told him that we have simply got to do something, especially now with Trudeau's fireside chats. We cannot remain silent. Eventually he relented."

On December 30, 1982, "The National", the CBC's news broadcast, announced that "the Bishops of Canada's Roman Catholic Church have decided to speak out on the economy." On New Year's Eve, the *Toronto Star* scooped the nation with the complete publication — largely through the eager intervention of Tom Harpur — of the Social Affairs Commission's "Ethical Reflections on the Economic Crisis." Carter was dumbfounded. De Roo was ecstatic. The bishops became instant celebrities.

The document follows the pattern of the CCCB's social justice statements in that it argues its case at the level of general principle and avoids explicit endorsement of any political strategy, thereby guaranteeing its treasured non-partisanship. But a careful reading of "Ethical Reflections" indicates that the suggested "alternative ways of looking at our industrial future and organizing our economy" bear a

striking similarity to positions advocated by Canada's social demo-
crats, the New Democratic Party. Bishops not inclined to a socialist
critique of a Liberal government with its mixed economy baulked at
the new boldness of their Social Affairs Commission when the writers
asked rhetorically, "What would it mean to develop an alternative
economic model that would place emphasis on: socially useful forms
of production; labour-intensive industries; the use of appropriate
forms of technology; self-reliant models of economic development;
community ownership and control of industries; new forms of worker
management and ownership; and greater use of the renewable energy
resources in industrial production? As a country, we have the resources, the capital, the technology and, above all else, the aspirations
and skills of working men and women required to build an alternative
economic future. Yet the people of this country have seldom been
challenged to envision and develop alternatives to the dominant
economic model that governs our society."[7]

Carter was infuriated, not only by the partisan tone of the statement, but by what he perceived as the patently undemocratic manner
of its publication. He said so and in a manner which startled the
nation and pleased his friend the Prime Minister, Pierre Elliott
Trudeau. He called a press conference on New Year's Eve and issued
the following statement: "It is my duty to point out that the Bishops of
Canada have not made a statement on economic policy as reported in
the media. This statement emanates from the Social Action Office of
the Conference and there was no consultation of the collectivity of the
Bishops. Speaking personally I must state that I saw the text of the
declaration only yesterday, December 30, 1982. I have serious reservations concerning some of the material and attitudes contained
therein while not contesting the right of the office to express its
opinion." As Trudeau remarked, "The fox is now among the
chickens."

While many in the national media were centring their attention on
Bishops Remi De Roo, Adolphe Proulx (Hull) and John O'Mara
(Thunder Bay) or reacting to the Carter press release with a flurry of
far-from-impartial editorials, Carter pressed ahead, behind the
scenes, seeking clarification and remonstrating with a besieged
Légaré. He wrote to the President of the CCCB on January 10, clearly
irritated, forthright, but respectful of episcopal decorum. He noted
that his "first inkling of a Statement on Economic Affairs was while I
was watching the National newscast at 10 P.M. December 30th. . . .

Since I am a Canadian bishop and since I have never heard of such a decision nor participated in such a stand, I was mystified. Had I overlooked a consultation or a series of them? Had a vote been taken at the Plenary which did not appear in the minutes? I telephoned a few bishops that night and the next morning and received the same reply from all, 'No, there had not been any general consultation.' Yet the thrust of the newscast was clearly to implicate all Canadian Bishops. We were in full flood of attribution without consultation, responsibility without participation, conclusion without dialogue."[8]

He made his point in the letter that his reservations, at the moment, were procedural. He said that he would gladly debate his substantive concerns at a later time, though he never in fact did so. Disturbed by what he saw as a pack of zealots riding roughshod over established procedure, he left his most pointed criticism to the end when he attacked the centralizing trends of the CCCB's middle management. He drew on his council experience to drive home the point with added force and authority: "Some of us, along with 2,000 of the 2,500 bishops present, carried forward a lively, fruitful and sometimes contested project to oppose exaggerated centralization in the Church. We objected to decisions and positions being taken on matters concerning us all by a small group of persons who then handed down their dicta for our digestion. We haven't entirely succeeded in Rome and we still, all too often, receive position papers and declarations when it would be better if we were permitted some input in the first instance. Must we now envisage an Ottawa Curia that does not consult us? Everything said and done I think I prefer the Roman. There is more chance of worldwide expertise and a balanced view. But why should we have to choose? Can't we truly believe in dialogue, in co-responsibility, in sharing? In a matter like economics, of all subjects, don't our people get to say anything *before* the bishops speak out? Or are we so decided on our opinions and our course that we are blocking our ears?"

Carter ended his letter with a dramatic flourish, likening his unpopular stand, made in conscience and good faith, with the redoubtable Martin Luther's concluding peroration at the Diet of Worms: "I am sorry if my position has disturbed anyone but as has already been said in ecclesial history, 'I can do no other.' "

It was the kind of extravagant analogy that would appeal to the history-loving Conrad Black.

Légaré stood firm. He acknowledged Carter's longstanding apprehension over the politics of composition concerning CCCB documents and the nature of their authority, particularly those statements that emanate from one of the episcopal commissions. But he insisted that the Code of Procedure as approved by the Executive Committee of the CCCB in 1976 had not been violated in the instance of "Ethical Reflections". He also insisted that all decisions regarding the substance and publication of the document were taken by elected or appointed members of the Conference itself. There was no Ottawa Curia.

Légaré, in an adroit move, quoted from a letter he had just written Alex Carter, in which he demonstrated the continuity of argument and style of the "Ethical Reflections" document with previous CCCB statements. "Ethical Reflections" was not essentially new, he said. Had there been the extensive consultation Carter was demanding, how is it possible that the episcopate would have dissociated itself from a position it had been consistently arguing since its 1977 document, "A Society to be Transformed?" It would not have been possible without a dramatic reversal of position.

But Carter disagreed. He wrote to Légaré arguing that "even a superficial examination coupled with a re-reading of the previous statements by the Conference leads one to the conclusion that there are indeed many points of economics which we have never addressed *ex professo* on any previous occasion. I refer specifically and generically to the question of wage restraints; to the taxation of capital investment; to the preference of certain kinds of industry over others, etc., etc. . . . The evangelical principles were certainly invoked on previous occasions and faultlessly repeated here. But the economic stance was assuredly novel."

Légaré did not concede to Carter his argument that "Ethical Reflections" offered something substantially new. To do so would mean that the Executive of the CCCB had been derelict in its duty, failing dismally in its mandate to consult widely and at length with all the bishops concerning official CCCB policy. But he did grant to Carter the point that the document could have been more explicit in distinguishing between offical CCCB policy and various suggestions and questions advanced for public discussion. Carter was still not satisfied, but he shifted ground to concentrate on the signal role played by De Roo and Proulx regarding the time and place of issuance. He also made clear, in his last letter to Légaré on the subject, his conviction that "the failure in the collegial spirit which I perceive, independently of any technical observances, will leave bitterness for many of us."

Carter received a strong measure of criticism from several quarters for his open dispute with the Social Affairs Commission, from *Globe and Mail* columnist Orland French to the Senate of Priests of the Diocese of Antigonish, and he weathered it all, steadfast of purpose. He has always liked a good fight; it was the Irish in him, his mother would have said. He was also persuaded, he said in a letter to his old friend Joseph MacNeil, Archbishop of Edmonton, that he could not "accept that we shook off the yoke of an overly centralized bureaucracy in Rome to create a similar one in Ottawa. I remain of the opinion that after our stand, it will not likely occur again in the near future."9

Carter's response to "Ethical Reflections" was not confined to a behind-the-scenes correspondence with Canada's bishops. Aware that the public perception of his reaction to "Ethical Reflections" consisted largely of a press release clarifying the authority of the statement with all the attendant negative vibrations, he decided, ever conscious of the publicity factor, that he now needed a positive approach to offset the negative. He found his opportunity to do so in the person of a Canadian Jesuit with a Harvard doctorate in economics, the English-language General Secretary for the CCCB, William Ryan.

A one-time Director of the Social Action Department of the Canadian Catholic Conference, Ryan provided a reasoned analysis of the weaknesses, particularly in terms of its international perspective, of "Ethical Reflections" in an article for the *Globe and Mail*. Carter read it, saw his chance and grabbed it. Ryan had sterling liberal credentials, and he had received some funding in the past from both Emmett and Alex when he was launching his Washington-based, socially progressive Center for Concern some fifteen years earlier. He was the ideal man to contact. As Dr. Tony Clarke tells it, "Cardinal Carter was not recovering very well from the media bashing he took over his opposition to 'Ethical Reflections', and he needed something to get him off the hook. Ryan hit on the idea of a panel or commission that could provide a serious follow-up to "Ethical Reflections", holding hearings and issuing a report. Carter bought the idea."

Ryan met with Carter, Leonard Wall and a few other officials to decide how to conduct the public hearing and whom to appoint to sit on the panel. Ryan recounts that "there was no fear in Carter, he had no problem with the panel's being independent, and he was keen on the panel conducting its hearings away from the chancery office, employing its own secretariat and preserving in every visible way its utter impartiality. He never interfered in the proceedings, never attempted to compromise the panel, nor applied any pressure on the panel members. He simply wanted to establish the fact that he was not being small-minded or petty in his criticism of "Ethical Reflections", and that he could offer something more constructive than a terse press release dissociating himself from the position of the Social Affairs Commission."

The panel's composition was representative of the wide spectrum of political and economic opinion and religious persuasion that characterizes Toronto. It consisted of Ryan (Vice-Chairman); Judge Lucien Beaulieu, a senior judge of the Provincial Court (Family Division); Dr. Reva Gerstein, psychologist, educator and policy advisor; John Fraser, National Editor of the *Globe and Mail*; and Dr. George Ignatieff, diplomat, scholar and Chancellor of the University of Toronto (Chairman). They held their hearings for three full days in June 1983 and reviewed over one hundred written submissions, with over half making representation at the hearings. A summary of the written submissions and of the hearings was subsequently published under the title *Canada's Unemployed: The Crisis of Our Times*.

But the criticism continued. Mary Jo Leddy observed that "the panel was a waste of time and money. The hearings were conducted at the plush Ramada Renaissance Hotel miles from the city core, which you could only get to by car. The locale said everything. Why, for instance, could the hearings not be conducted in parish halls, accessible to everyone?" Still, Carter had made his contribution in his way, bearing his stamp, and he felt that he had acquitted himself well. After all, the decision as to where to hold the hearings, like so many other initiatives, was exclusively a panel decision.

He made his mark in other ways as well. Convinced that the procedures were not followed adequately at the time of "Ethical Reflections", Carter lobbied for change, and according to Clarke, "a new set of codes and procedures, with stringent guidelines, was put in place to control us. For example, all statements now had to go to the bishops in advance of being made public and in a specified timeframe. In addition, there . . . now must be consultation with Toronto, Montreal, Quebec City, and one other diocese before any of the drafts could proceed apace."

But the drama of 1983 was replayed in 1985 with many of the same actors, including the principals, Emmett Carter and Remi De Roo. On the Feast of St. Joseph the Worker, May 1, 1985, the Social Affairs Commission under the chairmanship of De Roo issued a statement entitled "Defending Workers' Rights — A New Frontier". Because of one reference to the T. Eaton Company, at the time involved in a labour relations dispute, the document was dubbed the "Eaton's Statement", and almost immediately, precisely because of the Eaton reference, Carter wrote to De Roo reminding him that bishops "are not trained to be economists, nor are we trained in the contests of the marketplace. As a member of the National Economic Conference held recently in Ottawa I was privileged to observe the tendencies towards intransigence and closed minds which characterize both the majority of managers and business leaders and also the majority of union leaders. Neither seems very willing to listen to the other and any approach which we make to this situation should be guided by a very obvious even-handedness. In a word we should make very sure that we are getting both sides of the question before we come out with individual and particular judgments."[10]

Carter was annoyed by the singling out of Eaton's for special mention by the commission, and he was concerned that once again the Social Affairs group had compromised its moral neutrality by taking one side against another. Carter contacted the Eaton people directly to get their version of the dispute, and provided their documentation for De Roo's enlightenment, noting that Eaton's labour relations record was not as suggested in the Social Affairs May 1st statement. He faulted the commission for failing to do what he so easily did: get both sides of the story. In Carter's mind, the commission had made a "preferential option for the unions" and had thereby jettisoned its moral right to mediate. He scolded De Roo for his misplaced zeal, and for not appreciating the simple truth that "taking up a strong position almost necessarily and inevitably involves exaggerations and the slanting of views. Certainly the truth seldom lies in the extremes in which it is presented. For instance, no one in his right mind would pretend that in the past few decades no single labour union has been guilty of excess. In the human condition a totally unbiased neutrality is impossible. This is true. But when any group is either mandated or sets itself up as a judge, it must make every effort to be as neutral as possible. . . . My statement was and is that the Commission made a judgement, found certain parties guilty and yet never heard the defence. . . . A single phone call to the proprietors of the T. Eaton Company would have brought you the information which would have anchored your statement. This omission remains to me incomprehensible."

De Roo attempted to answer Carter's queries by providing documentation of his own and by reminding the Cardinal that there are certain instances when "unbiased neutrality is impossible." This Carter could not accept. Yet it would be hard to prove Carter's own neutrality in the matter, given his personal friendship with John Craig Eaton and his limited sympathy for unions.

A year after the "Eaton's Statement", De Roo lost his position as Chairman of the Social Affairs Commission, at which point Conrad Black took up the cudgels to beat the leftist De Roo. Carter was now a mere spectator of a rhetorical donnybrook of savage and entertaining dimensions.

Black, a director of the T. Eaton Company and a highly articulate public advocate of free-market economics, launched one of his verbal broadsides against the social justice positions of the Canadian episcopal left. It *is* surprising that he should have done it first in the left-leaning Jesuit journal, *Compass*, but it is wholly predictable that he should have followed the *Compass* piece with another one in the *Globe and Mail*'s *Report on Business Magazine*. In his column piece, "Unholy Economics", Black castigates the bishops for their hopeless naivete in relying on one specific ideological critique of the socioeconomic order as if it were holy writ. He says he has little stomach for the socialist cliches of Bishop De Roo, and is downright contemptuous of the episcopate's suicidal thrust to embrace the secular at the expense of the transcendental. "With passing years, the bishops have become more trendy, biased, misleading and desperate for attention. Of course, the church has the right, and often the obligation, to speak out on secular issues that have moral implications. I am not so convinced that the local successors of the Apostles have an unarguable right to do violence to the credibility of their venerable institution by identifying it with a sophomoric mishmash of false prophecies, factual errors, reflexive prejudices and naive velleities.

Their reckless guilt-mongering has given new meaning to Malcolm Muggeridge's description of the 'great liberal death-wish.'"[11]

Reserving the full impact of his vitriolic sting for the last paragraph, Black applauds the "sacking" of De Roo and speculates that a modicum of reason may again resurface in episcopal ranks. "In 1971, the bishops despised 'the official support, especially financial, given to the Church by bourgeois society.' The sacking of the egregious Bishop De Roo from the chairmanship of the Social Action Commission in 1986 raises the hope that the episcopate has thought better of forsaking the ancient sources of sincere adherence, while aligning the Canadian Catholic Church with the indifferent, the skeptical and the contemptuous attitudes that many of [their social justice] documents unwittingly incite."

De Roo struck back immediately and in Black's backyard. In Toronto to receive an honorary degree conferred by Ryerson Polytechnical Institute in the same month that Black's column on the bishops appeared in *Report on Business Magazine*, De Roo denounced in his convocation address Black's political and economic thinking as neither christian nor "authentically human." De Roo admonished the corporate elite for its survival-of-the-fittest capitalism and its failure to put people before profits. Black was never far from his thoughts. De Roo's address occasioned a lead editorial in the *Toronto Star*, which charged both men with the facile and dangerous use of "stark, simplistic images". It went further to note that in place of the strategy "to paint the morality of the marketplace in starkly contrasting shades of Black and De Roo, these gentlemen would do well to recognize that the canvas can be improved with various shades of gray."[12]

Within three days of this editorial Black had a letter to the editor published rebuking the editorialist for misrepresenting his socioeconomic position. He proceeded then, no doubt smarting from De Roo's Ryerson volley, to strike back at Vancouver Island's "Red Bishop". He wrote: "I have criticized a number of absurd, reckless and mendacious statements of his and of an unrepresentative group of his Episcopal brothers. I appear to have struck a sensitive point, and The Star should not be gulled by Bishop De Roo's hollow shrieks of indignation into believing that I hold the views that he unjustly imputes to me. . . . Whenever Bishop De Roo is called to account for his more fatuous and inflammatory remarks, he skulks back to the recitation of platitudinous red herrings. Most bishops or occupants of comparable positions of authority and leadership accept the obligation to speak responsibly and sensibly. The fact that Bishop De Roo has frequently shirked his responsibility and behaved like a publicity-crazed mountebank is assumedly one of the reasons why the Canadian Council [read Conference] of Catholic Bishops did not re-elect him to head its Social Action [read Affairs] Commission."[13]

Emmett would agree entirely, although he would never debate with a brother bishop in public to the extent that he would threaten collegial unity, nor would he employ the kind of vituperative prose that Black relishes. He held his peace. But De Roo's friend Gregory Baum did not, and when the opportunity presented itself to respond to Black's attack in a public venue, he did so — minus the vituperation. In his CBC Massey Lectures, "Compassion and Solidarity: The Church for Others", which were first aired in November 1987, Baum accused Black of distorting the social justice teaching of the Canadian bishops and of rejecting the spirit of dialogue in favour of invectives. "What Mr. Conrad Black completely overlooks is that the identification with the poor is not an invention of the Canadian Catholic bishops but represents an international movement in the Catholic Church and in the other Christian churches."[14]

As much as he may have found himself in agreement with his friend Black, and as much as he may have disliked the sociological meanderings of the dissident Baum, Carter was unwilling to appear in any way critical of the socially progressive thinking of the man who made him Cardinal, Pope John Paul II. And both Baum and the Social Affairs people were adept at quoting the Pontiff in support of their "pastoral methodology" and pro-labour thinking. Carter kept his distance on this point, happy to comply with papal teaching as long as it stayed at the level of general, *a priori* principles.

But when it came to practical and administrative advice, John Paul himself did not hesitate to draw on Carter's financial expertise, and Carter was only too willing to offer it. On the matter of annual financial statements, fiscal accountability and the sorry state of Vatican investments, Carter was vigorously blunt. Appointed to the powerful Council of Cardinals for Study of Organizational and Economic Problems of the Holy See, and following the disastrous collapse of the Banco Ambrosiano in 1982 and the loss of millions, coupled with an incalculable loss of face for the Vatican, Carter urged immediate and drastic reforms. He deplored the Roman obsession with secrecy and insisted that unless they broke out of that centuries-old style of thinking they could not raise the necessary funds from those prosperous countries accustomed to open books and open budgets. Along with like-minded cardinals, including Philadelphia's Krol and New York's O'Connor, he eventually succeeded. In a news item published in *The Tablet* following a fall 1989 meeting of the Council of Cardinals, Carter announced "that for the first time the figures were being independently audited and a certified financial report would be sent to every diocese in the Church. His council, he said, had fought 'quite a battle' with Vatican officials over that: 'Every year we were pounding on at the same thing, and finally we got it done.' "15

Carter's Toronto Chancellor, Leonard Wall, himself a financial wizard, admits, "He can read a financial statement faster than I can." No small prize for the son of a Montreal unionist.

However, Carter's financial prowess and his demonstrated ability to negotiate comfortably with the brokers and dealers of the temporal world made him the target, especially during the Toronto years, of severe criticism from those who felt that a bishop is a pastor first and foremost. Carter did not deny that a bishop is a pastor, nor did he dispute the view that a bishop's primary job is to be among his people, consoling, sanctifying, leading. But, he argued, those who govern, and those in positions of power and wealth, are just as likely to need spiritual comfort as the disadvantaged, the *petite bourgeoisie*, the intellectuals and artists, and others. In short, the Conrad Blacks and Hilary Westons of our society are as entitled to the benefits of religion as the poor and powerless. Carter's way was never with the rag pickers; he was not an enthusiast of liberation theology, political theology or any other kind of theology that he understood to be potentially divisive of the believing community. His realm was the spiritual realm and in that he was supreme. It was one thing for the secular press to criticize the Canadian bishops on certain policy proposals that directly affected the socioeconomic order, for that was fair game — If you can't take the heat stay out of the kitchen — but it was quite another thing for the media to attack the church on matters of doctrine and internal governance, particularly when the media dispensed with the *sine qua non* of its credibility: objectivity.

Following the widely reported allegations of clerical sexual abuse and the hearings and sentencings that took place from 1988 to 1990, the Canadian episcopate found itself on the defensive in a way it had not been since the *Humanae vitae* affair of 1968. Their position was only made more difficult after the often lurid judicial and ecclesiastical investigations of similar allegations involving the Irish Christian Brothers and their Mount Cashel Orphanage in Newfoundland. Fully aware of the seriousness of sexual abuse by priests, of the need for justice for the accused and, for the first time, of a full recognition of the primary rights and needs of the victim by the institutional church, Carter moved quickly to establish interim procedures to guarantee justice for the aggrieved and the accused. Appalled by the enormity of the revelations and keenly aware of the damage these revelations have caused the church, Carter was quick to initiate various canonical measures of correction or containment. But, as he feared, the media would have its way, and the church was particularly vulnerable on this issue.

During what would be his last Cardinal's Dinner as the Archbishop of Toronto, Carter struck a melancholy, spirited, but rather incoherent note when he covered leadership, hierarchical competence and media persecution in one sour diatribe. He excoriated the media for failing to appreciate the demands of leadership and for paying servile attention to that most ephemeral of idols — popularity. "The media, particularly the CBC, spearheaded by 'The Journal', have been having a field day with scandals in the Church. I have commented in other ways on the scandals themselves. But I am equally distressed by the ravenous hunger to exploit them in order to denigrate the leadership in the Church. Recently 'The Journal' held a panel of several people, one a priest who had deserted his life commitment twenty years ago, another a woman who obviously had an axe to grind, and so on. No one person was invited who was prepared to point out some obvious facts in defense. A kangaroo court and not the first on the CBC. Among other things, the Church was described on the programme as a 'Gulag'. In twenty-seven years as a bishop in the Church, I have never observed repressive measures. There are consultative organisms in every step of our governance, much more than in civil government. True, the Church is not a democracy in the sense that our leaders are elected by popular vote. They are chosen by the pope after a wide consultation which includes lay people. And all in all, with due humility, when I look at the bishops and compare them to the House of Commons, I don't feel any inferiority."[16]

He made his point to a captive and respectful audience and all applauded sympathetically, including the politicians present, but the defensive posture lacked the elan and sense of fairplay that had characterized the early Carter. He was tired that night in the late fall of 1989, tired of the attacks or perceived attacks over episcopal negligence regarding clergy accused of sexual abuse, a negligence that entailed legal, fiscal and moral culpability. He was tired because he knew that he was largely powerless to arrest the damage being inflicted upon the church, tired because he knew that he and his brother bishops were guilty of at least a negligence born of ignorance and tired because he had been recently fighting another battle over an unfair portrait of his heir apparent.

When Judy Steed, a features writer for the *Toronto Star*, wrote a largely unsympathetic treatment of Aloysius Ambrozic ("A Cardinal for Conservatives", *Saturday Star Magazine*, July 29, 1989), Carter felt obliged to defend the media-shy Ambrozic with a letter to the editor: "Your article is ungracious because you go out of your way to portray the archbishop in an unfavourable light. The opening words are 'fear and loathing', which you postulate as a general and dominating note in the Archdiocese of Toronto. Anyone close to the scene could have told Steed this is arrant nonsense, but one senses that a more moderate and more accurate summation would not have fit into the sensationalism she was evidently seeking. There will always be a few people who won't like any bishop of any diocese. But 'fear and loathing' of Aloysius Ambrozic in Toronto? Come off it, Steed."[17]

Carter went on to rebuke Steed for prejudging Ambrozic, given that Ambrozic has yet to have "his hands on the wheel" of the ship. Carter was still captain, and it was the job of the captain to defend his mates, although in his own career Carter had known otherwise: "Without bitterness looking back on my own life I have always been rather intrigued by the fact that so few people ever came to my defense when I got a bum rap. And I got quite a few. It is interesting to speculate as to the reason — I mean for the absence of defenders."[18] But Ambrozic was not lacking for a defender. He had one of the best in Carter.

Very much a man of the church, Carter felt compelled to rally around his coadjutor archbishop for several reasons. First of all, he was eager to put to rest the view, and a prevalent one at that, that he had reluctantly acceded to Rome's imposition of Ambrozic. It was at Carter's request that a coadjutor was appointed in the first place, and whether Ambrozic was Carter's first choice or not, he willingly complied with the Holy See's appointment. The notion that he was being gradually usurped, that he had lost Rome's confidence to some degree and that with the nomination of Ambrozic a more loyal son of Rome would be securely ensconced in Canada's premier English See, was repellent to him. The Steed piece gave him an opportunity to defend his successor in full public view. But he was also bothered by the unprovoked nature of the attack, for he clearly saw it as an attack. Relying, in his estimation, on almost exclusively disaffected Catholic sources, like teacher and social activist Ted Schmidt of *Catholic New Times*, and without any primary data (Ambrozic had declined an interview), Carter could see no reason for the piece at all. Unschooled in ecclesiastical politics and theology, Steed, the biographer of New Democratic Party leader Ed Broadbent, was most likely not inclined to sympathize with the anti-socialist, Slovenia-born, scholar bishop of Toronto. She may well have used the piece on Ambrozic to strike out at the increasingly right-wing directions of the diocese and the universal church.

Carter thought Ambrozic was getting a "bum rap" too. He knew that his coadjutor was not popular in several circles in the Toronto church, that his reputation as more Roman than Rome preceded him, that he had little time for polemics and for the dangerous intermingling of politics with religion and that he lacked the *savoir-faire* of the professional prelate. But his strengths were considerable, and Carter knew them well. Carter preached the homily at the consecration mass when Ambrozic became an auxiliary bishop for Toronto, he consulted with him over the vexatious issues of women and ministry, he knew and valued his multilinguistic accomplishments and sound biblical scholarship and he knew him to be Rome's man. Ambrozic was inducted as Coadjutor Archbishop on June 25, 1986. Carter preached at the induction and noted "that in the eight years that I have known him as my senior Auxiliary Bishop and Vicar General, I've learned to respect his qualities of mind and heart to the highest degree. A scripture scholar and educationist, a linguist and a man of deep pastoral sense. What has impressed me most has been his dedication to the Church, to orthodoxy and to loyalty in its best and broadest sense. He's never hesitated to express his opinions and his opinions have always been guided by the common good."[19]

Like Rome, Carter prizes loyalty and obedience. Whatever his personal preferences or misgivings, Rome gave him Ambrozic. Ambrozic would be welcomed and he would be defended.

But if there was one "bum rap" that Carter found singularly distressing, it was the accusation occasionally levelled at him that he was prone to a mild, socially acceptable but utterly distasteful form of anti-Semitic humour. Many of his Jewish friends, including the former mayor of Toronto Phil Givens, repudiate the accusation. He is no more anti-Semitic than he is anti-Irish. Still, thanks mostly to the press who have covered the various dinner speeches that have provided the occasion for the accusation, the label sticks. A careful examination of Carter's interfaith record, especially as it concerns Catholic-Jewish relations, reveals that Carter is no ecclesiastical Archie Bunker.

A "Sabbath Gentile" as a child, he lit the candles of the Orthodox Jews on the Sabbath (as they were forbidden to engage in such labour) and through such an activity he breached the bounds of his narrow English-Catholic ghetto in French Montreal. It was the first of many illuminating encounters with Jews. As an educator, canon and bishop, he had frequent opportunities to meet and collaborate with Jews — fired as he was by the emancipating and revolutionary Vatican Council Decree on Non-Christian Religions (*Nostra aetate*), as well as by his personal relations with Jews in Montreal, London and Winnipeg, the latter being the home of his sister Mae's personal physician, a Manitoban Jew of deep sensitivity.

But his public addresses and initiatives in Toronto defined more clearly his personal convictions regarding the Jewish community and the Roman faith. He began most auspiciously with his Lenten Pastoral of 1979, a "milestone Lenten message which demanded an honest and proper interpretation of the Easter message."[20] Written with the assistance of Toronto theologian Father Dan Donovan, the pastoral letter addresses with commendable bluntness the christian roots of anti-Semitism, especially in the wake of the Holocaust, and exhorts Catholics that they must spurn the deadly allure of stereotypes and always remember that the "Jews are still the people of [God's] covenant."[21]

Dr. Jordan Pearlson, Senior Rabbi of Temple Sinai Congregation in Toronto and the Canadian representative of the International Jewish Committee for Interreligious Consultation, has been an admirer of the Cardinal since Carter's arrival in Toronto. Long a member of the interfaith luncheon group founded in Toronto during the Pocock years by Anglican priest and parliamentarian Roland de Corneille and Catholic layman and college principal William Dunphy, Pearlson values the great candour and intelligence Carter has brought to these informal but top-level discussions. In his view, Carter is not a two-dimensional man, not given to a "preference of political theatre over *realpolitik*. In his Lenten message of 1979, in his behind-the-scenes support for Israel, in his willingness to sit down with rabbis, other clergy and scholars from different faiths on a regular basis, unlike any other cardinal in the world, in these things and in others we see the true measure of Emmett Carter."

Carter has also strenuously underscored the Catholic roots in Judaism. In a talk given in Temple Emmanu-El in Toronto he informed the congregation of their common heritage: "I am probably more familiar with Isaiah and Jeremiah than many of you here present. Our liturgy and even our dress has frequently been derived from Jewish tradition. You may have noticed that I am wearing a yamulka. We don't call it that but that's where it comes from. The mitre which we wear on ceremonial occasions in the liturgy is a direct descendant from the head dress of the high priests of the Temple in Jerusalem. We should cherish our similarities and recognize the unity of the origins of our religions."[22] He was not reluctant to address the differences or, indeed, the flashpoints of contemporary disagreement between Judaism and Catholicism, such as the nonrecognition of the state of Israel by the Vatican and the protracted debate over the presence of a Carmelite convent on the grounds of Auschwitz, which had been simmering for several years.

On the matter of the Carmelites at Auschwitz, Carter chose a path that met with public criticism from Ian J. Kagedan, the Director of Government Relations for B'nai Brith Canada, who observed in the *Globe and Mail* that when Carter was approached to support the international agreement reached by cardinal-representatives and delegates from international Jewry over the removal of the convent from its present Auschwitz site, Carter demurred, preferring a "made-in-Poland solution." Eventually, the Vatican did intervene and the principal Polish prelates involved, Jozef Glemp of Warsaw and Franciszek Macharski of Krakow, got their marching orders from high command. In the process, the principle of collegiality suffered, that principle which had long been dear to Carter's heart. As he told a no doubt surprised congregation at an interfaith event at Holy Blossom Temple, "the idea that the Church is a monolithic structure and that nothing can be done unless the Pope does it is the one which some of us have combatted for many years."[23]

Carter's stance ably illustrated the fiercely independent streak that runs through this perfect company man. Carter knows when to obey, when to bend and when to stand firm. He is not one to pander to popular opinion, though the blows and barbs he receives at the hands of the media and disagreeing Catholics affect him more than his Irish nature will allow him to admit. The fight is in him still.

But he has wearied; age is taking its toll. His energy is more easily sapped. Rome gave him three years after his automatic resignation offer at seventy-five. He served, he waited, he obeyed.

Then, at the first hour of the Feast of St. Patrick's, March 17, 1990, he relinquished his authority as Ordinary to Aloysius Ambrozic. The Canadian church will not be the same again. The Carter era has ended.

Epilogue

It was an impressive ovation by any yardstick. Minnie would have been proud.

In addition to the stellar cast of bishops and politicians, there were business executives of the calibre of Conrad Black, John Craig Eaton, Galen Weston, bank presidents like William Mulholland and real estate magnates of the stature of Joseph J. Barnicke. They were all there. And so was the media. Emmett liked that. They could see for themselves the influence the church could still wield in the person of a leader like himself.

The triple anniversary celebration was an event unique in recent Canadian history. It had been some time since such prominent figures of state and high society had paid such public tribute to a churchman in what has become an increasingly pluralistic Canada. Bernard Cardinal Law, the blustery Irishman from Boston, looked on with transparent awe and envy. Perhaps, just perhaps, the halcyon days of ecclesiastical influence exercised by his predecessor and national celebrity, Richard Cushing, could be recaptured. It seemed as if they had been in Carter's Toronto. The entire proceedings smacked of the triumphalist, pre-conciliar Catholic Church in style, if not in substance, and there could be no doubt that there was but one prelate in Canada who could pull it off without appearing either anachronistic or ostentatious: Gerald Emmett Carter.

Surrounded by power, reverence and the acclaim of the mighty and the opinion makers, Carter had been reminded earlier in the day of his mortality at the St. Michael's Cathedral mass by no less a knowledgeable dignitary than his brother Alex: "In a period when Bishops are fair game for critics, some of them often ill-informed and sometimes uncharitable and mischievous, he continues to serve with calm, with decision and even with humour. Healthwise he paid dearly for any honours that came his way, including his appointment to the College of Cardinals. Despite the sudden stroke which nearly ended his life, he fought back and continues to serve the church with vigour, determination and distinction. To quote a final teaching of the wisdom of *Ecclesiasticus*: 'Cling to the Lord and do not leave Him, so that you may be honoured at the end of your days.' "

Having overcome the worst features of his infirmity, Carter stood resplendent, honoured at the end of his days, comfortable in his leadership. Minnie's son held sway that late spring day, his power secure, his reputation unassailed in the quarters that mattered to him, his confidence supreme. But he is Tom's son, too, the son of a man who paid dearly for his convictions, who suffered at the hands of one of the press lords, who knew what it meant to challenge industry. Was the spectre of Tom to be found in the small protesting band of Christian Workers standing outside the Convention Centre? He turned his attention to the demands of the moment. The witty and purposeful son of Minnie Carter brought the multitude to its feet.

It was, after all, his hour. It was her hour too.

LIST OF PERSONS INTERVIEWED

Below is a list of persons interviewed in the preparation of this book. Reference to observations by the following will be made without formal citation and will be to these interviews, unless otherwise noted.

Sebastiano Cardinal Baggio
Mr. Joseph J. Barnicke
Joseph Cardinal Bernardin
Mr. Conrad Black
Ms. Bonnie Brennan
Bishop Colin Campbell
Bishop Alexander Carter
Gerald Emmett Cardinal Carter
Sr. Lenore Carter, SP
Sr. Mary Carter, RSCJ
Dr. Tony Clarke
Fr. Brian Clough
Bishop Robert B. Clune
The Honourable William Davis
Bishop Remi De Roo
Mr. Gerry Duggan
Mrs. June Duggan
Ms. Lenore Duggan
Fr. Joseph Finn
Dr. Thomas Francoeur
Mr. John Fraser
Edouard Cardinal Gagnon
Archbishop Louis Garnsworthy
Paul Cardinal Grégoire
Archbishop James Hayes
Fr. Edward Jackman, OP
Count Robert Wendelin Keyserlingk

Franz Cardinal Koenig
Bishop M. Pearse Lacey
Sr. Mary Jo Leddy, NDS
Fr. Robert Liddy, C.R.
Fr. Massey Lombardi, OFM
Mr. Ron Locas
Dr. John MacPherson
Archbishop Paul Marcinkus
Fr. Brad Massman
Fr. James McConica, CSB
Fr. Ambrose McInnis, O.P.
Ms. Margaret McLaughlin
Msgr. Dennis Murphy
Dr. John O'Farrell
Fr. Sean O'Sullivan
Rabbi Jordan Pearlson
Archbishop Joseph-Aurèle Plourde
Bishop William Power
Joseph Cardinal Ratzinger
Mrs. Madeline Reiter
Fr. William Ryan, SJ
Bishop John Sherlock
Fr. Cornelius Siegfried, CR
Fr. Joseph Snyder
Mr. Charles Wayland
Mrs. Galen Weston

ENDNOTES

Preface

1. "Child Study in Relation to the Curriculum: The Adolescent Period." An unpublished paper by the Very Reverend Canon Emmett Carter, Ph.D.

Prologue

1. This and the following quotation are from Carter's Metro Convention Centre address, May 26, 1987.
2. John Fraser, *Telling Tales* (Toronto: Collins, 1986), p. 211.

Chapter One

1. Kildare Dobbs, "Ireland and the Irish Canadians," *The Untold Story: The Irish in Canada*, eds. R. O'Driscoll and L. Reynolds (Toronto: Celtic Arts of Canada, 1988), pp. 4–5.
2. *Constitution and By-Laws of the St. Patrick's Society of Montreal* (Montreal: Printed by John Lovell, St. Nicholas Street, 1864), pp. 10–11.
3. G.E. Carter, homily at the funeral mass of his sister Margaret, April 13, 1981.
4. Sister Mary Lenore Carter, "Quis ut Deus," (unpublished), p. 3.
5. Mother Mary Carter, "Sister's Story: Life with Emmett," *Catholic Register*, May 23–29, 1987, p. CC7.
6. Betty Paproski, as recorded in Douglas Fisher's column, *Toronto Sun*, July 19, 1979.
10. This and the following quotation are from John Brehl, *Sunday Star*, July 1, 1979.

Chapter Two

1. Walter M. Abbott, s.j., ed., *The Documents of Vatican II* (Piscataway, N.J.: New Century Publishers, 1966), p. 734.
2. From a speech entitled "Spirituality of Marriage," dated December 1951.
3. *Montreal Gazette*, July 4, 1979.
4. *A Shepherd Speaks: Occasional Writings, Sermons and Papers by Gerald Emmett Cardinal Carter* (Toronto: Mission Press, [undated]), p. 10.

5. Walter Pornonovich, "Two of a Kind," *Madonna Magazine* 36 (January 1963): 9.

Chapter Three

1. Steve Markell, "Education Problems His Strength," a *Monitor* profile.
2. Very Reverend Canon G. Emmett Carter, *The Catholic Public Schools of Quebec* (Toronto: W.J. Gage, 1957), pp. 23–26.
3. Reference to this information can be found in various newspaper articles, and is contained in Chapter 7 of *The Catholic Public Schools of Quebec*.
4. *The Catholic Public Schools of Quebec*, p. 20.
5. Very Reverend Canon G. Emmett Carter, *Psychology and the Cross* (Milwaukee: Bruce Publishing, 1959).
6. Very Reverend Canon G. Emmett Carter, *The Modern Challenge to Religious Education* (New York: William H. Sadlier, 1961).
7. Letter from Gladys E. Neal, Manager, School Book Department, The Macmillan Company of Canada Limited, addressed to Very Reverend G. Emmett Carter, March 3, 1954.
8. Letter to Miss Gladys E. Neale, Manager, School Book Department, The Macmillan Company of Canada Limited, March 23, 1954.
9. The Very Reverend G. Emmett Carter, *The Modern Challenge to Religious Education* (New York: William H. Sadlier, 1961), p. 1
10. *Lumen Vitae* 1:2 (1946): 399.
11. Correspondence between Johannes Hofinger and Walter M. Abbott, s.j., published as an interview in *America*, December 2, 1961, p. 335.
12. G.E. Carter, address given at a banquet held in Carter's honour at the Windsor Hotel, Montreal, October 12, 1961.

Chapter Four

1. Letter from George B. Flahiff, December 15, 1961.
2. Letter from Philip F. Pocock, December 6, 1961.
3. "Thoughts on an Anniversary — Part I," *Catholic Register*, penned in 1973.
4. As recorded in the *Canadian Register*, February 17, 1962, p. 11.
5. Letter to Claude Ryan, April 20, 1978.
6. Francis J. Leddy, "May There Be No Dust Upon Our Banner," speech to the Canadian Association of the Knights of Malta, Ottawa, April 29, 1978.
7. The founding fathers of the Canadian body were: Chief Justice Thibaudeau Rinfret of the Supreme Court of Canada, Colonel Thomas Guérin, Colonel J.D. LeMoyne, Desmond Clarke, Quintin J. Gwyn, Count Robert W. Keyserlingk and Daniel de Yturralde.
8. Letter to Olivier Maurault, January 6, 1961.
9. Francis J. Leddy, "The Keys of St. Peter and the Cross of Malta," address to the Canadian Association of the Knights of Malta, Ottawa, May 5, 1979.
10. G.E. Carter, Conventual Chaplain ad Honorem, address to the Canadian Members of the Knights of Malta, Ottawa, December 5, 1970.

11. Letter to Francis J. Leddy, March 20, 1979. The letter quoted immediately below is dated November 30, 1979.
12. Referred to in a letter from Baggio to Carter, September 11, 1959.
13. Letter to Sebastiano Baggio, December 20, 1972.
14. Peter Hebblethwaite, *The New Inquisition?* (London: Collins, 1980), p. 73.
15. Letter to Sebastiano Baggio, February 28, 1973.
16. Peter Hebblethwaite, *In the Vatican* (London: Oxford University Press, 1987), p. 120.
17. John J. Wright, "The Impact of the Ecumenical Movement," in *Dialogue for Reunion*, ed. Leonard Swidler (New York: Herder and Herder, 1962), p. 30.
18. Letter to John J. Wright, March 22, 1972.
19. Note to John J. Wright, undated.
20. Letter to John J. Wright, June 22, 1971.
21. Editorial, *Globe and Mail*, November 9, 1971.
22. Letter to Philip F. Pocock, September 1, 1962.
23. Emmett Carter, unpaginated "intervention" on Religious Freedom.
24. Emmett Carter, *Catholic Register*, February 10, 1973.
25. Letter to A. Bugnini, March 21, 1967.
26. *Confidential Report* on the meeting of the Consilium, Rome, April 10-20, 1967, p. 4.
27. Letter to Pope Paul VI from Gordon J. Gray, August 1, 1967.
28. Letter to Gordon J. Gray, August 8, 1967.
29. Letter to James Knox, April 25, 1974.
30. Letter to James Knox, June 14, 1974.
31. Letter to James Knox, August 13, 1974.

Chapter Five

1. *Hansard*, Ontario Legislature, February 21, 1963, p. 916.
2. Letter to Premier John Robarts, March 23, 1964.
3. Letter from John Turner, May 22, 1964.
4. Letter to Prime Minister Lester B. Pearson, March 7, 1964.
5. Letter from Michael Patrick, February 27, 1964.
6. "Spadina" referred to the Spadina Expressway controversy in which numerous residents' associations vigorously opposed a major freeway through part of downtown Toronto. Davis solved the latter problem but left the former for *his* successor.
7. Statement of the Honourable William Davis, Prime Minister of Ontario, on the Question of Extended Public Assistance to the Separate School System, Queen's Park, Tuesday, August 31, 1971.
8. *Windsor Star*, October 6, 1971.
9. OECTA Address, March 19, 1974.
10. From an early 1940s Montreal *Gazette* report entitled "The Idea of a Catholic Women's College Designed to Meet the Needs of Modern Women."
11. *Casti connubii*, in *7 Great Encyclicals*, ed. William J. Gibbons (1939; rpt. New York: Paulist Press, 1963), p. 98.

12. *The Documents of Vatican II*, ed. Walter M. Abbott, s.j. (Piscataway, N.J.: New Century Publishers, 1966), p. 635.

13. *The Documents of Vatican II*, pp. 639–40.

14. Letter to John Cardinal Wright, January 7, 1975.

15. Letter to Paul J. O'Byrne, November 27, 1974.

16. *Catholic Register*, October 15, 1977.

17. "The State of Catechetics in the World," an intervention by Bishop G. Emmett Carter to the Synod of Bishops, Rome, October 1, 1977.

18. Information on the history of King's College is drawn largely from Patrick Phelan's *Studium et Hospitium: A History of King's College* (London: King's College, 1979). Unless otherwise noted, reference to Bishops Carter and Sherlock is derived from our personal interviews with them.

19. *Studium et Hospitium*, p. 49.

20. References are to a mimeographed copy of the "Report of the Commission to Study the Catholic Character of King's College," bearing the note "reproduced in the office of the Principal, King's College, January, 1975."

21. *UW Gazette*, May 10, 1989, p. 2.

22. G.E. Carter, address given at Windsor meeting of OECTA, March 22, 1970.

Chapter Six

1. T.S. Eliot, "Thoughts after Lambeth," *Selected Essays* (London: Faber and Faber, 1969), p. 375

2. John G.J. O'Driscoll, "Divorce, Abortion, and Birth Control," in *Brief to the Bishops: Canadian Catholic Laymen Speak Their Minds*, ed. Paul T. Harris (Toronto: Longmans, 1965), p. 38.

3. "Final Report of the Pontifical Commission on Population, Family and Birth," included in Robert Blair Kaiser's *The Encyclical That Never Was* (London: Sheed and Ward, 1987), p. 10.

4. "Statement on the Synod of Bishops," issued October 19, 1969.

5. Arthur McCormack, "Light on *Humanae vitae*," *The Tablet*, December 12, 1987, p. 1346.

6. Brocard Sewell, *The Vatican Oracle* (London: Duckworth, 1970), p. 97.

7. Francis X. Murphy, *The Papacy Today* (New York: Macmillan, 1981), p. 131.

8. John Horgan, ed., Humanae vitae *and the Bishops: The Encyclical and the Statements of the National Hierarchies* (Shannon: Irish University Press, 1972), p. 8.

9. As quoted in *The Encyclical That Never Was*, p. 248.

10. Anne Roche, *The Gates of Hell: The Struggle for the Catholic Church* (Toronto: McClelland and Stewart, 1975), pp. 131-2.

11. Anne Roche Muggeridge, *The Desolate City: The Catholic Church in Ruins* (Toronto: McClelland and Stewart, 1986), pp. 97–98.

12. Letter to John Cardinal Dearden, December 14, 1973.

13. Letter to John Cardinal Wright, December 14, 1973.

Chapter Seven

1. The Flahiff intervention and the Vatican Declaration are to be found in Michael W. Higgins and Douglas R. Letson, eds., *Women and the Church: A Sourcebook* (Toronto: Griffin House, 1986), pp. 173-75 and 126-38, respectively.

   The question raised in Flahiff's intervention recurs in Canadian Synod presentations. It is worth noting, too, in this context that the Canadian interventions result from rigorous advanced planning and shared consensus. See Michael W. Higgins and Douglas R. Letson, "Canadian Participation in Episcopal Synods, 1967-85," *The Canadian Catholic Historical Association: Historical Studies*, 54 (1987): 145-57.

2. "Study Commission on Woman in Society and in the Church," a report presented to the Synod of Bishops, October, 1974, p. 4.

3. See, for example, Douglas R. Letson, "The Fruit of Solidarity: The Social Justice Teachings of John Paul II," *Conrad Grebel Review* 7 (Winter 1989): 25-40.

4. Letter to John Cardinal Wright, October 7, 1975.

5. Letter from Aloysius M. Ambrozic, December 1, 1975.

6. Letter to Aloysius M. Ambrozic, December 23, 1975.

7. Letter from Aloysius M. Ambrozic, December 31, 1975.

8. *Canadian Register*, December 14, 1968, p. w-1.

9. On May 9, 1973, Carter concluded a talk entitled "To Love is to Serve" and delivered to the Catholic Women's League in Chatham, Ontario, with the summary observation that it is the "particular gift of women for both love and service."

10. G.E. Carter, talk given in Woodstock, Ontario, on September 16, 1970. The following extracts are taken from talks on similar themes given in Chatham, Ontario, on October 4, 1975; at St. Peter's Cathedral in London on December 8, 1974; to the Sisters of St. Joseph at Mount St. Joseph in London, on August 12, 1974; and at St. Joseph's Oratory in Montreal on March 17, 1977.

11. *Women and the Church: A Sourcebook*, p. 127.

12. *Summa theologica* (3 vols.), translated by the Fathers of the English Dominican Province (New York: Benzinger Brothers, 1947, 1948). (IIa, IIae, Q. 177, art. 2)

13. *Summa theologica*, Question 39, art. 1: "Whether the Female Sex Is an Impediment to Receiving Orders." See also IIa, IIae, Q. 177, art. 2.

Chapter Eight

1. G.E. Carter, "The Responsibility of the Press to the Church," address delivered at the Canadian Managing Editors' Conference, Mount Royal Hotel, Montreal, February 11, 1955.

2. G.E. Carter, "Responsibility of the Press in the Modern World," address delivered at the Canadian Church Press Convention, Toronto, March 30, 1973.

3. Letter to Robert G. Vezina, October 13, 1972.

4. Letter from Robert G. Vezina, October 23, 1972.
5. Letter to Robert G. Vezina, November 9, 1972.
6. Anne Roche, "What Do You Do When Your Church Leaves You?", *Saturday Night*, June 1972, p. 28.
7. Letter from Robert G. Vezina, December 5, 1972. Carter's reply is dated December 8, 1972.
8. G.E. Carter, *Catholic Register*, January 20, 1973.
9. Letter to Stan Koma, August 2, 1973.
10. John K. O'Farrell, Review of *The Gates of Hell*, *The Chelsea Journal* (November-December 1975): 287.
11. Letter to Larry Henderson, January 28, 1976.
12. Michael W. Higgins and Douglas R. Letson, *Portraits of Canadian Catholicism* (Toronto: Griffin House, 1986), pp. 81-82.
13. Letter from Alex Carter to Philip Pocock, January 24, 1978.
14. Walter M. Abbott, s.j., ed., *The Documents of Vatican II* (Piscataway, N.J.: New Century Publishers, 1966), pp. 407-8.
15. G.E. Carter, "Christian Humanism," address given in Hartford, Connecticut, October 16, 1969, and at the Divine Word Centre, London, October 13, 1971.
16. G.E. Carter, "Outline for Parliamentary Session," address given to the Diocesan Council, London, November 13, 1971.
17. G.E. Carter, "Living Tradition and Faith," address given at the Religious Education Congress, Louisville, Kentucky, October 13, 1972.
18. G.E. Carter, address to the Synod, April 6, 1968. The following quotation is from his address to the Synod, November 30, 1968.
19. G.E. Carter, column for *Catholic Register*, May 27, 1974.
20. Michael W. Higgins, "Synod Diary," *Grail: An Ecumenical Journal* 2 (March 1986), p. 89.
21. This and the following quotation are from Carter's letter to Guy Poisson, September 6, 1977.
22. Letter to Charlotte H. Tansey, November 30, 1977.
23. Michael W. Higgins, "Church in Canada," *New Catholic Encyclopedia* (Washington: The Catholic University of America, 1989), vol. 18, p. 58.
24. Letter to Jean Villot, Papal Secretary of State, June 2, 1977.
25. G.E. Carter, Sermon for Twenty-Seventh Sunday, St. Peter's Cathedral, October 13, 1976.
26. G.E. Carter, *Catholic Register*, September 10, 1977.
27. G.E. Carter, "The Sacred Magisterium: Foundation for Renewal and Evangelization," address given at the CUF Congress, London, April 28-30, 1978.
28. G.E. Carter, address given at the Ontario Bishops' Meeting, April 1978.

Chapter Nine

1. Carter's installation address, June 5, 1978.
2. G.E. Carter, Letter to the Priests, Religious and Laity of the Archdiocese of Toronto, May 8, 1979.
3. Letter to Richard J. Doyle, March 12, 1979.

4. G.E. Carter, address given to the Ontario Catholic Supervisory Officers, April 4, 1979.

5. G.E. Carter, *Globe and Mail*, January 19, 1980.

6. G.E. Carter, "Vatican II — 20 Years After: A Pastoral Letter," October 1985, p. 12.

7. G.E. Carter, "The Forthcoming Synod and the Role of the Laity in the Church: a Pastoral Letter," September 1986, p. 2.

8. G.E. Carter, "The Universal Church, the Local Church, and the Papacy," address given at Michaelmas Conference, June 22, 1979, pp. 10-11.

9. G.E. Carter, "The Gospel according to John Paul II," *Saturday Night*, August 1984, p. 13.

10. G.E. Carter, August 15, 1984.

11. As quoted by reporter Michael Burke-Gaffney, *Catholic Register*, June 9, 1979.

12. Jack Costello, "Carter Named Cardinal: 'An Opportunity for Wider Service,' " *Catholic New Times*, June 3, 1979, p. 1.

13. Quoted in *Catholic Register*, February 22, 1969.

14. George Bull, *Inside the Vatican* (New York: St. Martin's Press, 1982), pp. 92-93.

15. As quoted by Larry Henderson, *Catholic Register*, July 21, 1979.

16. Tom Harpur, *Toronto Star*, July 13, 1979.

17. G.E. Carter, "Montreal Dinner Address," October 21, 1979, pp. 7-8.

18. G.E. Carter, address given at Ontario Provincial Dinner, Harbour Castle hotel, Toronto, Ontario 22, 1979, p. 12.

19. As quoted by Stan Oziewicz, *Globe and Mail*, November 1, 1979, p. 1.

20. As quoted by John Cruickshank, *Globe and Mail*, November 5, 1983, p. 18.

21. G.E. Carter, "Participatory-Democracy: Both or Neither," an address given to the Canadian Institute of Chartered Accountants, Harbour Castle Hotel, Toronto, September 15, 1979, p. 20.

22. G.E. Carter, *Globe and Mail*, May 10, 1982, p. 7.

23. This and the following quotations are from G.E. Carter, "Pastoral Letter to the Clergy, the Religious and the Faithful People of the Archdiocese of Toronto," June 21, 1981.

Chapter Ten

1. Claire Hoy, *Bill Davis: A Biography* (Toronto: Methuen, 1985), pp. 264-65.

2. G.E. Carter, address given at the Ontario Provincial Dinner, October 22, 1979.

3. G.E. Carter, address given at the Cardinal's Dinner held at the Harbour Castle Hotel, Toronto, November 3, 1983. The following quotation is from the following year's event, November 8, 1984.

4. Michael W. Higgins and Douglas R. Letson, "An Interview with Lewis Garnsworthy," *Grail: An Ecumenical Journal* 5 (September 1989): 28.

5. From a talk given to an Ontario Separate School Trustees Association meeting, Toronto, January 15, 1983.

6. This letter was reprinted in *Body Politic*, November 1984, p. 8.

7. See, for example, a talk given at Brennan High School, Windsor, Ontario, January 10, 1972, and his homily at the Deanery meeting of the Diocese of Stratford, January 9, 1975.
8. *Globe and Mail*, June 24, 1988.
9. Homily for St. Augustine's Seminary, 75th anniversary, October 26, 1988.

Chapter Eleven

1. Letter to Dr. Mary Malone, January 22, 1987.
2. G.E. Carter, homily given at St. Peter's Cathedral on March 25, 1970. The same theme was developed in a number of other sermons at St. Peter's on April 7, 1971; September 9, 1975; and on March 20, 1978.
3. "The Power and the Glory of Emmett Cardinal Carter," *Saturday Night*, April 1983, p. 23.
4. Notes for the Red Mass, Ottawa, September 12, 1983.
5. G.E. Carter, homily given at the Chrism Mass, St. Michael's Cathedral, Toronto, April 15, 1987.
6. G.E. Carter, homily given at St. Michael's Cathedral, Toronto, October 31, 1981.
7. G.E. Carter, homily given in Newmarket, October 31, 1987.
8. John Mable, *Catholic Register*, December 10, 1978.
9. "The Power and the Glory of Emmett Cardinal Carter," *Saturday Night* (April 1983), p. 23.
10. *Communio* 5 (Spring 1978): 228–51.
11. Notes for after-dinner address to the Catholic Women's League, June 2, 1988.
12. Letter from Donald J. Keefe to Monsignor Alan McCormack, Carter's Chancellor for Spiritual Affairs, dated November 5, 1984.
13. Correspondence from Chauncey Stillman to Donald J. Keefe, dated December 3, 1984.
14. Letter from Brendan Walsh, Assistant Editor, Catholic Truth Society, London, England, and dated December 12, 1984.
15. Letter from Chauncey Stillman to Donald J. Keefe, dated December 3, 1984.
16. *Catholic New Times*, February 12, 1984.
17. Letter to Anne Roche Muggeridge, May 11, 1984.
18. Letter from Father Anthony Durand, February 15, 1984.
19. Letter to Douglas Letson dated January 21, 1987.
20. Letter to Mary Malone, September 3, 1985.
21. The twelve recommendations and analyses of the progress of women in the church can be found in the June 1985 issue of *Grail*.
22. *Catholic Register*, April 27, 1985.
23. Carter's intervention to the annual plenary assembly of the Canadian Conference of Catholic Bishops meeting in Ottawa, October 15, 1984 (it had been prepared in advance).
24. "Bishops Adopt Softer Tones to Reopen Talks with Women," *Edmonton Journal*, October 26, 1984.
25. Denys Horgan, *Globe and Mail*, October 25, 1984.
26. *Edmonton Journal*, October 27, 1984.

27. *London Free Press*, October 26, 1984.
28. Notes for an after-dinner address to the Catholic Women's League, [n.l.] June 2, 1988.

Chapter Twelve

1. These articles were reprinted in and have been quoted from *A Shepherd Speaks: Occasional Writings, Sermons, and Papers by Gerald Emmett Carter* (Toronto: Mission Press, [undated]).
2. Pastoral letter issued by Carter on August 15, 1984, during the federal election campaign.
3. From a statement sent by Carter to William F. Ryan, s.j., General Secretary of the Canadian Conference of Catholic Bishops on April 18, 1985, as the CCCB prepared to respond to the crisis generated by the Morgentaler clinics.
4. G.E. Carter, address given at the Cardinal's Dinner, October 30, 1986.
5. G.E. Carter, homily given at St. Peter's Cathedral, September 26, 1971.
6. G.E. Carter, address given at First Friday Club of Detroit, March 2, 1973.
7. G.E. Carter, public address given in honour of John McIlhone, October 29, 1973.
8. G.E. Carter, address given to graduates of St. Joseph's School of Nursing, London, June 21, 1974.
9. G.E. Carter, Good Friday sermon delivered at St. Peter's Cathedral on March 28, 1985. The following excerpt is from a homily delivered at the same location on December 12, 1976.
10. Letter to Larry Henderson, March 20, 1978.
11. Pastoral letter, August 15, 1984.
12. Michael Cuneo, *Catholics against the Church: Anti-Abortion Protest in Toronto, 1969-1985* (Toronto: University of Toronto Press, 1989), pp. 75-77.
13. G.E. Carter, presentation dated March 8, 1987.
14. G.E. Carter, address delivered on February 25, 1990.
15. Michael W. Cuneo, pp. 47-52.
16. Letter to Prime Minister Brian Mulroney, February 29, 1988.
17. Document dated April 11, 1985, and mailed to William Ryan on the same date.

Chapter Thirteen

1. G.E. Carter, "The Techniques of Communism," unpublished, 1947.
2. G.E. Carter, "Community and Democracy," address given at the Canadian Club, London, Ontario, December 14, 1977, pp. 5-6.
3. G.E. Carter, "Is Marxism the Answer for Christian Social Justice?" address given at the Canadian Club, Toronto, October 18, 1982, pp. 6, 7.
4. *Globe and Mail*, June 25, 1982.
5. G.E. Carter, "Is Marxism the Answer for Christian Social Justice?", address to the Canadian Club, Toronto, Oct. 18, 1982.

6. "Unemployment: the Human Costs," January 4, 1980, reprinted in *Do Justice! The Social Teaching of the Canadian Catholic Bishops*, ed. E.F. Sheridan, s.j. (Toronto: The Jesuit Centre for Social Faith and Justice/Editions Paulines 1987), p. 355.
7. "Ethical Reflections on the Economic Crisis," December 22, 1983, *Do Justice!* pp. 406–7.
8. Letter to Henri Légaré, January 10, 1983. This was followed up by successive letters to Légaré dated February 21, 1983, and April 5, 1983.
9. Letter to Joseph MacNeil, April 5, 1983.
10. Letters to Remi De Roo, May 7, 1985 and August 6, 1985.
11. This quotation and the following one are from Conrad Black, column in the *Globe and Mail*'s *Report on Business Magazine*, October 1987.
12. Editorial, *Toronto Star*, October 28, 1987.
13. Conrad Black, letter to the editor, *Toronto Star*, October 31, 1987.
14. Gregory Baum, *Compassion and Solidarity* (Toronto: CBC Enterprises, 1987), p. 40.
15. *The Tablet*, November 4, 1989, p. 1283.
16. G.E. Carter, Cardinal's Dinner Address, Metro Convention Centre, November 8, 1989, pp. 5–6.
17. G.E. Carter, Letter to the editor, *Toronto Star*, August 5, 1989.
18. Letter to Michael Higgins and Douglas Letson, August 9, 1989.
19. G.E. Carter, "Words at the Aloysius Ambrozic Induction," June 25, 1986, p. 2.
20. Rabbi Jordan Pearlson, Opinion Column, *Toronto Star*, May 20, 1989.
21. G.E. Carter, "Lenten Pastoral, 1979."
22. G.E. Carter, address given to the Congregation of the Temple Emmanu-El, Toronto, April 15, 1988, pp. 12–13.
23. G.E. Carter, address given at the Interfaith Event, Holy Blossom Temple, Toronto, November 27, 1989.

INDEX

Abbott, Walter, 51, 72
"A Cardinal for Conservatives"
  (Steed), 226–27
Adams, Jack, 62
"A Dialogue of Trust" (Cenerini,
  Clough, Murphy and Reilander), 176
Alanus de Insulis, 27, 28
Alfrink, Cardinal (Archbishop of
  Utrecht), 65
Altiburo, See of, 58, 60
Ambrozic, Aloysius (Archbishop of
  Toronto), 2, 117–19, 177, 183, 188,
  203, 226–27; as Auxiliary Bishop for
  Toronto, xiv, 151, 227, 230
Ancient Order of Hibernians, 8
Anglican Church, 101, 122
Anti-Semitism, 228–29
Apologia (Newman), 129
Aquinas, Thomas, 21–24, 42, 52; views
  regarding women, 41, 116, 120, 122–
  23
Aristotle, 22, 23
"A Society to be Transformed"
  (CCCB), 217
Augustine of Hippo, 27, 43, 52, 129
Auschwitz, 229
Ave Maria, 160

Baggio, Sebastiano Cardinal, 58, 66,
  68, 71, 149; friendship with Carter,
  66–69, 70, 73, 160
Baltimore Catechism, 90
Barnicke, Joseph J., 211, 231

Basilica of St. James, 24
Bassett, Douglas G., 211
Baudoux, Maurice (Archbishop of St.
  Boniface), 107
Baum, Gregory, 109, 143, 153, 223
Beaulieu, Lucien, 219
Beaulne, Yvon, 161
Belloc, Hilaire, 9
Bernardin, Joseph (Archbishop of
  Toronto), 142, 143
Bernier, Sandra, 195
Bishop, role of, 133–34, 144–45
Bishops' Brief, 84
Black, Conrad, 38, 162, 173, 203–4,
  216, 221–23, 231
Blue Kit, 192
Brehl, John, 17
Brennan, Bonnie, 190–91
Brescia College, 96
British North America Act, 79, 81, 83–
  84
Brunelle, René, 160
Buchanan, Judd, 212
Bugnini, A., 74

Campaign Life, 202, 203
"Canada's Unemployed: The Crisis of
  Our Times" ("Ethical Reflections"
  panel), 219
Canadian Broadcasting Corporation,
  74, 202–3, 214, 223, 225
Canadian Catechism, 90–95

Canadian Catholic Conference, 105–10, 132; *See also* Canadian Conference of Catholic Bishops

Canadian Catholic Organization for Development and Peace, 207–9

Canadian Catholics for the Ordination of Women, 182

Canadian Catholics for Women's Organization, 184

Canadian Catholic Trustees Association, 86

Canadian Conference of Catholic Bishops, 139, 141–43, 192–94; Social Affairs Commission, 213–20; *See also* Canadian Catholic Conference

Canadian Register, The, 45

Caprio, Giuseppe Cardinal, 159

Carney, James, 111

Carrigan, Owen, 97

Carson, Ray, 39–40

Carter, Alex (Bishop of Sault Ste. Marie), 20–21, 71, 81, 175, 191, 193; clerical career, 13–14, 16, 58; relationship with Emmett, xiv, xvi, 8, 21, 35, 103, 160, 161, 231–32; and Winnipeg Statement, 105, 107, 110

Carter, Cyril, 8, 10–11

Carter, Frank, 8, 11

Carter, Gerald Emmett: administrative style, xiv-xv, 108, 125, 136–38, 142, 150, 151; appointed Cardinal, 158–62; attends Synods of Bishops, 94–95, 138–41; attends Vatican II, 71–73; Archbishop of Toronto, 145, 149, 151–52; Auxilliary Bishop and Bishop of London, 53, 58–61, 80, 87, 95–99; boyhood, 9, 11, 14–21, 49; Canon of the Basilica of Our Lay of the World, 31; *Catholic Public Schools of Quebec, The,* 34, 40–43, 48, 79, 88; chairman of ICEL, 75–77; Coat of arms, 59; Consilium for the Implementation of the Constitution on Sacred Liturgy, 73–75; director of Catholic Action, 30–31; director of Jacques Cartier Normal School, 35; *Do This in Memory of Me,* 184–88; Ecclesiastical Inspector, 25, 32–35, 37–40, 49, 50–51; elected to Permanent Secretariat of Synod of Bishops, 141; founds Thomas More Institute for Adult Education, 37; and funding debates, 81–85, 172–75; homiletical skills, 27; influence of Aquinas on, 21–24, 42, 52, 120, 123–24; joins Knights of Malta, 62–66; *Modern Challenge to Religious Education, The,* 43, 44, 50–51, 91; motto, 59; Newman Clubs Chaplain, 25–27; on executive of CCCB, 141–43; ordination as priest, 24–25; pedagogy and catechetical training, 42–46, 49–50, 86, 88, 90, 92–94, 99, 175–76, 178; *Psychology and the Cross,* 43–49; Rector of St. Lawrence College, 31, 52, 57–58; relationship to siblings, 13, 18, 160; scholastic awards, 31; and "Screwball Letters", 28–30, 48; sense of humour, xiii, xv-xviii, 2–3, 30, 52, 228; seventy-fifth birthday and anniversary, xiv, 1–3, 231–32; suffers stroke, 167–70; theory of self-realization, 46–48; view of church's role in social justice, 207–26; view on lay-cleric relationship, 46–48; view on papacy and Roman secrecy, 75–76, 154–55, 156–58, 229; view on politics and the church, 29, 61–62, 80–81, 151, 163–67, 200–201; view on abortion, 198–205; view on theological dissent, 87, 125, 132–33, 143–44, 153; view on individual freedom and conscience, 111–13, 129, 130, 134–35, 155–56; view regarding women's role in home and church, 23–24, 28–29, 88–89, 116, 117–19, 120–21, 123, 181–82, 185–92, 196–98; visits Poland, 143–45; *See also* Catechetics; Celibacy, clerical; and Women

Carter, Irene, 8, 9–10; *See also* Mary Lenore, Sister

Carter, Mae, xv-xvi, 8, 10–13, 16

Carter, Margaret, 8, 9, 198

Carter, Mary: *See* Carter, Mae

Carter, Michelle, 9, 11

Carter, Minnie, 8, 14, 15–17, 23, 59, 232

Carter, Nora, 11

Carter, Peggy, 11

Carter, Tom (father), 7–8, 13, 14, 16–17, 53, 232

Carter, Tom (son), 8, 11

Carter, Tom (grandson), 9, 11

Casaroli, Agostino Cardinal, 159

Casey, Paul C., 60

Casti connubi (Pius XI), 101

Catechetics, 49–50, 90–95, 139–41, 175–78

Cathedral Church of St. Michael, 1

Catholic Central High School, 85

Catholic New Times, 3, 188, 189, 207

Catholic Physicians' Guild of Manitoba, 109

Catholic Public Schools of Quebec, The (Carter), 34–35, 40–43, 46, 48, 79, 88, 90

Catholic Register, 90–91, 111, 126–33, 190, 192, 197

Catholic School Commission of Montreal, 37–40

Catholics against the Church: Anti-Abortion Protest in Toronto, 1969–1985 (Cuneo), 199

Catholics in Dialogue, 109

CCCB: *See* Canadian Conference of Catholic Bishops

CELAM. *See* Latin American Episcopal Conference

Celibacy, clerical, 47, 70–71, 92, 117, 118–19, 127–28

Cenerini, M., 176

Champagne, Andrée, 16

Charbonneau, Joseph (Archbishop of Montreal), 23, 26, 30–31, 38

Charter of Rights and Freedoms, 202

Chelsea Journal, 130

Chesterton, G.K., 2, 9, 64, 156

Christian Education of Youth (Pius XI), 40, 88

Christian Workers, 3, 232

Christ the King College: *See* King's College

Christus dominus: *See* Decree on the Bishops' Pastoral Office in the Church

Civardi, Ernesto Cardinal, 159

Clarizio, Archbishop Emmanuele, 103, 108

Clarke, Tony, 212, 213–14, 218

Clement, Mimi, 16

Clough, Brian, 167, 176

Clune, Robert, 180

Coderre, Gérard-Marie, 103

Cody, John C. (Bishop of London), 58, 61, 66, 80, 83–84, 98, 173

Come to the Father catechism: *See* Canadian Catechism

Commission on Education (Ontario), 83

Commission of Inquiry into the Catholic Character of King's College, 98–99

Committee of the Council of Education (Quebec), 35

Commonweal, 65

Communism, 208–9

Compass, 221

"Compassion and Solidarity: The Church for Others" (CBC Massey Lectures), 223

Conference of Catholic Teachers, 86

Congregation for Divine Worship, 76

Congregation for the Doctrine of the Faith, 130

Congregation for Sacraments, 76

Congress on the Theology of the Renewal of the Church, 135–36

Consilium for the Implementation of the Constitution on the Sacred Liturgy, 73–75

Contraception, 99, 101–13, 159

Convent of the Sacred Heart, 26

Conway, Sean, 165

Corneille, Roland de, 228

Cotter, Father, 9

Couglin, Charles, 208

Council of Cardinals for Study of Organizational and Economic Problems of the Holy See, 223–24

Council of Trent, 134
Cuneo, Michael W., 199, 201
Curran, Charles, 153
Cushing, Richard Cardinal, 231

Dailey, Thomas, 105, 176
Daly, Bernard, 105, 190–91
D'Angelo, Mary R., 184
D'Arcy McGee High School, 37
"Dare to Be a Priest Like Me" campaign, 181–82
Davis, Charles, 153
Davis, William: and funding for Catholic schools, 82, 84–85, 172–75; friendship with Carter, 2, 81, 162, 163–64, 165, 171–74, 211
Dearden, John (Archbishop of Detroit), 2, 112, 142
Declaration on Certain Questions Concerning Christian Ethics (1976), 143
Declaration on Christian Education (Vatican II), 88-90
Declaration on Religious Liberty (Vatican II), 72–73, 89
Declaration on the Question of the Admission of Women to the Ministerial Priesthood (1976), 115, 121–22, 124, 181, 185, 195
Decree on the Bishops' Pastoral Office in the Church (Vatican II), 134
Decree on Ecumenism (Vatican II), 89
Decree on Non-Christian Religions (Vatican II), 228
"Defending Workers' Rights — A New Frontier" (CCCB Social Affairs Commission), 220–23
DeGroot, Paul, 194
DeKonick, Charles, 156
De Lubac, 7, 153
Democracy in the church, 156–58
De Roo, Remi (Bishop of Victoria), 105, 107, 110, 194, 214, 215, 217, 220–23
Desaulniers, Omer-Jules, 39, 40
Deschamps, Alphonse-Emmanuel (Bishop of Montreal), 13, 24

De Smedt, Emile (Bishop of Bruges), 71–72
Desolate City: The Catholic Church in Ruins, The (Muggeridge), 110
De Valk, Aphonse, 130
Dewar, Marion, 194
Dewart, Leslie, 109
Dignitatis humanae: See Declaration on Religious Liberty
Di Santo, Odoardo, 165
Dissent in the church, 134–35, 143–45, 152–55
Divine Word (catechetical centre), 93–94, 99
Divini illius magistri: See Christian Education of Youth
Dobbs, Kildare, 7
Documents of Vatican II, The (Abbott), 51
Dogmatic Constitution on the Church (Vatican II), 157
Dolores, Sister, 90
Donato, Andy, 171
Donovan, Dan, 228
Dooley, David, 192
Do This in Memory of Me (Carter), 119, 184-89, 193–94
Doyle, James (Bishop of Peterborough), 175
Doyle, Richard J., 152–53
Ducet, Eugene, 39
Duggan, Gerry, 9
Duggan, Lenore, 9
Duggan, Wilfrid, 9
Dunphy, William, 228–29
Duplessis (Black), 38
Duplessis, Maurice, 37–40, 81–82
Duquesne University, 70
Durand, Anthony, 92, 93, 189

Eaton, John Craig, 211, 221, 231
"Eaton's Statement" (CCCB Social Affairs Commission), 220–23
Echebarria, Araceli, 191
École Normal Jacques Cartier, 35
Education system: in Ontario, 79–99, 172–75; in Quebec, 31, 33–53

Eliot, T.S., 101
Elizabeth I, 64
Ellis, John Tracy, 129
Emmett Club, 8
Ensign, The, 63
Episcopal Commission on Liturgy
  (English Sector), 74-75
"Ethical Reflections on the Economic
  Crisis" (CCCB Social Affairs Com-
  mission), 214-20
Evangelization (1974), Synod of
  Bishops on, 138

Fallon, Michael, 132
Family: role of in education, 41;
  women's role in, 197-98
F.J. Brennan High School, 85
Flahiff, George Bernard, xvi, 58, 106,
  115
Francoeur, Thomas, 51, 90-95, 99, 198
Fraser, John, 3, 174, 219
French, Orland, 218
Freud, Sigmund, 29, 45
Frost, Leslie, 82, 164

Gagnon, Edouard, 171
"Gang of Five", xvi
Garnsworthy, Lewis, 172
*Gates of Hell: The Struggle for the
  Catholic Church* (Muggeridge), 109,
  127-28, 130-32
Gaudium et spes: See Pastoral Constitu-
  tion on the Church in the Modern
  World
Gauthier, Georges, 25, 33, 35
Gerard, Warren, 150
Gerstein, Reva, 219
Gervais, Marcel, 176, 194
Gillespie, Alistair, 212
Gilson, Etienne, 156
Givens, Phil, 228
Glemp, Archbishop Jozef, 229
Globe and Mail, 151-52, 154-55, 194-
  95, 209, 218, 229
Globe and Mail's Report on Business,
  221
Godfrey, Paul, 166

Gough, E.-St.-J., 35
Graham, Ron, 182, 184
Grand Séminaire de Montréal: *See*
  Grand Seminary
Grand Seminary, 14, 19-24
Gravissimum educationis: See Declara-
  tion on Christian Education
Gray, Gordon J. (Archbishop of Edin-
  burgh), 75-76, 77, 108
Great Siege (1565), 64
Greeley, Andrew, 94
Greene, Graham, 156
Green Kit, 120, 192-95
Grégoire, Paul Cardinal, 20, 21, 66

Hamer, Jerome Cardinal, 185
Haring, Bernard, 153
Harpur, Tom, 150, 214
Hayes, James, 91, 93, 122
Hebblethwaite, Peter, 69
Hegel, G.W.F., 208
Henderson, Larry, 132-33, 200, 203
Hermaniuk, Archbishop Maxim, 138
Herr, Dan, 129
Higgins, Paul, 211
Hofinger, Johannes, 50-51, 93
Homosexuality, 143, 176, 177
Hosek, Chaviva, 166
Hoy, Claire, 171
Humanae vitae (Paul VI), 99, 101-13,
  153, 159
Humphrey, Hubert, 74

Ignatieff, George, 219
Inter insignores: See Declaration on the
  Question of Admission of Women to
  the Ministerial Priesthood
International Commission on English
  in the Liturgy (ICEL), 75-77
International Consultation on English
  Texts (ICET), 76
Irish Canadians, 7
Irish Christian Brothers, 225
"Irish Humour is Analyzed", 30

Jackman, Hal, 211
Jackson, R.W.B., 83

Jahnke, Grant, 188
Jerome, Brother, 49
John XXIII, 52, 71, 101–2, 134
John Paul II, 68, 116, 130, 158, 213;
relationship with Carter, 42, 158–59,
161–62, 223; *See also* Wojtyla, Karol
Johnson, Albert, 166
Judaism, 185
"Justice Demands Action" (CCCB),
212

Kagedan, Ian J., 229
Keane, E.C., 98
Keating, Mary Frances, 167, 185, 191
Keefe, Donald J., 185–88
Kelly, Senator, 172
Kennedy, John F., 74
Kerr, Mary Agnes: *See* Carter, Minnie
Keyserlingk, Robert, 2, 63, 92
King's College, 95, 96–99
Knights of Malta: *See* Sovereign and
Military Order of St. John of
Jerusalem of Rhodes and of Malta
Knox, James, 76, 77
Koma, Stan, 130
Krol, John Cardinal, 138, 224
Küng, Hans, 129, 130, 153, 154–55

Laborem exercens: See On Labour
Lacelle, Elisabeth, 194
Lacey, Pearse, 180
Lalonde, Marc, 212
Lambeth Conference (1930), 101
Langevin, Gilles, 140
La Rocque, Eugene, 97
Latin American Episcopal Conference,
68, 212
Latin Mass Society, 73
Law, Bernard Cardinal, 2, 231
Leddy, Francis J., 62–63, 65–66
Leddy, Mary Jo, 184, 209–11, 219
Légaré, Henri (Archbishop of
Grouard-McLennan), 214–20
Léger, Paul-Émile Cardinal, 31, 57,
59, 72
Leo XIII, xix, 21, 41, 163, 212
Leonard, Ellen, 184

"Lepanto" (Chesterton), 64
Lestapis, Stanislaus de, 101
Letter to the Bishops of the Catholic
Church on Certain Questions Con-
cerning the Minister of the Eucharist
(Ratzinger), 186
Lewis, C.S., 28
Liddy, Bob, 95
Locas, Ron, 51, 198
London Free Press, 194
London (Ontario), See of, 53, 61, 62,
136–37
London Synod (1966), 136–37
Lonergan, Bernard, 37, 134, 153
Loyola College, 37
Lumen gentium: See Dogmatic Consti-
tution on the Church
Lumen Vitae, 49, 50
Lumen Vitae (catechetical centre), 93–
94
Lyng, Jim, 34

McAuliffe, John W., 98
McClellan, Ross, 164
McConica, James, xv, 177
McCormack, Alan, xv
McCormack, Arthur, 104
McCracken, E.J., 35
MacDonald, Donald, 82
MacDougall, Angus, 149
MacEachen, Allan, 212
McGee, Thomas D'Arcy, 7
McGibbon, Pauline, 162
McGill University, 25–27, 36
McGrath, Marcos, 72
McGuigan, James Charles, 61, 151
McGuigan, Mark, 157
Macharski, Franciszek, 229
McIlhone, John, 86
McInnis, Ambrose, 150
Mackasey, Bryce, 212
McLaughlin, Margaret, 190
McManus, Joe, 62
McManus, Michael, 34
McManus, Ora, 105
Macmillan of Canada, 44
McNalley, W.J., 168

MacNeil, John, 143
MacNeil, Archbishop Joseph, 192, 218
McNight, Richard, 183
McNulty, James A. (Bishop of Buffalo), 104–5
McShane, Msgr. Gerald J., 14–15, 19, 25–26, 52, 63
Magisterium, Carter's views on, 144, 155–56
Malley, E.R., 98
Malone, Mary, 179–80, 192
Marcinkus, Paul, 67, 73
Marian teachings, and Carter's view regarding women, 23–24
Maritain, Jacques, 156
Marshall, John, 101
Martel, Charles "The Hammer", 64
Martel, Eli, 164
Martelet, Gustave, 187
Martin, Paul, 61
Martinez, Luis Aponte (Bishop of San Juan), 138
Marx, Karl, 208–9
Marxism, 208–9
Mary Jackson, Sister, 92
Mary Lenore, Sister, 9–10, 50; *See also* Carter, Irene
Mary Zimmerman, Sister, 167
Massman, Brad, xv, xvii, 167–68, 188, 190, 191
Maud, André, 105
Maxwell, Grant, 132
Medellín (Columbia), 68, 212
Media, Carter's relations with, 72, 125–33, 139, 152–55, 224–26, 228
Mertens, Clement, 101
Mertens de Wilmars, Jacques, 102
Metropolitan Toronto Police, 166
Michaelmas Conference (979), 157
Missionaries, 207–9
Modern Challenge to Religious Education, The, 43, 44–45, 50–51, 91
Montreal Beacon, The, 30
Montreal Catholic School Commission, 31
Montreal College, 19, 49–50
Montreal Daily Star, 18

Montreal Star, 30
Moore, Vern, 150
Morgentaler, Henry, 200, 201
Mounier, Frederic, 156
Mount Cashel Orphanage, 225
Muggeridge, Anne Roche, 109–10, 127–28, 188–89
Muggeridge, Malcolm, 222
Mulholland, William D., 211, 231
Mulroney, Brian, 2, 202
Munro, John, 212
Murphy, Dennis, 142
Murphy, J., 176

National Catholic Register, 133
National Catholic Register, 65, 102–3
Newman, John Henry, 108, 112, 129, 162–63
Newman Club, 25–27
Nixon, Robert, 164
Nostra aetate: See Decree on Non-Christian Religions
Notre Dame Basilica, 59
Noyes, Alfred, 156

O'Boyle, Patrick Cardinal, 104–5
O'Byrne, Paul J. (Bishop of Calgary), 92–93
O'Connor, John Cardinal, 224
O'Connor, R. Eric, 37
O'Driscoll, John, 102
O'Farrell, John, 130–32, 150
O'Mara, John (Bishop of Thunder Bay), 215
On Human Life: *See Humanae vitae*
On Labour (John Paul II), 213
On New Things (Leo XIII), 212
Ontario English Catholic Teachers Association, 10, 86
Ontario Foundation Tax Plan (1964), 79–83
Ontario Separate School Trustees' Association, 81
Ontario Teachers' Federation, 10
Options on Life Committee, 205
O'Sullivan, Sean, 180, 181–82, 184
Ottaviani, Alfredo Cardinal, 71–72

Ouellet, Gilles, 213
Our Family, 92
Our Life with God (Sadlier), 90

Packer, David, 201
Palmas, Angelo, 2, 142
Paproski, Steve, 160
Pastoral Constitution on the Church in the Modern World (Vatican II), 44, 89
Patrick, Michael, 81
Paul VI, 65, 67, 68, 74, 115–16, 138, 145; and *Humanae vitae*, 99, 103, 104, 108
Pearlson, Jordan, 228
Pearson, Lester B., 80–81
Pegis, Anton, 156
Phelan, Patrick, 97–98
Pinsonnault, Pierre-Adolphe (Bishop of London), 58
Pius XI, 40, 41, 46, 48, 88, 101, 116
Pius XII, 13, 45, 101, 208
Playboy, 181
Plourde, Joseph-Aurèle (Archbishop of Quebec), xvi, 66, 103, 142–43, 187, 194
Pluralism, philosophy of, 86
Pocock, Philip Francis (Archbishop of Toronto), 72, 106, 133, 149, 150, 159; and funding of Catholic schools, 172, 175; relationship with Carter, xvi, 58, 59, 83, 103; and ShareLife, 203, 210
Poisson, Guy, 140
Pontifical Commission on Population, Family and Birth, 102–3
Power, William (Bishop Emeritus of Antigonish), xiv, 27, 72, 121
Priesthood: clerical morale, 180–82, 184–89; power and the, 182–84
Progressive Conservative Party (Ontario), 164–66
Proulx, Adolphe (Bishop of Hull), 215, 217
Psychology and the Cross, 43–44, 45, 48–49, 50
Puebla (Mexico), 68, 212

Racism, and Metropolitan Toronto Police, 166
Rahner, Karl, 153
Ratzinger, Joseph Cardinal, 186, 187, 189
Reding, Paul F. (Bishop of Hamilton), 175
Regulation 16/64, 82–83
Reilander, D., 176
Reiter, Madeline, 51–52
Religious of the Sacred Heart of Jesus, 12–13
Rerum novarum: See On New Things
Riedmatten, Henri de, 102
Righi-Lambertini, Egano Cardinal, 159
Robarts, John, 79–83, 164
Robinson, Paul Anthony, 210–11
Roche, Anne: *See* Muggeridge, Anne Roche
Roche, Douglas, 109
Rogers, Arnold, xv–xvi
"Roman Catholic Church and Sexism, The" (Leonard and D'Angelo), 184
Rosalie Hall, 205
Roy, Maurice (Archbishop of Quebec City), 57, 59
Rubin, Wladyslaw Cardinal, 159
Ryan, Claude, 61–62
Ryan, Joseph (Bishop of Hamilton), 83, 107
Ryan, William, xiii, 204, 218–19

Sacramental sexuality and the ordination of women" (Keefe), 185
Sacred Congregation for Bishops, 68–69
Sacred Congregation for the Clergy, 69
Sacred Congregation for Divine Worship, 74–75, 76, 77
Sacred Congregation for the Doctrine of the Faith, 115, 143
Sadlier Publishers, William H., 91
St. Anne's High School, 85
St. Augustine's Seminary, 176–78, 179, 184

St. Clare's Church, 61
St. Hippolyte de Kilkenny, 25
St. Joseph's Teachers' College, 36, 51–52
St. Lawrence College, 31, 36, 52, 57–58
St. Michael's Hospital, 167
St. Onge, Charles, 105
St. Patrick's Church, 8, 15, 26
St. Patrick's School, 49
St. Patrick's Society of Montreal, 8
St. Peter's Basilica, 61
St. Peter's Seminary, 95–96
Santa Maria in Traspontina, 161, 195
Saturday Night, 127, 128, 158, 174, 184
Saturday Star Magazine, 226–27
Scarboro Foreign Mission Society, 207
Schmidt, Ted, 227
Schorsch, Alexander, 90, 93
Scorsone, Suzanne, 191–92
Screwtape Letters (Lewis), 28
Second Vatican Council, 2, 23, 46, 71–73, 131, 155, 212
Secretariat of Catholic Action, 31
Separate School Act (1863), 79
Seton, Elizabeth, 117
Sewell, Brocard, 104
Sewell, John, 162, 163
Sexual abuse, alleged clerical, 224–26
ShareLife, 203–4, 207, 209–11
Sharp, Mitchell, 212
Shaw, J.G., 45
Sheen, Bishop Fulton, 208
Sheridan, Edward, 105
Sherlock, John (Bishop of London), 136, 175, 194; and King's College, 96, 98, 99; views regarding Carter, xv, xvii, 151
Shook, Lawrence K., 117
Sisters of Providence, 9–10
Snyder, Joe, xv, xvi, 95–96, 137, 180
Société de St. Sulpice, 14
Somerville, Janet, 188
Sovereign and Military Order of St. John of Jerusalem of Rhodes and of Malta, 62–66, 67, 87
Speck, Paul, 151–52

Stanford, J.J., 24
"Statement on the Formation of Conscience" (CCC), 111–13
Status, 184
Steed, Judy, 226–27
Stern, Karl, 45
Stillman, Chauncey, 187, 188
Stong, Alfred, 164
Study Commission on Woman in Society and in the Church, 116, 117
Suenens, Leo, 65, 71, 72
Summa theologica (Aquinas), 21, 22, 42
Supreme Court of Canada, 202
Synod of Bishops (1971), 71
Synod of Bishops (1974), 137–39
Synod of Bishops (1977), 139–41
Synod of Bishops (1980), 141

Tablet, The, 102–3, 104
Tansey, Charlotte, 37, 140–41
T. Eaton Company, 220–23
Telling Tales (Fraser), 3
Textbooks, 36, 39; *See also* Education
Theologo '67: *See* Congress on the Theology of the Renewal of the Church
Theresa, Mother, 122
Thomas More Institute for Adult Education, 33, 37
Thompson, Francis, 9, 156
Toronto Pastoral Missionary Council, 207–8
Toronto School of Theology, 188
Toronto, See of, 145, 149–70
Toronto Star, 151, 166, 209–10, 214, 222
"To Speak as a Christian Community" (CCCB), 195
"Training of Teachers of Religion, The" (Carter), 49
Trudeau, Pierre Elliott, 2, 202, 212, 213, 215
Trujillo, Alfonso Lopez (Auxiliary Bishop of Bogota), 68
Tulk, John, 176
Turner, John, 80, 157, 162
Twin Circle, 65

Unemployment: The Human Costs" (CCCB), 213

"Unholy Economics" (Black), 221–22

Unitatis redintegratio: See Decree on Ecumenism

United Irish Society, 8

United Way, 203, 210

University of Montreal, 20, 25, 36, 37, 43

University of St. Michael's College, 96–97

University of Toronto, 177

University of Waterloo, 30, 98–99

Vachon, Bishop, 194

Van Horne, Ron, 164

Van Hove, Brian, 187

Vanier, Georges, 74, 80

Van Rossum, Pierre, 102

Vatican II: *See* Second Vatican Council

Vatican Oracle, The, 104

Vezina, Robert, 127–28

Viens vers le Père catechism: *See* Canadian Catechism

Violence en héritage (Assembly of Quebec Bishops), 195

Walker, Gordon, 160

Wall, Leonard (Auxiliary Bishop of Toronto), 193, 210, 219, 224

Wanderer, The, 133, 188

Waugh, Evelyn, 156

Wayland, Charles, 16, 20, 21, 27, 49

Weekend Magazine, 151–52

Welan, Lawrence, 19–20

Wells, Tom, 160

Wescott, Ed, 34

Western Canadian Conference of Priests, 109

Western Catholic Reporter, 109

Westhues, Ken, 98–99

Weston, Galen, 231

Weston, Hilary, 211

Who is My Mother? (Malone), 192

Wilhelm, Joseph (Archbishop of Kingston), 107

Wilson, John Killoran, 167

Winnipeg Statement (1968), 105–10, 159

Wintermeyer, John, 82

Wojtyla, Karol, 143, 144; *See also* John Paul II

Women: ordination of, 115–24, 182–96; role in the church, 36, 116–24, 179–96; women's liberation movement, 120–21, 183, 197

Women for Life, Faith, and Family, 192

Women's Committee on the Role of Women in the Church, 192–94

Wright, John, 60, 69–71, 73, 92, 108–9, 112, 117

Wyszynski, Stefan Cardinal, 143

Young Christian Workers, 27

Zilboorg, Gregory, 141